JOHN QUINCY ADAMS
AND THE POLITICS
OF SLAVERY

JOHN QUINCY ADAMS

AND THE POLITICS

OF SLAVERY

Selections from the Diary

DAVID WALDSTREICHER
& MATTHEW MASON

OXFORD
UNIVERSITY PRESS

OXFORD

UNIVERSITY PRESS

Oxford University Press is a department of the University of Oxford. It furthers
the University's objective of excellence in research, scholarship, and education
by publishing worldwide. Oxford is a registered trademark of Oxford University
Press in the UK and certain other countries.

Published in the United States of America by Oxford University Press
198 Madison Avenue, New York, NY 10016, United States of America.

© Oxford University Press 2017

Library of Congress Cataloging-in-Publication Data
Names: Adams, John Quincy, 1767–1848. | Waldstreicher, David, editor. |
Mason, Matthew, 1968- editor.
Title: John Quincy Adams and the politics of slavery : selections from the diary /
David Waldstreicher, Matthew Mason [editors].
Description: New York, NY : Oxford University Press, 2017. |
Includes bibliographical references and index.
Identifiers: LCCN 2016028236| ISBN 9780199947959 (hardback) |
ISBN 9780190624613 (ebook epub)
Subjects: LCSH: Adams, John Quincy, 1767–1848—Diaries. |
Adams, John Quincy, 1767–1848—Political and social views. |
Slavery—Political aspects—United States—History—19th century. |
United States—Politics and government—1783–1865. | BISAC: HISTORY / United States /
19th Century. | HISTORY / United States / Revolutionary Period (1775–1800).
Classification: LCC E377 .A3 2017 | DDC 973.5/5092—dc23
LC record available at https://lccn.loc.gov/2016028236

3 5 7 9 8 6 4 2
Printed by Sheridan Books, Inc., United States of America

To our advisors
David Brion Davis and Ira Berlin

CONTENTS

INTRODUCTION

The Diary, the Life, and the Politics of Slavery

John Quincy Adams kept diaries for most of his long adult life. Thanks to two printed editions (edited in twelve volumes by Charles Francis Adams in 1874–77 and condensed to one volume by Allan Nevins in 1928), the diary has long been one the most quoted sources for the political history of the early American republic.[1] Now that the entire fifty-one manuscript volumes totaling fourteen thousand pages are online courtesy of the Massachusetts Historical Society, however, it is more widely appreciated that the very length of the diaries has made both systematic analysis and leisurely reading something of a challenge.

1. Massachusetts Historical Society (MHS), The Diaries of John Quincy Adams: A Digital Collection, http://www.masshist.org/jqadiaries/php/; Charles Francis Adams, ed., *The Memoirs of John Quincy Adams, 1795 to 1848*, 12 vols. (Philadelphia: J. B. Lippincott, 1874–77); Allan Nevins, ed., *The Diary of John Quincy Adams, 1794-1845* (1928. Repr. New York: Scribner's, 1951). For the publication history, see "Introduction," in David Grayson Allen et al., eds., *Diary of John Quincy Adams. Vol. 1: November 1779-March 1786* (Cambridge, MA: Harvard University Press, 1981), xxii–xxxv. The second volume of the Harvard University Press edition contains the diary from 1786 through 1788; these portions were not included at all by Charles Francis Adams, whose edition begins in 1794, after a gap of several years in the diary.

For examples of recent histories that rely extensively on the diary, see Sean Wilentz, *The Rise of American Democracy: Jefferson to Lincoln* (New York: Norton, 2006); Daniel Walker Howe, *What God Hath Wrought: The Transformation of America, 1815-1848* (New York: Oxford University Press, 2007). Howe's volume is dedicated to Adams, as if in a riposte to Wilentz, who much prefers Andrew Jackson and often uses the diary to mock Adams and his politics, except where it concerns Adams's antislavery, which earns his grudging admiration.

This has become only more true as historians have come to grant more attention and significance to the problem of slavery. Adams's behind-the-scenes comments on the Missouri Crisis, which remained private during his lifetime, are often quoted by political historians and have long established him as a keen, and honest, prophet of war over slavery—if a man who confines prophecy to his diary can be so honored. During his postpresidential, congressional career, he chronicled his battles with the "Slave Power" as he turned his private pique to public action, overcoming his own fears of aging and irrelevance to fill a new role as "Old Man Eloquent," the conscience of the nation. A selective reading of the diary can support the increasingly prevalent sense of Adams as the only president before the Civil War to get the slavery question right. But there are costs to emphasizing the sunny side or happy ending according to our current preferences. It has become easier to celebrate Adams's second career as an antislavery stalwart in Congress than to understand how and why it took him so long to get there.

The diary would seem to be the best place to look to answer that question, since the rightly famous quotations suggest both a record of private thoughts and an insider's account of the halls of power in light of public and controversial events. What did African slavery mean to John Quincy Adams? When did he begin to think of himself as antislavery? When or how did he act on those beliefs politically? The diary provides many answers—but also complications. The answers and the complications derive from both the nature of the diary and the nature of slavery as a political problem in the early United States.

The diary has informed several different kinds of approaches to John Quincy Adams's life and legacy, which seem to appear in successive waves of praise and critique—sometimes in response to earlier studies, and perhaps even more consistently in relation to the rise or fall in the reputation of Adams's adversaries, especially Andrew Jackson. Those who see Adams as a heroic figure—a learned, thoughtful statesman whose inevitable ambitions (he was a son of a president, after all) were leavened by an intense sense of duty and patriotism—find in his diary a constant, and inspiring, struggle to improve himself and his country. For Samuel Flagg Bemis, his most thorough and most important biographer, the diary was "a secret tuning fork for his pent-up emotions" and "a process of self-discipline and introspection." Similarly, the incisive political historian

George Dangerfield, writing of the years when Adams was secretary of state and then president, described the diary as a place where Adams rehearsed not only his conscience but also public arguments.[2] Leonard L. Richards, the first historian to focus on the "second career," argued that the diary became a workshop not only for Adams's well-established character but also for the refashioning of his self, especially as he transitioned from the executive branches to Congress, and toward a politics that ultimately emphasized rather than tried to suppress the slavery issue.[3]

In introducing his one-volume edition in 1928, Allan Nevins maintained that the emotionalism in the diary could humanize the public man who himself readily admitted that some saw him as cold and forbidding. More recently, however, sympathetic biographers have noticed that Charles Francis Adams did not just edit out the dross, as he intended to do: he worked as a quintessential Victorian, expurgating most evidence of family and intimate life to focus on the public persona. The unedited diary reveals a much-better-rounded person who cared deeply about people and politics.[4] It might be fairer to say that much of the emotion in John Quincy Adams's diary remains in his son's edition, but it is the emotion directed toward public questions and career goals. As a result, sometimes the relationship between his private life and his public actions has been obscured.

On the other hand, much like his father, Adams's tendency to scribble about his doubts, faux pas, and failures (especially on his birthday) left

2. Samuel Flagg Bemis, *John Quincy Adams and the Foundations of American Foreign Policy* (New York: Knopf, 1949), viii; Lynn Hudson Parsons, *John Quincy Adams* (Madison, WI: Madison House, 1998), 18; George Dangerfield, *The Awakening of American Nationalism, 1815-1828* (New York: Harper Torchbooks, 1965), 27–29; for an earlier version of Dangerfield's interpretation, see his prize-winning study *The Era of Good Feelings* (New York: Harcourt Brace, 1952), 7–9. Dangerfield went so far as to assert that Adams always "intended it for publication" someday. There is no quotable evidence for this claim, but it seems plausible by the time of his presidency or afterward, given that the existence of the diary became quite well known in Washington circles, so much so that he was asked to consult it and report back during controversies about past events.
3. Leonard L. Richards, *The Life and Times of Congressman John Quincy Adams* (New York: Oxford University Press, 1986), 5–6.
4. Phyllis Lee Levin, *The Remarkable Education of John Quincy Adams* (New York: Palgrave Macmillan, 2015), 5–7; Fred Kaplan, *John Quincy Adams: American Visionary* (New York: Harper, 2014), xi–xii.

more than enough evidence for a more critical view. Dangerfield laid out the problem in the language of another era, when psychology was on the rise: "He was, above all, a moral man. . . . But it was the morality of a man who was also corroded by meanness, suspicion and fear. It was a torturous, not to say tortured morality, which for years did his reputation great disservice. Every reader of his Diary recognizes, respects, and recoils from it." The diary reveals at every turn his "passion for the truth" and "the brilliance of his insights. But when it comes to the interpretation of motive, then the passion turns into a mania: Mr. Adams' unhappy ego peers out across the world in an agony of suspicion; everything seems to be transformed into a conspiracy against Mr. Adams."[5] Dangerfield's remarks, which are also of the mid-century period during which Samuel Flagg Bemis recovered Adams as a major statesman from the condescension of pro-Jackson historians like Arthur Schlesinger Jr., remain valuable insofar as they index the contrary (and contrarian) nature of both the diary and the uses to which it has been put.[6]

During the 1980s and 1990s, Paul C. Nagel built a skeptical and tragic psychological interpretation out of the self-doubts and family

5. Nevins, "Introduction," xii; Dangerfield, *Awakening of American Nationalism*, 28–29.
6. The Progressive ascendancy in the historiography traces to Frederick Jackson Turner and culminated in Schlesinger Jr.'s *The Age of Jackson* (1945), in which Adams and his presidency were at best the "last chance" of the "business community." He showed "few evidences of statesmanship." Adams's fight against the gag rule did not require more than a brief acknowledgment, quoting the Diary, that Adams had foreseen the irrepressible conflict in 1820. Adams's complicity, Schlesinger implied, made him an ineffective if not irresponsible spokesman against slavery when the matter "occasionally flare[d] up for a moment in an exchange on the floor of Congress (often around Adams, who knew his responsibility)." Schlesinger, *The Age of Jackson* (Boston: Little, Brown, 1945), 35, 424. "Looking back, I think I did Hamilton, Adams and Clay a good deal less than justice in *The Age of Jackson*," Schlesinger wrote in a 1989 essay he incorporated into his memoirs in 2000. Arthur M. Schlesinger, "The Age of Jackson," *New York Review of Books* (December 7, 1989), 50; Schlesinger, *A Life in the Twentieth Century* (Boston: Houghton Mifflin, 2000), 366. For early and incisive critiques of the biases of the Progressive historians with respect to slavery and the Jacksonian era, see Alfred A. Cave, *Jacksonian Democracy and the Historians* (Gainesville: University Press of Florida, 1964); Staughton Lynd, *Class Conflict, Slavery, and the U.S. Constitution* (1967. Repr. New York: Cambridge University Press, 2011), 3–24, 135–84.

It is worth considering also that the Adams Trust routinely denied access to the unpublished materials, including the diary, between 1910 and 1951, except to Bemis. Allen et al., "Introduction," xxxiv–xxxv; George A. Lipsky, *John Quincy Adams: His Theory and Ideas* (New York: Crowell, 1950), ix, 5n4.

tragedies on display in the diary and the private writings of other family members.[7] One problem with this interpretation is that the political issue of slavery begins to appear as mainly a matter of repression and, eventually, career therapy for a disappointed one-term president. In the conventional terms of late twentieth-century "new" political history voiced by Robert Remini, antislavery politics was a dubious substitute for the party politics Adams was too slow to embrace as the American way. In a sense, this interpretation should instruct us as the obverse of the optimistic one, now back in fashion, that Adams had all the answers at the right time.[8] Where skeptics, in other words, make of Adams's obsessive journaling both a historian's dream and an example of his limitations as a person and a politician, his champions see in the diary the hallmarks of Adams's wisdom and leadership—the virtues that won out in the end, even (perhaps especially) with respect to the politics of slavery, and which should now guide how we interpret his life and era.

Not coincidentally, Adams optimists or partisans like Senator Bennett Champ Clark tend to see him as "singularly consistent" in opposing slavery. This tack may have something to recommend it compared to the countervailing tendency to downplay the slavery issue altogether or treat it as a mere screen for resentment or partisanship.[9] But

7. Paul C. Nagel, *Descent from Glory: Four Generations of the John Adams Family* (New York: Oxford University Press, 1983); Nagel, *John Quincy Adams: A Public Life, A Private Life* (New York: Knopf, 1997); for a critique of Nagel, see especially Edith B. Gelles, *Portia: The World of Abigail Adams* (Bloomington: Indiana University Press, 1992), 16–21, and Gelles, "An American Dynasty," in David Waldstreicher, ed., *A Companion to John Adams and John Quincy Adams* (Malden, MA, and Oxford: Wiley-Blackwell, 2013), 534.
8. Robert Remini, *John Quincy Adams* (New York: Times Books, 2002), 137–55. For a review of interpretations of Adams's life, see David Waldstreicher, "John Quincy Adams: The Life, The Diary, and the Biographers" in Waldstreicher, ed., *A Companion to John Adams and John Quincy Adams*, 241–62.
9. Bennett Champ Clark, *John Quincy Adams: Old Man Eloquent* (Boston: Little, Brown, 1932), 292. In 1956, John F. Kennedy, a young senator running for president and needing Southern votes, praised his New England predecessor in his best selling *Profiles in Courage* for bucking his own party and supporting the Louisiana Purchase and embargo—without saying a word about Adams's later courage in standing up to the slave power. John F. Kennedy, *Profiles in Courage* (1956. Repr. New York: Pocket Books, 1963), 27–44. Levin, for example, who sees Adams's antislavery as consistent, misremembers Senator Kennedy as having celebrated Adams's antislavery, which he never mentions: none of Kennedy's men of courage in US history are abolitionists, and half are Southerners. *The Education of John Quincy Adams*, 4.

the revived notion of a consistently antislavery (much less abolitionist) Adams does not stand up to the ample evidence in the diary that
there was much more to the politics of slavery. In a sense, these dueling perspectives continue to play the same American game of either
downplaying the politics of slavery as peripheral, as a narrow economic
interest, or as partisanship; or alternately highlighting it selectively to
prove the virtues of chosen founding fathers and the progressive nature
of American history.

Leonard Richards's notion of the diary as a workshop, or what we
would now call a journal, seems closer to the truth, and more in accord
with the seemingly contradictory assessments of the author himself.
John Quincy Adams regularly, even ritually, derided his diary writing as
"rubbish" or a waste of time. But he also, in his years of public service,
spent some of the same early morning hours that he devoted on other
days (and sometimes the same days) to official correspondence and writing projects, like his occasional and highly regarded orations, getting
the events of previous days right—for himself and for posterity—in the
diary. During his years as a diplomat, the diary expanded, serving as
both a place to reflect on conversations both official and off the record
(both being essential to the real work of diplomacy). As secretary of
state, he used the diary to break down the complex personal and fac-
tional politics of a one-party state, cataloging one cabinet meeting and
preparing for the next. This habit of Adams became so well known that
his colleagues began to ask Adams to consult his diary when memo-
ries or other documents failed. As president, he avoided putting his
decision-making process down on paper yet amply documented the
force field that froze him by recording his conversations with visitor
after visitor to the White House, with no end or answers in sight.
Afterward, the diary became a more active site of his vocational crisis,
as he transitioned from his first to second career—and from avoiding
to selectively embracing antislavery politics.

Even here, though, the diary makes it very clear that he always
abhorred not only proslavery but also antislavery positions that
rejected either the political process or a gradual approach. Although
his competing priorities may have sent him to different places on the
antislavery spectrum of belief and action in different contexts, as an
antislavery Northerner—and as a Whig—there were extremes on both

the antislavery and proslavery part of that spectrum to which he would never go. Given the place of slavery in the American political order as both an unavoidable and a highly politicized economic and diplomatic fact—as the elephant in the room that hardly any white people wished to notice—we might see Adams's diary as in part, and increasingly over time, an exercise in managing and working through the politics of slavery. Adams's transformation from seeing slavery as a political problem to be managed by wise, patriotic elites to thinking of it, and ultimately proclaiming it, as the root of American political evil was in significant measure developed, practiced, and performed in his diary. His most quotable pronouncements were as much desperate embraces of the political system he saw heading for apocalypse as they were the wailings of an antislavery conscience. Perhaps this explains why, unlike antislavery activists, he never testified to a conversion experience—nor can we find one in his diary. Only in far retrospect, nearing the very end, on October 31, 1846, did he conflate the stakes of his diary and his life with that of antislavery:

> If my intellectual powers had been such as have been sometimes committed by the Creator of man to single individuals of the species my diary would have been, next to the Holy Scriptures, the most precious and valuable book ever written by human hands, and I should have been one of the greatest benefactors of my Country and of mankind—I would, by the irresistible power of Genius, and the irrepressible energy of will and the favor of almighty God, have banished War and Slavery from the face of the earth forever—but the conceptive power of mind was not conferred upon me by my maker, and I have not improved the scanty portion of His gifts as I might and ought to have done. May I never cease to be grateful for the numberless blessings received through life at his hands—never repine at what he has denied—never murmur at the dispensations of Providence, and implore his forgiveness for all the errors and delinquencies of my life![10]

10. Diary of John Quincy Adams, MHS, October 31, 1846, http://www.masshist.org/ jqadiaries/php/doc?id=jqad46_83&year=1846&month=10&day=31&entry=entry &start=0.

This was John Quincy Adams's mindset in late 1846, but he would never have written anything like that in 1836, much less ten years earlier while president of the United States.

We should not see this as a failing or tragedy, even if Adams eventually did. Rather, it is an opportunity to understand the man and his times. The editors of this volume do not have as much invested in evaluating John Quincy Adams's character or championing or burying his reputation as his descendants or biographers have; we see value in, and draw on, both appreciative and skeptical approaches. We are part of a younger generation of scholars who are trying to find a middle ground between segregating slavery from the rest of US history and reducing everything to it. Figures like John Quincy Adams who struggled with the politics of slavery attract us because in their experiences and actions we might be able to discern how and why slavery became politicized and depoliticized and politicized again. We have used terms like "shifting," "complex," and "tangled" in trying to convey the nature of slavery's politics: how the history of slavery and antislavery cannot be separated from a range of issues politicians and citizens grappled with between the Revolution and the Civil War.[11] Though we have elsewhere tried to analyze these phenomena and tell the story more accurately, we also strongly believe that sometimes the best approach is to present the evidence—especially when the nature, extent, and eloquence of the evidence is part of the phenomenon we are trying to understand.

We also think that the search for heroes and villains in the past, for a too-easy resolution to the problem of the relation of slavery to the origins of the United States (which is sometimes engaged in even by those who excoriate others for the same sins), can be combatted by making the evidence more accessible. In this we have been inspired by path-breaking documentary histories that helped to open up the

11. Matthew Mason, "John Quincy Adams and the Tangled Politics of Slavery," in Waldstreicher, ed., *A Companion to John Adams and John Quincy Adams*, 402–21; Mason, *Slavery and Politics in the Early American Republic* (Chapel Hill: University of North Carolina Press, 2008); John Craig Hammond and Matthew Mason, eds., *Contesting Slavery: The Politics of Bondage in the New American Nation* (Charlottesville: University Press of Virginia, 2011); David Waldstreicher, *Runaway America: Benjamin Franklin, Slavery, and the American Revolution* (New York: Hill & Wang, 2004); Waldstreicher, *Slavery's Constitution* (New York: Hill & Wang, 2009).

conversation about the histories of antislavery and the fate of slavery in the Civil War.[12] Although at one point we imagined that we could present between two covers everything in the John Quincy Adams diary pertaining to the politics of slavery, the more than three hundred thousand words we identified (if one included the complete entry each time slavery-related issues appear) makes that neither desirable nor possible. So instead we have sought to provide key and representative passages, including many not in earlier published editions, with contextualizing and narrative bridges, in the hope that this volume can work as both a primary source and a narrative history of an enigmatic yet indispensable leader and his encounter with a central fact of American life and politics.

Several key themes emerged from our study of the diary as central to understanding Adams's relationship to the politics of slavery. These might be grouped under the larger rubrics of the Adams family legacy, his nationalism, his internationalism, and finally his development of an antislavery voice compatible with each of these overlapping aspects of his politics and identity. As with most American politicians, competing priorities, far more than ideological certainties, shaped his actions and words with regard to slavery.[13]

There has always been a tendency to explain Adams's eventual antislavery politics as simply the result of his having been an Adams. Even his grandson Henry Adams, a master ironist who avoided writing about John Quincy directly, indulged this genetic fallacy in his own memoir, describing antislavery as an inborn trait of his mother's family.[14] But the family legacy could mean much more. John Quincy Adams felt a great deal of pressure from his parents to succeed as a statesman. "You come into life with advantages which will disgrace you if your

12. See especially David Brion Davis, ed., *The Fear of Conspiracy: Images of Un-American Subversion from the Revolution to the Present* (Ithaca, NY: Cornell University Press, 1971); Willie Lee Rose, ed., *A Documentary History of Slavery in North America* (New York: Oxford University Press, 1976); Davis, ed., *Antebellum American Culture* (Lexington, MA: Heath, 1979); Ira Berlin et al., eds., *Free at Last: A Documentary History of Slavery, Freedom, and the Civil War* (New York: New Press, 1997).
13. A classic formulation to this effect is David M. Potter, *The Impending Crisis, 1848-1861* (New York: Harper Torchbooks, 1976), 43–45.
14. Henry Adams, *The Education of Henry Adams* (Boston, 1918), 25, cited in Levin, *Remarkable Education*, 61.

success is mediocre," exhorted father John. "And if you do not rise to the head of ... your country, it will be owing to your own Lasiness, Slovenliness, and Obstinacy." As historian Joseph J. Ellis has pointed out, "John Quincy spent his entire childhood hearing that anything less than the highest office in the land would be regarded as failure."[15] He also understood from early on that national statesmanship meant working with Southerners—a fact he could have observed as early as his father's service in the Continental Congress. Recent tendencies to depict John Adams as the great antislavery founding father in contrast to Thomas Jefferson notwithstanding, antislavery politics played little to no role in the first Adams presidency. Indeed, John Adams repeatedly deferred to Southern colleagues on slavery-related questions, despite his famous confidence in his own opinions. His son's diary suggests to us that for most of his life, the Adams family legacy, including its outsized yet in some ways realistic ambitions, added up to both private antislavery beliefs and public silence on the issue. Ambition and the example of his family seem to us to be important and underacknowledged factors in explaining the *lack* of engagement with the politics of slavery that Adams showed even as the issue heated up after 1800.

In a very real sense John Quincy Adams was the first American born into a national leadership class. To him, being national meant, among other things, not being sectional—a notion he makes explicit in the diary much earlier than he expounds on his objections to proslavery politics. His early political training as a diplomat—a specialist in geopolitical negotiation—may have reinforced his inclination to seek or expect sectional interests to be brokered, especially in the service of establishing the future of the nation. His distaste for political partisanship, and his belief in educated leaders standing above selfish particular interests, reinforced his association of political sections with political parties. When Massachusetts Federalists did turn, during Jefferson's administration, to a sectional brand of antislavery partisan politics, he was appalled, and he broke with the party even though he had participated—mostly anonymously, in the press—in developing some of their arguments against the Slave Power in 1802–3.

15. Joseph J. Ellis, *First Family: Abigail and John Adams* (New York: Knopf, 2010), 44, 92–93, 129, 242.

The uncomfortable truth that stymies fans and biographers is that John Quincy Adams's nationalism trumped any inclination he had toward antislavery politics as it actually existed. This remained the case for not just the beginning but rather for most of his political career, including his presidency. Historians have been quick to judge negatively Adams's nonpartisanship as president as a recipe for political failure. They rarely acknowledge that his transfer to the National Republican coalition two decades earlier, which is sometimes described as courageous dissent and conflated with his later maverick stand against proslavery Southerners, was the essential precondition for his triumphs as secretary of state and his rise to the presidency. It all relied upon the cooperation of Southerners. In other words, if he had been less politically astute, he might not have appreciated so well how much his nation-building policy agendas depended on Southern support. Later, Southern fears of Adams's supposed antislavery biases and Democratic partisan use of them became a structural problem of his presidency, despite his strenuous efforts to avoid the issue.[16]

Adams is rightly appreciated as a founder of an American style of foreign policy: a wary engagement with the world predicated on a sense of the United States as a young, expanding nation. His nationalism, of course, made him loath to see the United States as another colonizing or slave-driving nation, but some maintain that his exceptionalist statements provided a handy, even idealistic, cover for imperialism. Most recently, grand strategy historian Charles N. Edel has argued that Adams's late antislavery drew from his sense of the importance of the United States as a potential world leader—as an exemplar of international benevolence.[17] Yet during the years up to and including his tenure

16. Robert P. Forbes, *The Missouri Compromise and Its Aftermath: Slavery and the Meaning of America* (Chapel Hill: University of North Carolina Press, 2007), 9, 141, 186–87, 190–93; Samuel Flagg Bemis, *John Quincy Adams and the Union* (New York: Knopf, 1956), 26–27.
17. Compare Bemis, *John Quincy Adams and the Foundations of American Foreign Policy,* and Bemis, *John Quincy Adams and the Union*; William Earl Weeks, *John Quincy Adams and American Global Empire* (Lexington: University Press of Kentucky, 1992); James E. Lewis Jr., *John Quincy Adams: Policymaker for the Union* (Wilmington, DE: Scholarly Resources, 2001); Gretchen Murphy, *Hemispheric Imaginings: The Monroe Doctrine and Narratives of U.S. Empire* (Durham, NC: Duke University Press, 2005), 32–48; Richard H. Immerman, *Empire for Liberty: A History of*

as secretary of state, Adams resisted British initiatives against the international slave trade, and he vigorously pushed demands for reparations for slaves liberated during the War of 1812.[18] It would not be too much to say that he brought ample skills and energy to these tasks, as much as he brought to the Treaty of Ghent, the Transcontinental Treaty, or the Monroe Doctrine, and that the geopolitics of the slave trade were actually part of those "foundations of American foreign policy." His folding of slave trade suppression issues into the impressment of seamen controversy reflected both a desire to defend the United States from those who questioned its republican self-image in light of slavery and a particularly sensitive understanding of how slavery-related questions raised fundamental issues of sovereignty on which it would be perilous to compromise. In other words, John Quincy Adams's sense of how slavery-related issues implicated US foreign and domestic policy played a major role in his disinclination to support antislavery politics at home. There were career issues to be sure, but also much more than that.

In the end, it was partly through reinterpreting US foreign policy and its relation to domestic policy in the age of Jackson—as a decidedly proslavery expansionism that Jacksonians saw as continuity, not change—that he was able to fashion his influential antislavery nationalist politics after 1836. Finding an antislavery voice, for Adams, required him to be out of the White House and out of diplomacy. It may also

American Imperialism from Benjamin Franklin to Paul Wolfowitz (Princeton, NJ: Princeton University Press, 2010), 59–97; John Belohlavek, "John Quincy Adams, Diplomacy, and American Empire," in Waldstreicher, ed., *A Companion to John Adams and John Quincy Adams*, 281–304; Charles N. Edel, *Nation-Builder: John Quincy Adams and the Grand Strategy of the Republic* (Cambridge, MA: Harvard University Press, 2014); Andrew Bacevich, "In Search of Adams," *National Interest* (November–December 2014), 86–91. For Adams as an honest cosmopolitan and internationalist, see Bethel Saler, "John Quincy Adams, Cosmopolitan," in Waldstreicher, ed., *Companion*, 383–401; for the importance of union in the context of slavery, and an argument that the context changed more than Adams had, see David F. Ericson, "John Quincy Adams, Apostle of Union," in Waldstreicher, ed., *Companion*, 366–82.

18. For the background and Adams's role, see Matthew Mason, "The Battle of the Slaveholding Liberators: Great Britain, the United States, and Slavery in the Early Nineteenth Century," *William and Mary Quarterly* 3rd Ser. 59 (2002), 665–96; Mason, "Keeping Up Appearances: The International Politics of Slave Trade Abolition in the Nineteenth-Century Atlantic World," *William and Mary Quarterly*, 3rd Ser. 66 (2009), 809–32.

have required the forum of Congress. His conception of the role of the representative in a deliberative body also helped: a longtime student and fan of Cicero, he could play the scold and still be the patriot, especially as he himself carried so much institutional memory about what the American Revolution was supposed to mean, and what the federal government and its branches could and could not do.

The process by which Adams finally developed an antislavery political voice can be seen as a glass half empty and half full. On the one hand, it took an awfully long time. Far from an inevitable outgrowth of his beliefs, it was highly contingent upon his changing political roles, relationships, goals, and events far beyond his control. On the other hand, it was precisely because Adams had been around national politics for so long, carried the revolutionary nationalist tradition, and had worked within but fallen victim to the proslavery drift of the US government that he was in a position to contribute so forcefully to a new phase of antislavery politics.[19]

19. For an elaboration of this argument, see David Waldstreicher, "A Funny Thing Happened on the Way to the Amistad: John Quincy Adams, the Shutdown, and the Restart of Antislavery Politics, 1787-1836," in James Oakes and John Stauffer, eds., *The Antislavery Bulwark* (forthcoming).

A NOTE ON THE TEXT AND
EDITORIAL METHOD

THIS EDITION CONSISTS of a selection of John Quincy Adams's diary entries that deal directly or indirectly with slavery and the issues slavery raised in the early United States. We identified more than three hundred thousand words that fit this rubric, if one included all the words in each entry that would qualify as having some content related to slavery or the politics of slavery. To keep the text readable, we have chosen representative entries and have taken out some portions of entries that did not add context or important detail. When these deletions occur within an included passage, they are indicated by ellipses in the text. We have summarized and sometimes quoted from many other relevant diary entries in the headnotes and the introductions to each chapter. In all, we have sought to create an accessible yet comprehensive narrative of John Quincy Adams's engagement with the politics of slavery, using as much as possible his own words but also providing contextual information necessary to understand each individual diary entry.

The text is based mainly on Charles Francis Adams, ed., *Memoirs of John Quincy Adams, Comprising Portions of his Diary from 1975 to 1848*, 12 vols. (Philadelphia: J. D. Lippincott, 1874–77), and David Grayson Allen et al., eds., *Diary of John Quincy Adams*, 2 vols. (Cambridge, MA: Harvard University Press, 1981), which covers the years 1779 to 1788. We also consulted the diary manuscripts at the Massachusetts Historical Society, *The Diaries of John Quincy Adams: A Digital*

Collection, http://www.masshist.org/jqadiaries/php/, to find entries pertaining to the politics of slavery that Charles Francis Adams did not include, or which he edited.

Where we did decide to include such entries from the manuscript diary that have never been published, we retained the exact style of the manuscript diaries as much as possible; but for others we retain the style of the more readable 1874–77 edition of the *Memoirs*. Readers should be aware, however, that in addition to selecting entries and portions of entries for his twelve-volume edition, Charles Francis Adams did make corrections for style according to the norms of his era, including adding paragraph breaks and punctuation (he often substituted commas and periods for John Quincy Adams's frequent use of semicolons and dashes).

For versions of some of the entries here that reproduce the manuscript diary's orthography as much as possible, see the Library of America edition of *The Diaries of John Quincy Adams, 1779-1848*, 2 vols., ed. David Waldstreicher, forthcoming in 2017. Rather than focus on the question of slavery, that edition selects representative diary entries for their overall literary, historical, and biographical interest.

JOHN QUINCY ADAMS
AND THE POLITICS
OF SLAVERY

I

Rising Son of the Young Republic (1785–1809)

John Quincy Adams began his diary on November 12, 1779, while waiting to board a frigate for Europe. He accompanied, already for the second time, his father, John Adams, on a diplomatic mission to France. Keeping a diary had been his father's idea, but travelers often kept journals to pass the time and as an aid to memory. He began to write longer entries by 1785.

The first mention of American slavery in the diary recounts a conversation with Thomas Jefferson, one of the other American ministers in Paris. Jefferson had recently finished a version of his Notes on the State of Virginia, *a work of natural history in the form of responses to queries from a French ambassador to governors of the new states. Over the course of several chapters, Jefferson both criticized and defended African slavery. Two years later, upon publication of a small English edition of the* Notes *that Jefferson sent only to selected friends, Adams wrote that he "was very much pleased with them. There is a great deal of learning shown without ostentation, and a spirit of philosophy equally instructive and entertaining."[1]*

1. Diary, May 30, 1787; Thomas Jefferson, *Notes on the State of Virginia with Related Documents*, ed. David Waldstreicher (Boston: Bedford Books, 2002).

May 4, 1785—Mr. Jefferson, spoke concerning Virginia, a State, which he knows very particularly as it is his native Country. The blacks, he tells me, are very well treated there; and increase in population, more in proportion, than the whites. Before the War, he says the negroes, were to the whites, in the proportion of 3 to 4. Now they are as 10 to 11, which is a very material difference. He supposes about 500,000 souls in the State. He disapproves very much the Cultivation of Tobacco, and wishes, it may be laid entirely aside. He thinks wheat would be much more advantageous, and profitable, much less Laborious, and less hurtful to the ground: he is a man of great Judgment.

While Adams missed much of the glory, hardship, and turmoil of the Revolutionary War in the States, his time in Europe heightened his sense of national identity. He endorsed the notion of the United States as the fulfillment of Western traditions of freedom in a "slavish" world, despite the ubiquity of slavery for Africans. Sailing back to America on the Fourth of July, he turned the diary into a vehicle of celebration, adapting (with no sense of contradiction) some lines of the popular British patriotic poet James Thomson.

July 4, 1785—We still esteem ourselves 50 leagues East of the Bermudas. I wish'd very much to arrive in America before this day, which is the greatest day in the year, for every true American. The anniversary of our Independence. May heaven preserve it: and may the world still see

> A State where liberty shall still survive
> In these late times, this evening of mankind
> When Athens, Rome and Carthage are no more
> The world almost in slavish sloth dissolv'd.

After his return to the United States, John Quincy Adams enrolled in Harvard College. His distinctively political and diplomatic manner of analyzing human relations is apparent in this reflection on a town-gown dustup. If he believed that it is natural for members of a "well-ordered Republic" to unite when attacked by outsiders, he likely would have applied such thinking to the criticisms of American slavery that representatives of the new republic had faced in France.

April 3, 1786—This evening, there were it is said upwards of 100 Scholars out on the common, armed with Clubs, to fight the People, belonging to the Town. A few evenings since, Lovell, a junior, got quarreling with a man belonging to the Town, about a girl, two or three juniors being present took Lovell's part, and a few blows were dealt on both sides, Lovell, has told his story just as he pleased; and has raised almost all college; for this Society like most others thinks an insult offered to one member, must be resented by all, and as in a well ordered Republic, although, some of the Classes, have of late, been so much at Variance, yet immediately upon a foreign insult they all United. The only thing wanting, to make the scholars highly praise-worthy in this case, is a good Cause. It appears plainly that the first insult was from Lovell, and the original Cause of the quarrel an infamous girl. There would probably some very severe blows have past had not the Tutors and Professor Williams, interposed, this Evening. They perswaded both Parties to disperse; but this will perhaps be only a Suspension of arms: I doubt whether the matter will end here.

Adams participated in a debate about "Whether immortality of the human Soul be probable from natural Reason" and copied his prepared response into the diary. He happily took "the affirmative" and used slaves' beliefs in their freedom after death as a supporting example—but located the Africans rather safely in the West Indies rather than the United States.

May 16, 1786—That there is in Man, an interior Power, far different, and vastly superior, to that possess'd by any other being, of the animal Creation, no one I believe will deny to be highly probable from natural Reason. Indeed, it is so obvious, and there are such continual proofs of it, that all Nations seem to consider it as a moral certainty, rather than probability. Our bodies we have in common, with every other being of the animal Creation, and like them we are subjected to pain, disorders, and to final dissolution by Death. It is therefore natural to Conclude, that the faculty, which we alone possess, and which raises the vast distinction between man, and all other animals, is totally independent of the body; and if so, I know not of one reason, why we should suppose it began with the body, or that it will end with it. The Soul it is true, while it is in Connection, with the Body, has no natural proof of its own immortality. But the supreme Being, in all whose works, an infinite wisdom, is display'd, when he saw that it was best to leave the Soul, thus in Suspense, at the same time has made, all its hopes, all its desires to centre in immortality. We know of no animal in the Creation (man excepted) that has if I may so express myself an Idea of Immortality; man himself neither expects nor wishes, that his body might remain forever; there are indeed frequent instances of his being so weary of it, as to become himself, the willing instrument of its destruction. But, is there a man in Nature, who if he had it in his power, would annihilate his own Soul, unless a consciousness of its crimes, had joined the idea of eternal damnation, to that of eternal existence. For what Reason, can we suppose this abhorrence of a dissolution, and this fond desire for immortality has been implanted in the Soul, if there is no foundation for them?

Perhaps some one may say; if a man had nothing but natural Reason, to assist him in this Enquiry, he would not know, where to draw the line of distinction. There is perhaps a complete gradation of genius from a Newton, to the meanest insect in Creation; where than shall, we stop, or shall we also, grant immortality to the beasts? I answer, that I see not the necessity of this although I confess it will be difficult to distinguish aright. But would it not equally puzzle, the most skillful geometrician, to ascertain the limits between an angle, and a right Line. For although we can make an Angle, verging as near as we please, to a right line, yet a right Line never can be an angle. No two things can be more distinct, than these, yet no one knows where one begins, or where the other ends.

But the most convincing proof of the probability, natural Reason affords, that the human Soul is immortal, is the opinion, of those nations, which having never been favoured with the blessings of a divine Revelation, could have no other standard. The Greeks and Romans, undoubtedly, generally believed in the Soul's immortality; almost all the authors extant in these two Languages, are fully perswaded of it. It may be said, that the opinion of the whole Nation, and that the greatest parts of the Greeks, and Romans, might believe the contrary. Supposing this to be the Case, must we not confess, that men whose Reason was enlightened, and cultivated, were more proper judges of what is probable, than the common herd of mankind, who derive but little advantage, from the Soul, that is given them. But these men, were universally admired; their writings were sought for with the utmost eagerness. Homer and Virgil were considered as Oracles, and in many Places, they went so far even as to deify the Greek Poet. They do not raise a doubt concerning the immortality of the Soul: one book of the Odyssey, and one of the AEneid, are founded entirely upon this belief: there is no reason to think, that, when their Countrymen, consulted those Poems as Oracles, they excluded the 11th book of the Odyssey, or the 6th of the AEneid.

But this perswasion of an eternal future State, is not confined to the Greeks, and Romans: if we look among Nations where Reason had made, but little progress, we shall still find the same belief. The northern parts of Europe, were unknown to the Greeks, and to the Romans in the days of their Republic; they has a System of Religion, and gods peculiar to themselves. As they were continually at War, their delight was, to slaughter their fellow creatures, and they believed that after death, their Souls would enjoy an eternal happiness, in drinking the blood of their enemies, from their skulls. Even at this Day, in the west India islands, the enslaved African, bending under the weight of oppression, and scourged by the rod of tyranny, sighs for the Day, when Death, shall put a period to his woes, and his Soul again return to be happy in his native Country.

But to mention all the Nations that believe in the Soul's immortality from natural Reason, would be to enumerate, almost every People, that is or has been known on Earth. Happy the People, who confirm this Opinion, have been favoured, with a Revelation from above.

During the summer, Adams wrote a reflection on Shakespeare's Othello *to be recited at a meeting of a club. He had been reading Shakespeare regularly since he was fifteen, and this was the first of a series of critical writings on this play in particular, centering on the use of a dark-skinned man for the tragic hero (and love interest), all of which culminated in an article he published in a magazine a half century later.*[2]

2. See Diary, August 13, 1796; John Quincy Adams, "The Character of Desdemona," *American Monthly Magazine* (March 1836), 209–17; Fred Kaplan, *John Quincy Adams: American Visionary* (New York: Harper, 2014), 480–82.

August 28, 1786—This Play is by many considered as the most perfect of all, that we owe to the immortal Shakespeare, and if we attend merely to the conduct of it, we may readily confess that few dramatic performances are better; but the very foundation upon which the whole fabric is erected appears injudicious, disgusting, and contrary to all probability. Who can believe that the Senate of Venice, would give the government of an island belonging to the State, to a moor, when it is known how constantly the Venitian nobility have always enjoy'd every employment in the State? And how tenacious they have ever been of this Prerogative? And is it natural that a young Lady so virtuous and Chaste as Desdemona is represented would as Brabantio expresses it,

> Run from her guardage to the sooty Bosom
> Of such a thing as him, to fear, not to delight.

In short, I never could conceive what induced the Poet to take a negro for an example of Jealousy. But from this defect great beauties are derived.

After his graduation, Adams read law in the office of Theophilus Parsons. That location encouraged participation in the exciting debates over the new federal constitution: Parsons served as a delegate to the Massachusetts ratifying convention. In his Harvard commencement address published in the new Columbian Magazine, *John Quincy had argued that the failure of "national credit," the foundation of "national grandeur," constituted a "critical period" in the new nation's history—thus coining the term historians still use to describe the 1780s. Economic distress in Massachusetts could ultimately be understood as the "erosion of the bands of union which connected us to our sister states, [which] have been shamefully relaxed by a selfish and contracted principle," an unwillingness to pay taxes to retire the Revolutionary War debt. Localism was the problem, thinking bigger the solution. When Massachusetts folk abided by their agreements, the "radiant sun of our union" would not only reappear but also begin again to protect "the wretched object of tyranny and persecution in every corner of the globe." This was a call to republican virtue, to be sure, but one that deliberately*

emphasized national union over the rather specific events in Massachusetts
that summer of Shays's Rebellion.[3]

Nevertheless, he had doubts as to whether the proposed new national gov-
ernment would represent an advance or a retreat from liberty, and he recorded
his impressions several times in his diary. The provisions of the constitution
that favored slavery became controversial in Massachusetts and were brought
up repeatedly by Antifederalists, but Adams did not mention them as one of
his objections.

October 12, 1787—The day pass'd as usual, except that I had some political chat with Mr. Parsons. He favours very much the federal constitution, which has lately been proposed by the Convention of the States.
Nor do I wonder at all that he should approve of it, as it is calculated to
increase the influence, power and wealth of those who have any already.
If the Constitution be adopted it will be a grand point gained in favour
of the aristocratic party: there are to be no titles of nobility; but there will
soon be great distinctions; and those distinctions will soon be hereditary,
and we shall consequently have nobles, but no titles. For my own part,
I am willing to take my chance under any government whatever, but it is
hard to give up a System which I have always been taught to cherish, and
to confess, that a free government is inconsistent with human nature.

October 29, 1787—I went and spent the evening with Dr. Killiam
at his lodgings: he has made himself rather unpopular, by opposing
the submission of the federal Constitution, to a State Convention,
and I think he is perfectly right, in preferring his independency to his
popularity.

When word arrived that the Massachusetts convention had ratified the
Constitution, Adams's response to the majority's decision, and the demonstra-
tive celebrations of ratification that did so much to convey the sense that the
Constitution had the approval of the people, suggests his mixed feelings about

3. John Quincy Adams, "An Oration, Delievered at the Public Commencement in the
   University of Cambridge, in New England," *Columbian Magazine* 1 (Sept. 1787),
   625–28.

democracy. He did not mention the Constitution's protections for slavery, which had been controversial at the Massachusetts convention and in the press.

February 7, 1788—In this town the Satisfaction is almost universal: for my own part, I have not been pleased with this System, and my acquaintance, have long-since branded me with the name of an *antifederalist*. But I am now converted, though not convinced. My feelings upon the occasion have not been passionate nor violent, and as upon the decision of this question I find myself on the weaker side, I think it is my duty to submit without murmuring against what is not to be helped. In our Government, opposition to the acts of a majority of the people is rebellion to all intents and purposes; and I should view a man who would now endeavour to excite commotions against this plan, as no better than an insurgent who took arms last winter against the Courts of Justice.

February 8, 1788—This afternoon the delegates from Newbury, and from this town, returned home from the Convention. A number of respectable citizens, and a number, who were not very respectable, went out on horse-back to meet the members and escort them into Town; as they came along, the bells at the different churches were set to ringing, and this noisy expression of joy, was continued with some intermissions till 8 o'clock in the evening. The mob huzza'd and one would have thought that every man from the adoption of the Constitution had acquired, a sure expectancy of an independent fortune.

During the next spring term at Harvard, shortly before his graduation, Adams attended an oratorical exhibition at Harvard and was intrigued by a speech against the slave trade.

April 15, 1788—[Benjamin] Abbot closed with an English Oration, upon the slave-trade. The Composition was very good, and it was well-spoken, though, the natural disadvantage of a weak voice, injured the effect of his delivery. I do not recollect having heard any performances upon this subject, at College, and it will afford a fruitful source for declamation.

After a gap of several years, Adams resumed writing extensive diary entries on June 3, 1794, after he had been appointed by President Washington as minister to The Hague. Adams had impressed the president and his supporters with several series of newspaper essays supporting the administration's foreign policy. Yet he worried that his appointment at a young age (twenty-six) would be seen as nepotism or even another example of the creeping aristocracy that the emerging opposition party complained about, given the fact that his father served as vice president.

The voyage to Europe was especially rocky. Worse than the "tumbling and pitching" of the boat for Adams, though, was the sight of the ship's cook, a "black Fellow" he called an "animal" and thanked, sarcastically, for the fact that he had not overeaten during the ship's passage.[4]

Adams was in London when John Jay and his colleagues concluded negotiations for what became known as the Jay Treaty. He agreed with the negotiators that while the treaty could have been better for the Americans, it was still far better than another war. He listed among the benefits of the treaty "the commerce with their West India islands, partially opened to us," which would compensate "for the negroes carried away contrary to the engagement of the Treaty [of Paris in 1783]."[5] *Historians estimate that at least twenty thousand slaves were liberated by British forces during the war, and many had boarded British ships at the end of the war, contrary to the treaty.*

During these years Adams often found opportunities to test his ideas about government and liberty in conversations with fellow diplomats and other well-read foreigners. In March 1795, he recorded a conversation with Baron de Bielfeld, also the son of a famous diplomat and currently the minister from Prussia.

March 12, 1795—Mr. Bielfeld called on me this morning, and I took a walk with him round the town. Conversation with him upon a variety of subjects, principally political speculation. We talked much of the rights of man, the origin and foundation of human society, and the proper principles of Government. He says that in his opinion no consideration whatever can in any case justify a violation of truth. I told

4. Diary, October 14, 1794.
5. Diary, October 22, 1794.

him that such a sentiment was rather extraordinary coming from a diplomatic man. He declared his determination never to depart from it. We discussed the theory of human rights and of Government. We soon concluded that aristocracy, feudality, nobility, could not be reconciled with a Government founded upon *rights*. But whether man is so constructed as to be capable of living in society upon any plan of government clearly deducible from a theory of rights was then a question, which we debated until we found our walk at an end.

In late 1795, after the ratification of the Jay Treaty, Adams returned to London on an assignment to formally exchange the signed treaty documents while the American minister to Britain, Charles Pinckney, was in Madrid negotiating a treaty with Spain. In an interview with George Hammond, the British undersecretary for foreign affairs, he found himself on the defensive—and perhaps getting a lesson in the subtleties of diplomacy. He was particularly concerned with Hammond's attempts to probe American sectional conflict. Adams may have been increasingly sensitive to this issue because of Southern opposition to the Jay Treaty, which seemed to favor Northern and urban mercantile interests and did not secure payment for or the return of slaves taken during the Revolutionary War. At the time John Quincy had another reason to be particularly attuned to sectional differences in perception and reality. He was courting Louisa Catherine Johnson, the daughter of a Maryland tobacco merchant, for whom he had facilitated consignments of tobacco. Not long afterward he wrote to his parents of his plan to settle in the Southern states, probably on Georgia lands owned by Joshua Johnson. This plan never materialized, perhaps due to Johnson's bankruptcy soon after Louisa Catherine and John Quincy married in July 1797.

December 1, 1795—Called on Mr. Hammond at noon, as by appointment, and had considerable conversation with him. But his tone with me begins already to be different from what it was at first. His conversation was still such as if he thought my personal feelings or sentiments upon political subjects would have a tendency to make me complaisant. Asked if I had heard anything of the President's intending to resign. Told him no. He said he had heard such was his determination at the expiration of his present term, in case there should be no troubles in the country. What sort of a soul does this man suppose I have? He talked about the Virginians, the Southern People, the democrats; but I let him know that I consider them all in no other light than as Americans. They never shall be considered by me in any other light in treating with foreigners. He spoke again of Mr. Randolph's resignation. I told him I had seen an account from which, if true, it appeared clearly that there was nothing like bribery in the case. He said that the President, Mr. Wolcott, Mr. Pickering, and Mr. Bradford were all fully convinced that Randolph was guilty. I replied that, not having seen the papers, I could not be a competent judge of the facts; that the public officers he mentioned might think there had been improper conduct without believing there was any corruption. He said he had not the smallest doubt but Randolph was bribed by the French; and added, he had better be quiet on that score; for if he presumed to deny it, other proof, amounting to demonstration, would be produced. He said he would show me the next time I should see him the intercepted dispatches of Fauchet. But he promised me the same thing once before, and I question whether he means I shall see them. He says they abuse all the federalists very much, particularly my father (another address to my feelings, fruitless like all the rest); that they speak highly of Mifflin, Dallas, Jefferson, Madison, and Giles; of Randolph and Monroe. "Perhaps," said I, "this was because he thought those persons not much your friends." "Ah," said he, "but they are your enemies more than they are ours." "No, indeed," said I, "they are not in my opinion our enemies." "Yes, they hate us," said he, "because they owe us money, and they hate you because you will not let them owe you money." "Why, they do not owe you much money now; that matter is in a great measure settled already. The old debts are principally discharged; and as to all recent ones, we pay your people to admiration. Indeed, we are the best customers you have. What an immense quantity of your manufactures we take! You swallow up almost all the balance of trade in our favor that we get from every other quarter, and your trade with us supplies you principally with the means of supporting your war." "But we are the best customers you have, too. We take more articles of yours than anybody else does." "Ay, but in no proportion to what you sell us, and the balance in your favor is prodigious." "True, there is a balance, to be sure; but as to the old debts, you are mistaken in supposing them small. When that Commission comes to sit, you will find they amount to three or four millions sterling." "Well, the Commission will see; but I have no idea that the amount will be comparable to the sum you suggest."

This conversation was far from pleasant to him. At least it was very different from what he was doubtless disposed that I should hold.

He came at last to a language not less intelligible, but rather more of unqualified acid. "Well," said he, "Congress is to meet next Monday; and if they do not pass such laws as will be necessary to give effect to the Treaty, *we shall be all at sea again.* And I hear that the *Anti-federalists* threaten very high." This perpetual allusion to an American party, and affectation of an idea that our sense of injuries from this country is confined to that party alone, at length gave me an opportunity to touch another string. "Why," said I, "all Governments have their opposition, who find fault with every thing. Who has better reason to know that than you have in this country? But in America, you know, opposition speaks in a louder voice than anywhere else. Every thing comes out. We have no lurking disaffection that works in secret and is not seen; nothing that rankles at the heart while the face wears a smile. So that a very trifling opposition naturally makes a great show."

After the signing of the Jay Treaty, relations between France and the United States soured: now the French perceived US neutrality as aid to their enemy, much as Great Britain had earlier. The Adams administration made controversial war preparations but made peace with the French in 1799, much to the frustration of some Federalists. Between 1797 and 1801, Adams served as US minister to Prussia and as such avoided taking public stands on controversial issues during the Quasi War and the election of 1800. Watching US politics from his post in Berlin during his father's presidency, Adams remained aloof from the Anglophile and Francophile extremes in US politics and shared his father's pride in avoiding war with France: "You were not the man of any party, but of the whole nation," he wrote, in a turn of phrase that would become his mantra.[6]

6. John Quincy Adams to John Adams, November 25, 1800, in Worthington Chauncey Ford, ed., *Writings of John Quincy Adams* (New York: Macmillan, 1913–17), II, 271 (hereafter *WJQA*).

Yet in letters to a Federalist friend he complained about the enthusiasm of Southern "negro-keepers" for the French Revolution. News of Gabriel's Rebellion spurred him to write to his brother that "those absurd principles of unlimited democracy which the people of the Southern states . . . encouraged, are producing their natural fruits, and if the planters have not discovered the inconsistency of holding in one hand the rights of man and in the other a scourge for the back of slaves, their negroes have proven themselves better logicians than their masters." Nevertheless, he maintained that he hoped the "dreaded catastrophe" of Haiti would not recur: the eastern states should help put down any slave rebellion. While he imagined a black Haiti itself in a possible alliance with the United States, as indeed a kind of proof of the new dispensation—a postcolonial new world beyond "metropolis and colony, or in other words master and servant"—he saw Caribbean revolt in terms of its implications for American independence, not the future of African slavery. Slave revolt was most interesting insofar as it became another way to convince Southerners of the error of their political ways, though he believed that nothing short of actual insurrection would force "democratisers of the Old Dominion" to "feel their need of assistance from their sister states, nor the importance of the Union to them." He saw the need to "look coolly" at the possibility that the federal union might not last, though he did not think that Jefferson had disunion in mind. He scolded his brother Thomas, for example, for an article that sneered at Washington, DC's Southern sensibilities.[7]

After he returned to Boston in July 1801, Adams worked as a lawyer, but he found himself bored. He expressed interest in several political offices. "I feel strong temptation and have great provocation to plunge into political controversy," he wrote in his diary. "But I hope to preserve myself from it by the considerations which have led me to the resolution of renouncing. A politician in this country must be the man of a party. I would fain be the man of my whole country." Elected to the Massachusetts House of Representatives, he participated enthusiastically in the New England Federalists' nostalgia for better days, expressed most compellingly in the Boston Port-Folio, *where he published anonymously a parody of Thomas Jefferson's relationship with his slave Sally Hemings and his alleged paternity of her children.*

7. John Quincy Adams to William Vans Murray, March 20, July 14, August 14, 1798, to Thomas Boylston Adams, July 11, November 25, December 3, 1800, to William Vans Murray, December 16, 1800, April 7, 1801, *WJQA* II, 271, 349–50, 386, 398, 485-6n, 525–26.

Dear Thomas, deem it no disgrace
With slaves to mend thy breed,
Nor let the wench's smutty face
Deter thee from thy deed.

Prefaced by a quote from Notes on the State of Virginia *about a young country and its* "generative force of nature," *this Horatian ode mocked Jefferson
as a would-be emperor whose inflated sense of self-worth, like Nero, allowed
him to break his own rules ("Vice turns to virtue at his Nod").*[8]

*Soon after the Massachusetts House sent Adams to the US Senate, how-
ever, he identified against parties as much as with the Federalist Party. His
now-annual New Year's reflection at the end of 1803 associated his long-term
prospects and reputation with avoiding the extremes of partisanship.*

December 31, 1803—My election as a Senator of the United States, for
six years, has been the only important incident of my political career.
It has opened to me a scene in some sort though not altogether new,
and will probably affect very materially my future situation in life.
I have already had occasion to experience, what I had before the full-
est reason to expect, the *danger* of adhering to my own principles. The
country is so totally given up to the spirit of party, that not to follow
blindfold the one or the other is an inexpiable offence. The worst of
these parties has the popular torrent in its favor, and uses its triumph
with all the unprincipled fury of a faction; while the other gnashes
its teeth, and is waiting with all the impatience of revenge for the
time when its turn may come to oppress and punish by the people's
favor. Between both, I see the impossibility of pursuing the dictates
of my own conscience without sacrificing every prospect, not merely
of advancement, but even of retaining that character and reputation
I have enjoyed. Yet my choice is made, and, if I cannot hope to give
satisfaction to my country, I am at least determined to have the approbation of my own reflections.

8. Diary, January 28, 1802; John Quincy Adams to Rufus King, October 8, 1802,
   WJQA III, 7; "Original Poetry. For the Port Folio. Horace, Book II, Ode 4," *The
   Port-Folio* 2, no. 43 (October 30, 1802).

A major test of Adams's partisan and sectional identity occurred during the debates around the Louisiana Purchase and its ratification by treaty. Adams was the lone senator to vote both for admitting the territory and against limiting slavery there. Connecticut Federalist James Hillhouse offered amendments to the treaty calling for gradual emancipation, which failed by a vote of seventeen to eleven. According to Senator William Plumer, during the debates Adams said, "Slavery in a moral sense is an evil; but as connected with commerce, it has important uses. The regulations added to prevent slavery are insufficient." He also said that he did not think it was the place of Congress to change Louisiana's established institutions: "I am opposed to slavery but I have in this bill voted against the provisions introduced to prohibit and lessen it. I have done this upon two principles, 1. That I am opposed to legislating at all for that country. 2. I think we are proceeding with too much haste upon such an important question."[9]

January 24, 1804—The amendments to the Louisiana Government bill were taken up, and some progress made in them. Mr. Venable's amendment, to give them the beginning of a popular representation, failed for want of one vote. Yeas fourteen, nays fourteen. On the section prohibiting the slave trade, no question was taken. A letter from Governor Claiborne to the Secretary of State was received and read. It was sent with a *private* letter to the President of the Senate, which, however, Mr. Brown read. In the evening, the eleventh book of Raynal. It contains an account of the slave trade, and closes with the articles cultivated in the West Indies by slaves—cotton, coffee, sugar, and arnotto.

January 25, 1804—In Senate the debate continued all day upon the question of the admission of slaves into Louisiana. Mr. Hillhouse is to prepare a section to the same effect, but differently modified.

January 26, 1804—The section for prohibiting the admission of slaves from abroad into Louisiana was again debated all day. It was at last taken by yeas and nays—seventeen and six. The discussion of this question has developed characters. [James] Jackson [of Georgia] has opposed the section *totis viiibus*, in all its shapes, and was very angry when the question

9. Everett S. Brown, ed., *William Plumer's Memorandum of Proceedings in the United States Senate, 1803-1807* (New York, 1923), 119; Samuel Flagg Bemis, *John Quincy Adams and the Foundations of American Foreign Policy* (New York, 1949), 122.

was taken—called twice for an adjournment, in which they would not indulge him, and complained of unfairness. [Jonathan] Dayton [of New Jersey] has opposed the section throughout with equal vehemence, but happened to be absent when the question was taken. [Samuel] Smith, of Maryland, who has been all along extremely averse to the section, but afraid to avow it, complained bitterly that the yeas and nays were taken in quasi committee, instead of waiting to take them on the ultimate question in the Senate. But, finding his party on this point stiff to him as if he was in the minority, he left his seat, to avoid voting at all, in the yeas and nays. [Stephen Row] Bradley, of Vermont, after trying various expedients to give the slip to the real question, finally moved an amendment to prohibit the admission of slaves altogether, as well from the United States as from abroad. The object was to defeat the thing by its own excess, and made his abhorrence of all slavery the ground of his argument to oppose the partial prohibition. He therefore took the yeas and nays upon his own proposed amendment before they were taken on Mr. Hillhouse's section. The workings of this question upon the minds and hearts of these men opened them to observation as much as if they had had the window in the breast.

January 30, 1804—The Louisiana Government bill yet engrosses the attention of the Senate. The sections to secure the prohibition of the slave trade are still under discussion, and Mr. [John] Breckinridge [of Kentucky] has at length produced one which I suppose is to be the last. 'Tis to be printed for to-morrow.

January 31, 1804—The question upon striking out Mr. Hillhouse's proposed additional section to insert that of Mr. Breckinridge was debated *warmly*, until four o'clock; and passed finally against striking out—fifteen to thirteen. But the question on Mr. Hillhouse's proposition itself was not taken. Mr. Wright returned, after an absence of a month. In the evening we all attended at the ball given at Georgetown to celebrate the acquisition of Louisiana. It was very much crowded with company, but the arrangements and decorations were mean beyond any thing of the kind I ever saw.

Adams found himself newly in tune with an administration that seemed committed to both expansion and neutrality in order to best protect American interests and borders. He believed that a US senator should seek to represent the interests of the entire nation. While other New Englanders canvassed against Jefferson in the election of 1804, John Quincy Adams conferred at the White House about foreign affairs, explaining in letters to his father why his seeming apostasy made sense.

October 31, 1804—Paid visits to the President and Mr. Madison, both of whom I found at home. The President conversed with me respecting the impressments by the British frigates upon our coast, and respecting the trade carried on by some of the merchants with the blacks at St. Domingo. This he appears determined to suppress, and I presume a law will pass for the purpose at the approaching session.

Adams did not participate in efforts to limit or suppress the slave trade or slavery as a senator, with the exception of a probably unread draft speech, a set of resolutions, and an anonymous series of published essays spurred by the Ely amendment, a proposal to eliminate the three-fifths clause of the US Constitution (which made three-fifths of slaves count for representation and taxation). This proposal had originated in the Massachusetts state legislature. Adams tread carefully in trying to stake out a nationalist antislavery position and salvage his political base in Boston. As an electioneering piece that rakes New England Jeffersonians for kowtowing to Virginians, the "Publius Valerius" series is notable both for its structural analysis of slaveholders' political power in light of the three-fifths clause and its well-developed argument for constitutional adjustment in a permanent union. Adams did not try to argue his way out of the implications of the Louisiana Purchase, which he was known to have supported. New England's decline in power was "founded in nature." The real question was whether Southern power would be "enjoyed with moderation."[10] *In the meantime, he appears to have taken some satisfaction in the ban of the slave trade in the Louisiana Territory.*

December 15, 1804—I was so unwell and hoarse that I should have confined myself to the house this day; but Mr.[Timothy] Pickering

10. "Publius Valerius," *WJQA* III, 49–50, 59, 70–71, 73; "Proposed Amendment to the Constitution on Representation" [December 1804], *WJQA* III, 88.

yesterday invited me to dine with him, in company with the Louisiana deputies, Messrs. Sauvé, Derbigny, and Détréhan. I went accordingly, though the weather was very bad. The two former of these gentlemen speak English very well. The last, who is a native of Louisiana, speaks only French. They do not appear very sanguine of success in their present negotiation. They are, however, very much dissatisfied with the state of things in their country, and above all with Governor Claiborne, whom they most cordially detest. The prohibition of the slave trade is also an object of great discontent to them. If they could be quieted on these two points, I think they would return home well pleased. But it is not probable they will be gratified in either.

Congressional debates about the slave trade served as flashpoints, and Adams continued to observe them laconically. He also tried to avoid being quoted.

January 21, 1805—In Senate Dr. Logan presented the petition of certain Quakers, requesting the interference of Congress as far as they have power to check the slave trade. A question was made, whether the petition should be received, and very warmly debated for about three hours; when it was taken by yeas and nays—yeas nineteen, nays nine. A motion of reference to the committee who have the petition from Louisiana, in favor of the slave trade, before them—taken without yeas and nays—was negatived, fourteen ayes, thirteen nays; and the President [of the Senate, vice president of the United States], who has got over his scruple against voting, by forming a tie, prevented its passing. This same petition was presented to the House of Representatives, read, and referred to a committee without any objection. The reason for this difference of treatment to the same papers I take to be because the debates of that House are always published, and those of the Senate very seldom; nor were there any stenographers this day present.

December 17, 1805—A long debate was held in Senate this day on the question whether Mr. [Stephen Row] Bradley should have leave to bring in a bill to prohibit the importation of slaves into the United States after the 1st of January, 1808. The principal question was whether, consistently with the Constitution of the United States, Congress could pass any law upon the subject prior to that year. But some of the members, thinking it inexpedient to discuss the subject at this time, would have refused the leave to bring in the bill, and spoke to that purpose, until he asked or the yeas and nays on the question. Then Dr. [Samuel Latham] Mitch[i]ll [of New York] made a long speech to show why he should vote for giving leave though he had previously spoken against it. The Journal, he said, would be the record of his fame, and he could not suffer it to exhibit the appearance of his voting against the reception of a bill to the principles of which he was so friendly. Mr. [Robert] Wright [of Maryland], from a similar fear to vote as he wished, moved the previous question. But all would not do. The majority decided to take the question immediately, and then to receive the bill, which was read; and before the question was taken whether it should go to a second reading, Mr. Bradley moved an adjournment, which was carried.

For more than a year, the Senate considered various versions of a bill to officially ban trade with the revolutionary republic of Haiti. Adams did not express strong opinions on the issue in his diary; his longer asides on these occasions turned on matters of procedure.

February 20, 1806—The St. Domingo bill passed—twenty-one yeas and eight nays. Before its passage, Mr. [Samuel] White [of Delaware] delivered against it one of the most powerful and beautiful speeches I have ever heard made in Congress. Mr. [Andrew] Moore [of Virginia] and Mr. Wright were the only persons who ventured to oppose him, and they made but an indifferent figure.

Adams continued to avoid the issue of the slave trade when it returned to the Senate in anticipation of the lifting of the Constitution's twenty-year ban on legislation against the slave trade.

January 15, 1807—The Slave bill, which originated in Senate, was discussed in committee' of the whole, and occasioned a long debate. Mr. [Henry] Clay, the new member from Kentucky, made an ardent speech upon one of the sections. He is quite a young man—an orator— and a republican of the first fire. I took, and intend to take, no part in the debates on this subject.

The Federalist senator joined Boston Republicans in denouncing the British assault on the USS Chesapeake *in June 1807, a major incident that highlighted the increasingly controversial issue of impressment. During the years leading up to the War of 1812, Adams repeatedly compared impressment to the slave trade.*

July 11, 1807—I was at the Insurance Offices before dinner. J. Phillips told me I should *have my head taken off* for apostasy by the federalists. I have indeed expected to displease them, but could not help it. My sense of duty shall never yield to the pleasure of a party. I am this day forty years of age; and when I reflect how much in the course of that period I have received in blessings from Heaven, and how little I have returned in benefit to the world, I can neither look back nor forward with any satisfaction.

Adams supported the Jefferson administration's embargo policy: he was the only Federalist to do so. His opposition cost him his Senate seat, as Federalists in Massachusetts refused to renominate him. His passion on the topic of his principled stand is striking, especially given some Federalists' insistence that the embargo policy reflected proslavery interests. Adams countered that New England's opposition was disloyal and potentially fatal to American independence. Twenty years later he spent some of the waning weeks of his presidency writing a book-length corrective to denials of the existence of a New England secession movement, which he dated to as early as 1804. He even insisted that he himself deserved credit for the end of the embargo. He had gone directly to President Jefferson with news of the Yankee plot, arguing that the embargo be repealed to combat the secret Federalist–British negotiations. His efforts were particularly appreciated by Secretary of State James Madison, who compared Massachusetts's rapid unseating of Adams as senator to the backbiting he and Jefferson received from Senator John Randolph, their own home-state nemesis, who repeatedly called them soft on federal threats to the South and slavery.[11]

11. John Quincy Adams to Harrison Gray Otis, March 31, 1808, to Orchard Cook, November 25, 1808, to Nahum Parker, December 8 and 15, 1808, to William Plumer, October 16, 1809, *WJQA* IV, 193, 255–56, 258–59, 340–41; Henry Adams, ed., *Documents Relating to New England Federalism* (1877. Repr. Boston, 1905), 11–13, 107–330.

February 1, 1808—Mr. [Josiah] Quincy asked me to have some conversation with him; which I did, at his chamber. He enquired into the
motives of my late conduct in Congress, which I fully detailed to him.
He said my principles were too pure for those with whom I was acting, and *they would not thank me for them*. I told him I did not want
their thanks. He said they would not *value me* the more for them or
not. I told him I cared not whether they valued me for them or not.
My character, such as it was, must stand upon its own ground, and
not upon the bolstering of any man or party. I fully opened to him my
motives for supporting the administration at this crisis, and my sense
of the danger which a spirit of opposition is bringing upon the *Union*.
I told him where that opposition in case of war must in its nature
end—either in a *civil* war, or in a dissolution of the Union, with the
Atlantic States in subserviency to Great Britain. That to resist this I was
ready, if necessary, to sacrifice every thing I have in life, and even life
itself. I intimated to him that he would be called, perhaps ere long, to
make the election which side he would take, too. He said he did not
see the prospect in the same light, but, if he did, he should also be willing to meet that question when it came. He did not say which side he
should take. The result of the conversation was an opinion on my part
that he was too far pledged in opposition to retreat; and that his own
idea was rather that of reclaiming me from the *"error of my ways."* We
must wait with patience to see where the right is.

*Grateful members of the Jefferson administration proposed Adams for the US
Supreme Court, which he discouraged as not suiting his interests or tempera-
ment. But he did accept the diplomatic post of minister to Russia in the new
Madison administration.*

April 23, 1808—Mr. [Senator Nicholas] Gilman [of New Hampshire]
this day spoke to me, with intimations that it was the wish of several gentlemen with whom he had conversed to *bring me forward* in
some active and distinguished station; but that it was wished I would
take occasion, either in some speech or in some written publication, to
express my sentiments with respect to the practicability of our present
form of government, as, from some of my writings, published before

I went to Europe, there were persons who thought me inclined to favor a Constitution approaching nearer to the monarchical form. I told him I would reflect upon the suggestions, but my present impressions, which I did not think likely to change, were these. I was sworn to support the Constitution of the United States. I would support it to the utmost of my power, and with perfect sincerity. I had during the present session of Congress, to say nothing of preceding dates, pledged more to support it, in my own opinion, than any other man in the Union. I had sacrificed to it the favor of the party which had placed me in my present station. I had therefore not only the common stake of others who support the administration, but the responsibility of appearing to abandon my own party; and was liable to all the obloquy which such desertion carried with it. My motive for it was to support the Constitution as I had sworn. I had therefore taken an active part in the public affairs, both foreign and domestic; and to the best of my ability endeavored to "defend it against its enemies, external and internal." But I had not set one party at defiance, in this conduct, for the purpose of making myself the instrument of another. That as to my speculative opinions upon the practicability of our present Constitution, I had my doubts whether, in case of a war, it would get along in its present form. I believed it would become more democratic. With regard to the theory of government, I had not for many years read over any of the papers written by me and published before I went to Europe; but I was not aware of any one sentiment or opinion contained in them that I would now retract. That, as to my being brought forward in a conspicuous station, I certainly did not think it a desirable thing. There was not a place in the gift of the people, or of the Executive of the United States, or of my own State, for which I had the slightest wish. That to be dismissed from the place which I now am in would doubtless occasion a moment of personal mortification, for which, however, my mind was made up, and which would be more than compensated by the advantage of being released from the cares of the public service at such a time as this; but that as to any thing else, so far as my personal desires were concerned, I would not speak ten words, nor write two lines, to be President of the United States—nor, of course, to be any thing subordinate to that. He said this was standing on very independent ground indeed; but that for himself he was satisfied there ought to be that confidence in a man's principles and integrity not to require of him any pledge of opinions at all. I did not enquire, nor did he tell me, with whom he had conversed, or what the object was to which he referred as the conspicuous station of which he spoke in general terms. Mr. Gilman is, however, the particular friend of [Vice President George] Clinton, [governor of New York] as [Senator William Branch] Giles [of Virginia] is of Mr. Madison, with respect to the presidential election; and he some time since asked me which of the Departments I should prefer that of State or that of the Treasury. I answered him, laughingly, that I was about as well qualified for the one as for the other. He then said, in the same tone, that he thought so too; but he believed that the Department of State would suit me best, and when *he* should be President of the United States I should have it.

2

American Diplomat (1809–17)

John Quincy Adams's determination to be a statesman for the whole Union informed his years of varied service to that Union abroad. He served as the US minister to the Russian Empire from 1809 until late 1814, when the Madison administration sent him to Ghent to help negotiate the treaty that ended the War of 1812. From Ghent he proceeded to his country's prime foreign post as the US minister to Great Britain from 1815 to 1817. His strong commitment to his country's sovereignty and rights, and his view of the British Empire as the greatest threat to those rights, strongly conditioned his stances on international issues surrounding American slavery and the Atlantic slave trade. Though his job as a diplomat was to implement the policies of the Madison administration, he pursued these and surrounding questions with a vigor that revealed his hearty concurrence with those policies.

John Quincy Adams's diary entry for July 5, 1809, recorded his feelings upon accepting the appointment to the post of minister to Russia from the newly elected president, James Madison. He was the first credentialed US minister to serve in St. Petersburg. His years in Russia were a period in which the Russian Empire's fortunes were key to the balance of power in Napoleonic Europe, which was of obvious relevance to his own would-be neutral nation. This entry began with a list of personal and family reasons that tempted him to decline the nomination, but the following accounting of the counterbalancing

reasons to accept illustrated just how intertwined the patriotic, the political,
and the personal remained for the forty-two-year-old Adams.

July 5, 1809—To oppose all this, I have the duty of a citizen to obey the
call of his country signified by the regular constituted authority; the
satisfaction of being removed, at least for a time, and with honor, from
a situation where the deepest retirement has not sheltered me from the
most virulent and unrelenting persecution, and the vague *hope* of rendering to my country some important service, as intended by the mission; finally, the desire to justify the confidence reposed by Mr. Madison
in me, by assuming the station which *he* has chosen to assign me, and
by devoting all my powers to the support of his administration, so far
as it shall aim, as I am perfectly convinced it does and will aim, at the
welfare of this whole Union. These are my motives—and I implore the
blessing of Almighty God upon this my undertaking; that all its critical moments may find me in possession of myself—in possession of
the virtues which contribute all that human power can contribute to
success, and prepared alike for whatever event his Providence destines
for its termination. Finally, with the profoundest sense of gratitude for
that goodness which has so far rescued from its perils my beloved country, and from perils not less menacing my own person, and reputation
with the people of America, I humbly ask, from perfecting goodness, for
the extrication of my country from her difficulties and dangers, and for
myself, the continued consciousness of purity in my motives, and, so far
as it has been or may be deserved, the approbation of my countrymen.

The Europe to which Adams and his family sailed in August 1809 was entering
its third decade of the wars touched off by the French Revolution and Napoleon's
ascent to power in France. The Washington, Adams, and Jefferson administra-
tions had gone to extreme lengths to keep the United States from being pulled
into this series of wars on the side of either the nations allied with France or
those allied with Britain. Neither side's navy had a stellar record of respect for
the United States' self-proclaimed status as a neutral country, and seizures of
American merchant vessels caused serious diplomatic conflict as well as suffering
for those whose ships had been seized and detained. The British Royal Navy in
particular had violated Americans' touchy regard for their national sovereignty
by repeatedly boarding American ships to search for British nationals in the

crew, whom they would then impress into the Royal Navy. While Americans held that immigrants transferred their national identity and loyalties to their new nation upon emigrating, the British government upheld the doctrine of perpetual allegiance, or the notion that those born British subjects remained under obligation to their birth nation until death. All this background created tension when, on September 17, 19, and 25, British officers sought to board and search the ships on which Adams was sailing. These encounters added a specific menace to the generally perilous prospect of a wartime voyage from Boston to St. Petersburg, and such personal experience only fueled his hatred of the practice of searching American ships. On September 20, Adams encountered several Americans detained along with their ships in Christiansand, Norway, and these interactions led him to record the following vow.

September 20, 1809—The sight of so many of my countrymen, in circumstances so distressing, is very painful, and each of them has a story to tell of the peculiar aggravations of ill treatment which he has received. The desire of contributing to their relief is so strong in me that I shall, without waiting for express authority from the Government of the United States, use every effort in my power in their behalf, to however little purpose it may be as to its success.

Later diary entries reveal that he made good on this pledge. For instance, Adams asked Count Romanzoff, chancellor of the empire and foreign minister, to lean on the Danish government, which had seized the ships detained in Norway. Romanzoff's response resonated with and must have reinforced Adams's image of Britain as an arbitrary and malevolent world power. Further illustration of how Adams saw even slave-grown produce through the lens of the United States' standing on the world stage came in late December. The context for this interchange was a discussion of the commerce between the United States and Europe's colonies in the New World during this time of war.

December 26, 1809—[Romanzoff said] that nothing short of a general peace could probably put an end to these embarrassments, and that this general peace depended upon England alone; that he knew not why this general peace should not be made; that nothing would be asked of England, but, on the contrary, she would be left in possession of what she had acquired; that until she could be reduced to reasonable terms of peace, it was impossible that commerce should be free from rigorous restrictions, because it was by operating upon her commerce that she must be made to feel her interest in making peace. . . .

"But," said he [Romanzoff], "is not the produce of the United States in these articles of inferior quality? Cotton, for instance?"

I told him the United States produced the best of cotton, and in immense quantities; that in all the Southern States, as well as in Louisiana, the cultivation of this article within the last twenty years had flourished beyond imagination.

While in Russia, Adams made one of his first diary comments on slavery. It featured his reaction to reading the Mosaic decrees of feast days and other celebrations for ancient Israel in the book of Leviticus. This entry did not connect ancient slavery to the institution in the United States; indeed, he noted that the Jubilee, which every fiftieth year returned all property to its original owners and liberated all Israelite slaves and servants, was among those ancient practices that "have been considered as abolished by the Christian dispensation." But Adams's commentary on the Jubilee did reveal something of his embryonic thoughts on slavery in the abstract, and on the relationship between slavery and legislation.

April 5, 1812—The Jubilee was an excellent institution, which operated at once as an agrarian law and a law against slavery. The tenure of lands was equivalent at most to a lease of fifty years; nor could the service of a Hebrew be engaged for a longer time.

Slavery in the abstract was one thing, but given Adams's view of the British Empire's motives and impact, his reaction to ongoing British abolitionism was another thing entirely. By the time he wrote this entry, controversies including the impressment of American seamen had exploded into the War of 1812.

November 10, 1812—I read the remainder of Gisborne's Principles of Moral Philosophy,[1] and his remarks on a decision in the British House

---

1. Thomas Gisborne, *The Principles of Moral Philosophy Investigated, and Briefly Applied to the Constitution of Civil Society* (London, 1789).

of Commons, in April, 1792, on the abolition of the slave trade. He is a very zealous advocate for this abolition, which has been since legally decreed in England, as well as in America. Whether it will be eventually abolished in fact is yet a problem. The trade is beyond question an abomination, disgraceful to the human character, but there are so many powerful passions and interests concurring to support it, and the efforts to obtain its abolition are themselves so much composed of fashion and faction, that I still doubt whether the abolition will be accomplished. I say the motives of the abolitionists are in a great degree fashion and faction; for the impressment of seamen is to all intents and purposes a practice as unjust, as immoral, as base, as oppressive and tyrannical as the slave trade. It is in all its most heinous features identically the same crime; in some particulars it is more aggravated; and yet the same members of the British Parliament who have been the greatest zealots for abolishing the slave trade are not only inflexible adherents to the practice of impressments among their own people, but are now waging a rancorous war against the United States to support the practice of their officers in impressing men from American merchant vessels on the high seas. Every particle of argument that can bear against the slave trade bears with equal force against impressment. Dr. Gisborne is at least consistent. He admits that the impressment of seamen is a violation of the general principles of the English constitution; and he speaks of it, even as applied to British subjects, with disapprobation. He says nothing of the abuse of extending the practice to Americans and upon American vessels, and even his censure upon it as applied only to British subjects is very faint and cold compared with his fervor of passion against the slave trade.

In August 1814, Adams and other American and British negotiators arrived in the neutral Belgian city of Ghent to begin peace talks. Adams recorded an extensive preliminary conversation with Henry Goulbourn, the British undersecretary of state for war and the colonies. Adams found "the violence and bitterness of his passion against the United States" remarkable in this head of the British delegation, and ascribed it to Britons' "jealousy" of the "increasing strength and population" of the United States. They discussed a wide range of issues including the contested US–Canada border and relations with Native Americans, all vital context for the following conversation. While

Goulbourn accused the US government of official designs to conquer Canada,
Adams countered by asking whether the British government had sanctioned
Admiral Alexander Cochrane's wartime invitation to American slaves to fight
for the British and gain their freedom. Adams called this proclamation an
invitation to slave revolt. In the parry and thrust of this conversation Adams
also first introduced the popular American charge—made officially by the
Madison administration, as well as in partisan newspapers despite very sparse
and flimsy evidence—that British commanders had sold American slaves in
the West Indies rather than liberating them as promised.

September 1, 1814—[Goulbourn stated] that no proclamation encour-
aging the negroes to revolt had been authorized; but the proclamation of Admiral Cochrane, as referred to, gave no such encouragement;
there was nothing about negroes in it. It merely offered employment,
or a settlement in the British colonies, to such persons as might be disposed to leave the United States.

I referred him to the term free used in connection with that of settle-
ments, and observed that it was true the word negroes was not used in
it, but that no person in America could mistake its meaning; that it was
unquestionably intended to apply to the negroes, and that the practice
of many of their naval commanders corresponded with it; that it was
known some of them, under such inducements, had taken away blacks,
who had afterwards been sold in the West India Islands.

Upon this he manifested some apparent agitation, and said that he
could undertake to deny it in the most unqualified terms; that the character of British naval officers was universally known, their generosity
and humanity could not be contested; and, besides that, since the act
of Parliament of 1811, the act of selling any man for a slave, unless real
slaves, from one British island to another, was felony without benefit
of clergy.

I replied that, without contesting the character of any class of people
generally, it was certain there would be in all classes individuals capable
of committing actions of which others would be ashamed; that, at a
great distance from the eye and control of the Government, acts were
often done with impunity which would be severely punished nearer
home; that the facts I had stated to him were among the objects which

we were instructed to present for consideration if the negotiation should proceed, and he might in that case find it more susceptible of proof than he was aware.

He thought it impossible, but that it was one of those charges against their officers, of which there were many, originating only in the spirit of hostility, and totally destitute of foundation.

In his entries for November 28 and 29, 1814, Adams recorded a meeting of the American delegation at Ghent, which in addition to Adams and Jonathan Russell from Massachusetts included Henry Clay of Kentucky, James Bayard of Delaware, and Albert Gallatin of Pennsylvania. This regional balance was important given the various issues in negotiation that touched specific sectional interests. The debates that Adams recorded in these entries centered on what priority to give to securing a favorable Anglo-American boundary line for New England fishermen's rights within the waters in the North Atlantic, and to resisting the British push for a right for their commerce to navigate the Mississippi River. It is notable and consistent with Adams's overall stance in this phase of his career that he struck a more sectionally conciliatory note than did Henry Clay, who was later known as an arch-compromiser for union.

November 28, 1814—Mr. Clay lost his temper, as he generally does whenever this right of the British to navigate the Mississippi is discussed. He was utterly averse to admitting it as an equivalent for a stipulation securing the contested part of the fisheries. He said the more he heard of this the more convinced he was that it was of little or no value. He should be glad to get it if he could, but he was sure the British would not ultimately grant it. That the navigation of the Mississippi, on the other hand, was an object of immense importance, and he could see no sort of reason for granting it as an equivalent for the fisheries. Mr. Gallatin said that the fisheries were of great importance in the sentiment of the eastern section of the Union; that if we should sign a peace without securing them to the full extent in which they were enjoyed before the war, and especially if we should abandon any part of the territory, it would give a handle to the party there, now pushing for a separation from the Union and for a New England Confederacy, to say that the interests of New England were sacrificed, and to pretend that by a separate confederacy they could obtain what is refused to us.[2]

Mr. Clay said that there was no use in attempting to conciliate people who never would be conciliated; that it was too much the practice of our Government to sacrifice the interests of its best friends for those of its bitterest enemies; that there might be a party for separation at some future day in the Western States, too.

I observed to him that he was now speaking under the impulse of passion, and that on such occasions I would wish not to answer anything; that assuredly the Government would be reproached, and the greatest advantage would be taken by the party opposed to it, if any of the rights of the Eastern States should be sacrificed by the peace; that the loss of any part of the fisheries would be a subject of triumph and exultation, both to the enemy and to those among us who had been opposed to the war; that if I should consent to give up even Moose Island, where there was a town which had been for many years regularly represented in the Legislature of the State of Massachusetts, I should be ashamed to show my face among my countrymen. . . .

November 29, 1814—Mr. Gallatin had prepared his draft of a note to the British Plenipotentiaries, closing with the request for a conference, and his proposed article offering the navigation of the Mississippi as an equivalent for the fisheries within the British jurisdiction. This renewed our discussion of the whole subject, but it was now on all sides good-humored. I had some doubt whether it would be perfectly safe to ask a conference, while we were so far from being agreed among ourselves. Mr. Clay said he could put the subject of the Mississippi navigation upon principles to which it was impossible we should not all agree. I said that nothing like that had been apparent from our discussion hitherto; that he certainly would not be willing that I should be the

2. Gallatin here referred to a strong antiwar movement in New England that savored strongly of sectional grievances against the Southern-dominated federal government. While the peace delegations met in Ghent, Federalist representatives of aggrieved town meetings throughout New England met in the Hartford Convention to discuss a regional response to the ongoing war. The convention's report ended up calling only for amendments to the Constitution aimed at securing a better balance of power for New England within the Union, but many observers expected the Hartford Convention to be a New England secession convention.

spokesman of his sentiments, and I did not think it likely that he would very accurately express mine. . . .

I then told Mr. Clay that I would make a coalition with him of the East and West. If the British would not give us the fisheries, I would join him in refusing to grant them the navigation of the river.

He said that the consequence of our making the offer would be that we should lose both.

Both in meetings with the American mission and communications with the British delegation, Adams continued to press the canard about British officers enticing or kidnapping American slaves and then selling them in the West Indies. That he charged forward with the issue, even though the British were far more comfortable discussing it than the American delegation, underscored the depths of his Anglophobic nationalism. It is also somewhat remarkable that the two delegates from slave states would have been more cautious on this issue than Adams. After the signing of the Treaty of Ghent on December 24, the American delegation decided to provide an unofficial note about the allegations to the British delegation.[3]

November 30, 1814—I proposed also [to the American delegation] to send them [the British ministers] a copy of the deposition we have respecting the sale by their officers in the West Indies of negroes seduced from their masters in our Southern States by promises of liberty. The part of our instructions which asserts this fact has been noticed in both houses of Parliament in England. The [British] Ministers have pledged themselves to make strict enquiry into it, and I thought the communication of the proof furnished us by the Secretary of State might be useful, as it would certainly become thereby public, and by drawing the public attention to the practice might prevent its repetition hereafter. It would probably cease when the officers should no longer have the motive for stealing the negroes, in the opportunity to sell them. But all my colleagues objected against sending this paper. They said its tendency would only be to irritate, when we should make our note as conciliatory as possible; that the

3. See Diary, December 28–29, 1814; January 4, 1815.

proof was weak, being only a single deposition; that the charge as made in Mr. Monroe's instructions to us had more weight without this proof than it would have with it.

I replied that the fact was stated to be of public notoriety; that the deposition which we have is circumstantial upon one particular instance, with names and dates, and that it testifies also to the general practice; that no proof could be stronger, so far as one witness could afford proof. It was, however, determined not to send it.

December 7, 1814—Received from the British Plenipotentiaries . . . [a note] asking for proof of the assertion by the American Secretary of State that negroes taken by the British from the Southern States had been sold in the West Indies.

December 8, 1814—I made this morning a draft of an answer to propose to my colleagues to be sent to the British Plenipotentiaries to the note received yesterday from them respecting the seduction and sale of negroes taken from our Southern States by British officers. The note gives us an express assurance that any officer found guilty of such practices shall be punished in an exemplary manner. But it confounds together the two acts of seducing the slaves and afterwards selling them, and promises only to punish the whole. It is the seduction of the slaves that constitutes the offence against us. As to the sale of them afterwards, the British Government have no right to ask of us, and we have no sufficient motive to give them, proofs of the fact, unless they will disavow and pledge themselves also to punish the other.

I therefore in my draft offered to produce the proof if they would engage to indemnify the owners of the negroes for the loss of them; and for the proof of seduction, referred to Admiral Cochrane's proclamation of 2d April last, of which we have sent a copy with one of our former notes.

I requested a meeting of the mission at my chamber at noon. It was accordingly held; I read the draft I had made, but there appeared much diversity of opinion as to the proper mode of proceeding in this case. Mr. Bayard is afraid of irritating the British Government. Mr. Gallatin thinks our proof weak, and seems to have a doubt, though he does not exactly avow it, whether the fact can be proved. We have only one affidavit, but that is as strong—both to the general practice and to a particular instance in the knowledge of the deponent as any proof could be.

Hughes[4] remarked to me, however, that the deponent's Christian name was Patrick, which he did not like. I asked him, why? He answered, Irish. Mr. Gallatin was averse to requiring of the British Government to disavow and punish the seduction, because, he said, they would not only refuse to do it, but that all the opponents of the slave-trade would approve and justify the act. Mr. Russell said he had taken much the same view of the subject as that in my draft; but it was finally proposed and agreed to postpone the answer until we shall hear further from the British Plenipotentiaries on the main subject of the treaty.

December 9, 1814—Mr. Clay came into my chamber this morning and read to me the draft which he had been making of an answer to the negro note from the British Plenipotentiaries. It differed not much in substance from mine of yesterday, and was in a milder form, asking for explanation. I told him I was well satisfied with it, and only wished an addition noticing Cochrane's proclamation. . . .

Mr. Bayard spoke to me again about the negro note. He is for answering, that the indemnity for the loss of the negroes having been refused, we are not authorized to furnish our proofs, but will refer the note to our Government. He had not seen Mr. Clay's draft of an answer. I told him the substance of it, but he said he did not admire that course; he thought it calculated merely to produce irritation upon a collateral subject, which might tend to defeat the negotiation itself.

Britain's drive to secure American cooperation in abolishing the Atlantic slave trade played a much more central role in the negotiations than did the kidnap-and-sale side show. Adams's account revealed how the British raised that issue, and how it created mild divisions within the American delegation. Adams was far from the antislavery vanguard in these discussions.

December 10, 1814—They offered two new articles, one stipulating a concurrence of measures for abolishing the slave-trade, and the other, that the Courts of justice should be open in each of the two countries to the subjects and citizens of the other. Dr. Adams[5] observed of the

4. Christopher Hughes (1786–1849), the secretary for the American delegation.
5. British negotiator William Adams.

first that it was nothing at all, a matter of no consequence, binding to no particular act, and only sanctioning legislative acts which both had adopted. Mr. Gallatin said the Courts in England had actually proceeded to condemn American vessels for violations of the laws of the United States against the slave-trade; but that there would be a difficulty in the Courts of the United States to give a similar judgment against British vessels for the violation of the English statutes on the same subject; that it could be done only by a treaty in which the offence should be assimilated to piracy and it should be agreed to punish the offenders as pirates.

Mr. Bayard said that no such treaty could be made; that piracy was an offence against all nations, and punishable by every nation; that a nation might, if it pleased, make any other act of its own subjects punishable as piracy by its own Courts, but no nation, and no two nations, could make that piracy which is not recognized as such by other nations. Mr. Gallatin said he was aware of that, but they might assimilate it to piracy, and make it punishable in the same manner. Mr. Bayard denied that they could. . . .

After a conference of about two hours, they left us, and we continued another hour in session. We considered generally the subject of their proposals, and each of us made his remarks upon them. Mr. Gallatin was much in favor of the slave-trade article, and had originally drawn one up to be proposed on our part. I had some objections to it, as tending to give dissatisfaction to France, Spain, and Portugal, with whom Britain is now negotiating on the same subject, and who are very unwilling to yield to the British views upon it. The article for opening the Courts we considered as unnecessary and objectionable.

Given that the Treaty of Ghent evaded the issue of impressment and contained only a vague pledge to cooperate against the Atlantic slave trade, both of these remained outstanding (and intertwined) issues when Adams assumed the American ministry in London. The British and American governments also disagreed profoundly on whether the treaty placed an obligation on the British to return American slaves taken and freed by Cochrane and other commanders, or at least to compensate American masters for their lost human property. The British interpreted the wording of the first article of the treaty very narrowly, only recognizing this obligation with reference to slaves taken in American forts; Americans construed it to mean all slaves.

Among the many discussions of the fugitive slave issue, Adams's entry for August 16, 1815, stands out as especially revealing. It records an extended exchange between Adams and the prime minister, Lord Liverpool, over such questions as whether enslaved Americans should be considered foremost as humans or as property.[6]

August 16, 1815—[Liverpool granted that] with respect to the slaves they certainly construed very differently from the American Government the stipulation relating to them. They thought that it applied only to the slaves in the forts and places which, having been taken during the war, were to be restored.

I said that, independent of the construction of the sentence which so strongly marked the distinction between artillery and public property and slaves and private property, the process by which the article was drawn up demonstrated beyond all question that a distinction between them was intended and understood by both parties. The first projet [draft] of the treaty was presented by *us*. This had been required, and even insisted upon, by the British Plenipotentiaries. The article was therefore drawn up by us, and our intention certainly was to secure the restoration both of the public and private property, including slaves, which had been in any manner captured on shore during the war. The projet was returned to us, with a limitation upon the restoration of property, whether public or private, to such as had been in the places when captured and should remain there at the time of the evacuation. We assented to this so far as related to artillery and public property, which, by the usages of war, is liable to be taken and removed, but not with regard to private property and slaves, which we thought should at all events be restored, because they ought never to have been taken. . . . Our object was the restoration of all property, including slaves, which, by the usages of war among civilized nations, ought not to have been taken. All private property

6. See Diary, May 29, June 29, 1815; January 25, July 18, 1816, for discussions of this issue between Adams and Foreign Minister Lord Castlereagh. In the July 18, 1816, meeting, Adams suggested that a third nation arbitrate this issue.

on shore was of that description. It was entitled by the laws of war to exemption from capture. Slaves were private property.

Lord Liverpool said that he thought they could not be considered precisely under the general denomination of private property. A table or a chair, for instance, might be taken and restored without changing its condition; but a living and a human being was entitled to other considerations.

I said that the treaty had made no such distinction. The words implicitly recognized slaves as private property. They were in the article alluded to "slaves or *other* private property." I did, however, readily admit the distinction suggested by him. Most certainly a living, sentient being, and still more a human being, was to be regarded in a different light from the inanimate matter of which other private property might consist, and if on the ground of that difference the British Plenipotentiaries had objected to restore the one, while they agreed to restore the other, we should have readily discussed the subject. We might have accepted, or objected to, the proposal they would have made. But what could that proposal have been? Upon what ground could Great Britain have refused to restore them? Was it because they had been seduced away from their masters by the promises of British officers? It was true, proclamations from her officers to that effect had issued. We considered them as deviations from the usages of war. We believed that the British Government itself would, when the hostile passions of a state of war should subside, consider them in the same light; that she would then be willing to restore the property, or to indemnify the sufferers by its loss. If she felt bound to make good the promises of her officers to the slaves, she might still be willing to do an act of justice, by compensating the owners of the slaves for the property which had been irregularly taken from them. Without entering into a discussion which might have been at once unprofitable and irritating, she might consider this engagement only as a promise to pay for those slaves which should be carried away by paying the worth of them to their owners. Lord Liverpool did not reply to these observations, nor did he appear to take them in ill part.

Adams's solicitude for American sovereignty led him to at times surprising stands. At times it encouraged him to raise issues that would not otherwise have been issues, such as when he insisted to Lord Castlereagh that all future

Anglo-American treaties recognize their equality by the form in which the signatures appeared. And in the same meeting, he pushed for an accused mutineer to be protected in his due process rights in British military courts because "the man was a citizen of the United States." In February 1816, an even more telling case arose when the Royal Navy detained Bostonian George Cook for participating in the Atlantic slave trade on the west coast of Africa.[7] It was yet another case in which Adams's hatred of the Atlantic slave trade collided with his duty as an American ambassador and inclination as an American nationalist.

April 9, 1816—[T]he first subject upon which he [Castlereagh] wished to speak to me related to a note that I had sent him concerning a memorial to the Lords of the Treasury[8] from a man named George Cook, an American, and he wished to know precisely what the object of the note was. I said I had never seen Mr. Cook, and knew nothing of his case but what was set forth in his memorial to the Lords of the Treasury, a copy of which had been communicated to me by a Mr. Page, his agent, and likewise agent to several Spanish subjects, who had made complaints similar to that of Mr. Cook. The only ground upon which I had interfered in behalf of Mr. Cook was that he was a citizen of the United States, and as such entitled to all the assistance that in my official capacity I could give him. The only thing that I had been requested by Mr. Page to ask for him, and which I had asked by my note, was a *speedy* decision, and, presuming that I might speak in perfect confidence to him (Lord Castlereagh) on the subject, I would state to him the reason why the necessity that this decision should be speedy had been alleged to me by Mr. Page.

Lord Castlereagh said that he wished me to speak in perfect confidence, and that whatever was said between us on the subject should be private. I then said that Mr. Cook's memorial alleged a claim to be indemnified for great wrongs suffered by him in the form of judicial and executive proceedings by the Judge and Governor of a British

7. Diary, June 29, 1815; February 18, 1816.
8. A British commission of Treasury officials that adjudicated most cases related to economic matters.

settlement in Africa; that the Governor of that settlement was now here, but he had received another appointment to some foreign colonial establishment, and might be expected from day to day to embark for his new destination. It was the intention of Mr. Page, as Mr. Cook's agent, in case the decision of the Lords of the Treasury upon the memorial should not be satisfactory to him, to prosecute the Governor (Maxwell) in the proper Court of law, and he was anxious not to lose the opportunity of arresting his person. This was the motive upon which I had addressed to his Lordship the note concerning Cook. It was altogether distinct from the merits of the case, of which of course I could not judge. I had only asked for a decision.

Lord Castlereagh said the fact was that this Mr. Cook had been one of the greatest and most notorious offenders against the laws of the United States relative to the slave-trade, as well as against those of Great Britain. But the proceedings against him had been illegal, because his establishment had been upon the Rio Pongas, not within the territorial jurisdiction of Great Britain. If he had been taken at sea, his trial and condemnation would have been perfectly legal and regular; but he had been taken out of the British jurisdiction. The sentence of the Court that condemned him could not, therefore, be maintained, and that was the reason why it had been remitted here by a pardon. He then read me a letter from Mr. Goulburn to Mr. Cook, the Under-Secretary of State, in which he gives him the same account of his *namesake*.

I repeated to Lord Castlereagh that I could not judge of the merits of the case. Cook's memorial stated a case of great hardship and very severe treatment; he denied altogether having had any concern in the slave-trade, and averred that his establishment was of a commerce altogether different. He complained also of great partiality and oppression upon his trial—of not having been allowed to make his defence or to produce the evidence in his favor. But I was not competent to re-try the cause. He must find his remedy in the Government, or in the laws of England.

Lord Castlereagh said they would then determine whether the Government itself would make him indemnity, or whether they would leave him to his remedy, by suit in the Courts of law, against the individuals.

Adams's views on race are largely opaque during this period of his life. When he sailed for Russia his household included a free African American household servant Adams referred to only as "Nelson." In 1810, Nelson for some unknown reason joined the Russian Imperial household with Adams's recommendation, and in 1811 he was christened a Roman Catholic. These events make up the sum total of Adams's laconic entries in reference to Nelson.[9] Both in Russia and in Britain, he dealt with scattered pleas for help from black Americans abroad. He seems to have treated these cases much like those involving white Americans, giving help wherever he could. He never seems to have omitted the racial descriptor "black" when discussing these men, but he reserved that of "negroes" for references to American slaves as a group.[10]

In 1815, Adams met Prince Saunders, an African American educator and advocate for African American emigration to Haiti.[11] Saunders seems to have met Adams's sons George and John on their 1815 voyage to Britain, and his social call on them some months later was the occasion for the following entry. Adams's respectful interactions with Saunders himself (whom he calls "Sanders" in this entry), together with his condescending bemusement about the Haitian King Henri Christophe, captured the hesitant and ambiguous nature of his racial thought at this point in his life.

April 17, 1816—Mr. Prince Sanders, The Black Gentleman, came for the purpose of spending the day with my Sons; and being disappointed by not finding them at home, he stayed and spent it with me. . . . Mr. Sanders took a short walk of half an hour with me before dinner, and dined with me. I had much Conversation with him upon the subject of his visit to Hayti as he calls it, or St. Domingo,[12] and found he was in

---

9. Diary, August 5, 1809; June 3, 1810; April 20, August 3, 1811.
10. Diary, March 18–19, 1812; November 9, 1816.
11. Diary, June 2, 1815.
12. St. Domingue, or St. Domingo, was the name of this part of the Caribbean island of Hispaniola when it was a French colony. But in 1804 the victorious slave rebels there declared their independence as the nation of Haiti. The United States did not recognize Haiti's independence and send an ambassador there until the Abraham Lincoln administration. It is telling, therefore, that while Adams seemed impressed by Saunders personally, he was not inclined to exceed the normal American diplomatic language toward this new nation even in a diary entry.

the highest degree delighted with his new connection there, with king Henry (Christophe) of whom he spoke in high terms of praise and admiration; but he was very reserved, with me, in speaking of his own present mission, and of his future views. He gave me to understand however that his mission had reference to religious affairs. That King Henry was determined to admit no more Roman Catholic Priests into the Country; but that his intention was to introduce religious worship there according to the rites of the Church of England. Sanders says that King Henry was displeased with the State Coach that was built in this Country and sent out to him. It was too tawdry for him; and he sent word to the makers that he supposed he had taken him for a king of Congo, who was to be caught with Show. Sanders was just going away, when Mr. Joy[13] came in with the boys from their tour of Hampton Court. He then stopped an hour longer, and returned to town with Mr. Joy. He also persuaded me to give permission to the boys to go in to Town tomorrow to see him, and Captain Bronson of the new Packet who is now in London—It was with him that George and John, and Mr. Sanders came to England.

Like other diplomats in this era, Adams developed a personal seal authenticating his signature on diplomatic documents. The following entry featured reflections on including the lyre of Orpheus in his seal. This entry forcibly reiterated his self-image as a statesman for the whole Union, and also revealed the global stakes he thought were involved with the survival and prosperity of that Union.

September 7, 1816—In the Grecian mythology Orpheus is said to have charmed lions and tigers, the most ferocious wild beasts, and to have drawn after him the very trees of the forest and the rocks of the desert, by the harmony of his lyre. Its power was said to have triumphed even over the tremendous deities of the infernal regions. . . . Orpheus was a legislator, whose eloquence charmed the rude and savage men of his age to associate together in the state of civil society, to submit to the salutary restraints of law, and to unite together in the worship of their

13. We have been unable to identify this Mr. Joy, or perhaps Mr. Jay.

Creator. It was the lyre of Orpheus that civilized savage man. It was only in harmony that the first human political institutions could be founded. ...

The moral application of the emblem is, that the same power of harmony which originally produced the institutions of civil government to regulate the association of individual men, now presides in the federal association of the American States; that harmony is the soul of their combination; that their force consists in their union, and that while thus united it will be their destiny to revolve in harmony with the whole world, by the attractive influence of their union. It is the lyre of Orpheus that now leads the stars, as it originally drew after it rocks and trees. It is harmony that now binds in its influence the American States, as it originally drew individual men from the solitude of nature to the assemblages which formed states and nations. The lesson of the emblem is UNION.

In June 1817, Adams made an especially revealing record of and commentary on a conversation in which he articulated with candid clarity his dim view of British abolitionists and his priorities as an American foreign minister. It also showed the wide range of debates in which he found it useful to trot out the feeble charge of British officers trafficking in runaway American slaves. William Wilberforce, the leading British abolitionist and a member of the House of Commons, had sought out a meeting with Adams. Surely the savvy Wilberforce perceived that such a dialogue represented an opportunity to influence American foreign policy in a powerful way, given that Adams's household was that very day packing for his return to the United States as President James Monroe's secretary of state. Wilberforce's fellow abolitionist, member of Parliament Thomas Babington, also participated in this parley.

June 6, 1817—The suppression of the slave-trade was the subject of Mr. Wilberforce's wish to see me, and we had an hour's conversation relating to it. His object is to obtain the consent of the United States, and of all other maritime powers, that ships under their flags may be searched and captured by the British cruisers against the slave-trade—a concession which I thought would be liable to objections. ...

Probably this project originated in the brain of Master Stephen, the author of "War in Disguise,"[14] and brother-in-law to Wilberforce, one of the party called in derision the Saints, and who under sanctified visors pursue worldly objects with the ardor and perseverance of saints. Wilberforce is at the head of these Saints in Parliament, and is said to possess more personal influence in the House of Commons than any other individual. Lord Castlereagh has more than once thrown out this idea of a mutual stipulation that the cruisers of every nation which has passed laws for abolishing the slave-trade should be authorized to search and capture the slave-trading vessels of the other nations by whose laws the trade is prohibited. In substance, it is a barefaced and impudent attempt of the British to obtain in time of peace that right of searching and seizing the ships of other nations which they have so outrageously abused during war. I never discussed the subject with Castlereagh, because he never brought the point to an explicit proposal, and it was not necessary to sift the proposition to the bottom; but Wilberforce, after much lamentation at the inefficacy of the existing laws and measures for suppressing the trade, and asserting that it was now carried on with as much activity and inhumanity as ever, professed to be unable to devise anything that should effectually suppress it. And yet, he said, there was one thing that would accomplish the end if the nations would agree to it, and then came out with the proposal, and enquired whether the United States would agree to it: that all vessels, whatever nation's flag they should bear, but which might be suspected of being engaged in the slave-trade, should be liable to search and capture by the cruisers of any other nation.

I told him I thought there would be some objection to this. In the first place, no American vessel engaged in the slave-trade could use the American flag, for the trade was prohibited by law, and a vessel which should be captured while engaged in it could not obtain any interference of the American Government to rescue her. The flag could be no protection to her. The commander of the capturing vessel would only act at *his peril*, and if he seized a vessel not really concerned in the trade

14. James Stephen, *War in Disguise, or, the Frauds of the Neutral Flags* (1806), an attack on Americans' and other nations' assertion of neutral status during the Napoleonic Wars.

he must be responsible to indemnify the sufferer. Again, a stipulation of this nature, though nominally reciprocal, would be really one-sided. Cruisers against the slave-trade are in fact kept only by Great Britain. British vessels, therefore, would be liable to no search or capture but by officers under the authority of their own Government, while the vessels of other nations would be subject to seizure by foreigners not amenable or accountable to their own sovereigns. Some degree of prejudice must also be supposed to exist against the naval power of Great Britain, and particularly some jealousy of the exercise of an arbitrary power by her naval officers.

Mr. Babbington appeared to admit there was more foundation in these objections than Wilberforce was ready to allow. He suggested that in each cruiser there should be an officer of each power agreeing to the principle, and that he should be present at every search, and no capture be made without his consent. I objected to this, that it would lead to conflicts of opinion, and perhaps even of authority, between the officers of the different Governments; and Wilberforce did not like this expedient any better than I did. I also alluded to the misconduct of many naval British officers, to the manner in which they had taken slaves from the United States and had probably sold many of them. . . . Wilberforce was much struck by this information, of which I autho-rized him to make such use as he thought proper. He somewhat equivo-cally expressed his disapprobation of Admiral Cochrane's proclamation inviting the slaves to run away from their masters and join him, and said he knew too much of what had been the lot of those slaves. He added that there were very few of them in Halifax. I believe that Wilberforce was, on the whole, disappointed in the result of this interview; though we parted in perfect good humor and civility.

3

Secretary of State (1817–24)

To read Secretary of State John Quincy Adams's diary is to appreciate how slavery found its way into a multiplicity of related and seemingly unrelated issues, both domestic and foreign. To read it chronologically is to witness how often those issues interacted with one another to create a complex context in which Adams contemplated and acted on slavery-related matters. Aside from a few weeks in early 1820 in which the Missouri controversy took center stage in his thoughts, the multiple angles from which slavery approached his mind and desk in the State Department complicated his engagement with it. While he thought more deeply about slavery during these years—in particular due to the intensity and duration of the Missouri crises of 1819–21—competing priorities posed obstacles to translating his fervent private expressions of antislavery principle into policy.

Although James Monroe came to the presidency with overwhelming support from the Electoral College in 1816, Adams quickly discerned the deep political divisions stewing beneath that cover of national comity. In the following entry he analyzed the sources of the extant threats to national unity.

July 28, 1818—The truth is, that there is in this, and perhaps must be in every Administration in this country, a perpetual tendency to fall, as well as leaders of opposition always on the watch to trip them up or pull them down. Whatever their management may be, nothing but success can keep them up. Success is undoubtedly the effect partly of judicious management and partly of good fortune. The points upon which important interests in this country are depending, and upon which success or failure will affect the issue of the Administration, are the relations with Spain, those with Great Britain, and Indian affairs. The Spanish include those with South America. Now, upon neither of these points is any great and signal successful event to be expected, even if possible; and while opposition will be recruiting and mustering forces from every quarter, the Administration will be upon a perpetual defensive and constantly losing ground. Virginia is already lukewarm to the President, and shows a disposition to dictate to him his measures without scruple or delicacy. The Richmond Enquirer, which is the voice of Virginia, speaks to him like a master to his slave. As there is no present prospect that a citizen of Virginia can be raised to the next Presidency, the *pis-aller*[1] of Virginia will be to put in a native of that State residing in another, for which either Clay or Crawford[2] will serve the turn. An anonymous letter-writer has asserted that the intention of Virginia, after Mr. Monroe's turn, will be to set up John Randolph,[3] which I doubt; but that nothing less than a Virginian will satisfy Virginia is to me perfectly demonstrated. These reflections may be pursued hereafter.

In June 1818, Adams noted the return of an American whose unspecified mission to Haiti had failed because "King Christophe refused to receive him without a formal recognition of his royal title."[4] Adams received further support for this dim view of affairs in Haiti a few months later when he had another conversation with Prince Saunders. Saunders's manner in this conversation revealed his understanding of the implications Haiti's fate had for race relations in the United States.

1. Last resort.
2. Speaker of the House of Representatives Henry Clay, and Secretary of the Treasury William H. Crawford of Georgia.
3. John Randolph of Roanoke, an erratic but powerful Virginia representative and senator throughout the early nineteenth century.
4. Diary, June 5, 1818.

October 13, 1818—On returning to my lodgings I found there Mr. Prince Sanders the black man; who has returned from his establishments in the kingdom of king Henry of Hayti. I asked him if he intended to return thither, to which he did not think proper to give a direct answer; but said if he did it would be contrary to the advice of his friends. He appeared to be labouring however with the project of colonizing Hayti from the free people of colour in the United States. He admitted that the Government of King Henry was of rather an arbitrary character, and in respect to personal liberty and security was susceptible of some improvements. He spoke however very guardedly and with great reserve. I gave him my opinion of king Henry's government very freely.

As secretary of state, Adams continued parrying the British government's tireless efforts to secure American cooperation with its drive to abolish the Atlantic slave trade. Adams's record of a cabinet meeting to determine what instructions the administration should give to its ministers in Britain (Richard Rush) and France (Albert Gallatin) made it clear how his priorities put him in what may seem to us an unlikely alliance with Secretary of War John C. Calhoun of South Carolina. His record of this intense and prolonged discussion also showed how others questioned their own priorities regarding this thorny international issue that mixed so freely with domestic politics.

October 29, 1818—[Monroe] directed a Cabinet meeting at one o'clock, upon the instructions to be given to Messrs. Gallatin and Rush concerning impressment and the slave-trade. At one we met accordingly, and discussed the question upon impressment till four, without coming to any decision. Another meeting was appointed for twelve o'clock to-morrow. Rush, according to his instructions, made two successive proposals to the British Government upon impressment—one the 18th of April and the other the 20th of June last. The first was to restrict reciprocally the naturalization of sailors, the other was totally to exclude each other's seamen from the respective services, whether in public or in merchant vessels, with a positive stipulation against the impressment of men in any case. The British Government, in the first instance, rejected both, but afterwards, on the 13th of August, Castlereagh intimated to Rush, as a suggestion of his own, upon which he had not consulted the other members of the Cabinet, that the second proposition might be accepted with two modifications—one, that either party may withdraw from the engagement of the stipulation after three or six months' notice, as in the agreement concerning armaments on the lakes; the other, that if a British officer, after entering an American vessel for purposes admitted to be lawful, should find a seaman there whom he should suspect to be English, he should be authorized to make a record . . . of the fact, that it may be brought to the knowledge of the American Government, though not to take the man. The deliberation of this day was, whether Messrs. Gallatin and Rush should be instructed to agree to these modifications or not. Strong objections were urged against them both, particularly by Mr. Calhoun. Mr. Crawford inclined to accede to them both, and the President inclined to the same. Mr. Wirt,[5] without expressing himself very decidedly, thought like the President.

My own greatest objections were against the proposal as made by ourselves, to which I have always been utterly averse, thinking it an illiberal engagement, contrary to the free, generous, and humane character of our institutions, unjustly restrictive upon the rights both of our own and of British seamen, and having a tendency to excite the most violent animosities in their minds against one another, and especially among the British seamen against us. I thought it would be now peculiarly offensive and injurious to our commercial interests, doubted whether any such stipulation would be ratified by the Senate, was confident it would give universal dissatisfaction to the merchants, and, in the event of war, would be found impracticable in execution. As, however, we have made the proposal, we must abide by it, if accepted; but its own character may justly make us scrupulous against accepting any modifications which render it still more exceptionable.

Mr. Calhoun opposed the first of Lord Castlereagh's suggested modifications, as leaving it in the power of the British Government to make the stipulation itself nugatory to us at the very moment when it would begin to operate in our favor, and because, by consenting that the compact should thus be cancelled at pleasure, we should be understood to have given an indirect assent to the resumption of the British practice.

I concurred in this opinion, which was strenuously contested by Mr. Crawford and Mr. Wirt, the President leaning a little the same way.

5. Attorney General William Wirt of Virginia.

Mr. Crawford contended that the only object of these modifications, on the part of the British Ministers, was to make the stipulation itself palatable to their own people; that no British Ministers would dare to contract such an engagement without reserving to themselves some such apology to conciliate the public opinion of their own country; but that if the agreement should once be made, they would never use the privilege of giving notice that it should be cancelled. The practice being once abandoned, they would never incur the risk of resuming it.

Mr. Calhoun was also against acceding to the second proposed modification, which would allow a British officer to muster and pass under inspection the crew of every American vessel boarded by him. It would give rise to altercations, and expose the American master to the insolence of the British officer, scarcely less galling than the injury of impressment itself. Calhoun added that the result of the late war had been to raise the tone of feeling in this nation; . . . that any concession by the Administration which should tend to lower that tone of feeling would give great dissatisfaction to the nation, and would be used as a weapon against the Administration.

Crawford said he had mentioned the proposed modifications to Mr. Clay last Saturday, and he thought well of them.

"Ay," said Calhoun, "but what will the Kentucky and Western country newspapers say of them?" This question occasioned a general laugh, in which Crawford heartily joined. We all knew that Clay would think well of anything which might excite dissatisfaction with the Administration. It was past four o'clock when the meeting was adjourned till tomorrow. Calhoun took me home in his carriage, and I walked half an hour before dinner.

October 30, 1818—The adjourned Cabinet meeting was held at the President's from noon till four, and resumed after dinner till nine in the evening. We all dined there except Mr. Wirt, who at dinner-time went home and did not return in the evening. The question upon Lord Castlereagh's proposed modifications to our proposal for abolishing impressment from our vessels on the high seas was again resumed, and argued with much earnestness—Crawford and Wirt adhering to their opinions; Calhoun and I to ours. The President ultimately found a middle term upon which he concluded, after expressing his regret that he was obliged to decide between us, equally divided in opinion as we were. He determined to reject the second modification: first, because it implied that the boarding officer should have the power of mustering the crew of an American vessel and passing them individually under his inspection; and, secondly, because it implied a suspicion that we should not faithfully and sincerely carry our own laws into execution. He would do nothing to countenance such a distrust. He also should decline acceding to the proposal that the whole agreement might be cancelled at the option of either party, giving three or six months' notice, but would offer to limit the duration of the article to a shorter period than the remainder of the Convention. For he was convinced that if the British Government once brought themselves to contract the engagement not to take men from our ships, though it should be only for a year, they would never resort to the practice again. They had never before yielded so far as in this proposal. They had until now been inflexible in adherence to the principle of their pretended right to take men from our ships, and it would be the whole point gained on our part if we should once obtain (though for ever so short a time) an abandonment by them of the principle. It would come, too, so soon after the conclusion of the late war, that in the opinion of our people it would be considered as having resulted from it. There was a deep anxiety in their minds, from an apprehension that it would again give, rise to war. The British Ministry could not, in fact, abandon their pretended right without some reservation to conciliate the pride, the interest, and the feelings of their nation to the sacrifice.

I then suggested the expediency of proposing that it should be concluded as a separate article, to be acted upon by our Senate distinctly from the remainder of the Convention, which I thought would itself meet with much difficulty in passing through the Senate, unless there should be additional articles admitting us to the West India trade. I had found, upon conversation with Mr. King,[6] when I passed through New York, that he was averse to the renewal of the Convention in its present form, and his influence in the Senate was so considerable, and his knowledge upon commercial subjects so extensive, that I thought his opposition alone would operate strongly against the ratification. The stipulation to exclude all British seamen from our ships, which

6. Senator Rufus King, statesman from New York.

would have an immediate and certain injurious effect upon our commerce, for the distant, possible, but very uncertain boon of exemption from impressment in the next maritime war in which Great Britain shall be engaged and we neutral, will be so far from satisfying our people, that the general impression will be that we have been overreached in negotiation, and probably the ratification in the Senate will fail.

The President readily agreed that the stipulation, if agreed to, should be by a separate article, and directed that the limitation of its duration, to be proposed, should be four years. And, to avoid the immediate shock to our commerce by the exclusion of British seamen from our service, that it should commence from the first of October, 1820.

The next subject taken up was the proposal from Lord Castlereagh that we should join in the measures recently concerted, by treaties concluded with Spain, Portugal, and the Netherlands, for abolishing the slave-trade. The general character of these treaties is, that the commanders of armed vessels of each of these nations should be authorized to enter and search the merchant vessels of the other for slaves, and, when they find any, to carry the vessel into the nearest settlement of either of the two nations, where they shall be tried by a mixed court, consisting of a judge from each of the two nations and two arbitrators, also one from each nation, one of whom to be drawn by lot in each case upon which the two judges should be of different opinions; these mixed courts to be authorized to condemn all slave-trading vessels of either of the two nations, according to the penalties of their respective laws. In the treaty with the Netherlands there are some limitations as to the seas where this right of search in time of peace is to be exercised; but there is one article formally admitting that vessels under convoy may be searched as well as others. Lord Castlereagh, by a note to Mr. Rush, communicates copies of these treaties, inviting the United States to join in similar stipulations, and expressing the conviction that the abolition of the slave-trade cannot be effectually accomplished but by granting this power to the officers of one nation to enter and search the merchant vessels of another.

The opinion was unanimous that this proposal ought not to be acceded to.

1. Mr. Wirt thought there was no constitutional authority in the Government of the United States to establish a Court, partly

consisting of foreigners, to sit without the bounds of the United States, and not amenable to impeachment for corruption, and he cited the Constitution, Article 3, Section I. I thought there was sufficient authority by the Constitution, and likened it to the joint commissions which we have had by treaties with Great Britain and Spain, and to the Courts of Admiralty which it has been proposed to establish at Naples if we could have obtained the consent of that Government. Mr. Wirt pointed out distinctions between the two cases—between Courts constituted under the laws of nations and Courts to carry into effect our municipal and penal statutes. But, as the power of making treaties is without limitation in the Constitution, and treaties are declared to be the supreme law of the land, I still hold to the opinion that there is no constitutional difficulty in the way.

2. Another objection was, that we could not establish these Courts with reciprocity, as we have no possessions on the coast of Africa.

3. That we have suffered so much from the practice of foreign officers to search our vessels in time of war, particularly by its connection with a British doctrine that after an officer has entered for one purpose he may proceed to search for another, that we ought to be specially cautious not to admit of the right of search in time of peace.

4. That it is still more obnoxious as coupled with the provision that even vessels under convoy shall be subjected to it.

But, in declining the proposition, the President directed that an offer should be made to stipulate in general terms; that further laws should be made, if it should be found necessary, for carrying into execution those already enacted for the prohibition, of the traffic by our citizens, and that a copy of the Act of Congress of the last session to that effect[7] should be communicated to the British Government.

---

7. An 1818 law tightening enforcement of the United States' 1807 law banning American participation in the Atlantic slave trade or importation of slaves from abroad.

The following entry revealed both the limits and the persistence of Adams's Anglophobia. In May 1818, the British government agreed to refer the question of compensation for fugitive American slaves during the War of 1812 (among other outstanding issues) to an arbitrating nation, Russia. The "allowance" under discussion between Monroe and Adams here was the idea of adjusting American monetary claims for individual slaves upward to account not only for their property value but also for the value of their labor lost to their masters.[8]

December 24, 1818—Fourth anniversary of the signature of the Treaty of Ghent; a day that ought never to pass without recollections of my gratitude to Divine Providence for that great blessing to my country and myself—a blessing, great in itself, greater in its consequences, and which affords me a continual source of pleasure in the remembrance. I met Mr. Calhoun at the President's. . . . The President desired me to read over again all the papers in the case of the claim of bounty for captured slaves, in which his opinion is in favor of the allowance, and mine against it.

Adams put acquiring the territories of East Florida and West Florida from Spain near the top of his agenda as secretary of state. In the following entry he expounded on why signing a treaty to that effect with Spanish minister Luis de Onís y González-Vera made this day "perhaps the most important day of my life." This self-congratulatory entry spared no thought for the notion that this agreement—which would become the 1819 Adams-Onís Treaty—would annex slave territory to the United States.

February 22, 1819—The acquisition of the Floridas has long been an object of earnest desire to this country. The acknowledgment of a definite line of boundary to the South Sea[9] forms a great epocha in our history. The first proposal of it in this negotiation was my own, and I trust

8. See Diary, May 15, 19, 1818; November 3, 1819, June 26, 1820; Arnett G. Lindsay, "Diplomatic Relations between the United States and Great Britain Bearing on the Return of Negro Slaves, 1783-1828," *Journal of Negro History* 5 (October 1920), 416.
9. He seems to have meant that the treaty fixed the boundary between the United States and New Spain all the way to the South Pacific Ocean.

it is now secured beyond the reach of revocation. It was not even among our claims by the Treaty of Independence with Great Britain. It was not among our pretensions under the purchase of Louisiana—for that gave us only the range of the Mississippi and its waters. I first introduced it in the written proposal of 31st October last, after having discussed it verbally both with Onis and De Neuville.[10] It is the only peculiar and appropriate right acquired by this treaty in the event of its ratification. I record the first assertion of this claim for the United States as my own, because it is known to be mine perhaps only to the members of the present Administration, and may perhaps never be known to the public— and, if ever known, will be soon and easily forgotten. . . . The change in the relations with Spain, from the highest mutual exasperation and imminent war to a fair prospect of tranquillity and of secure peace, completes the auspicious characters of this transaction in its present aspect, which fills my heart with gratitude unutterable to the First Cause of all. Yet let me not forget that in the midst of this hope there are seeds of fear. The ratification of Spain is yet uncertain, and may, by many possible events, be defeated. If ratified, many difficulties will certainly arise to clog the execution of the treaty. . . . A watchful eye, a resolute purpose, a calm and patient temper, and a favoring Providence, will all be as indispensable for the future as they have been for the past in the management of this negotiation. May they not be found wanting!

The American Colonization Society (ACS) project of removing free African Americans to West Africa was gaining serious momentum by 1819. In that year its members started lobbying Congress and President Monroe to establish an American colony near the analogous British colony of Sierra Leone, to aid both the colonization of free blacks and the American drive to suppress the Atlantic slave trade. The latter effort itself received greater momentum in 1819 when Congress passed a bill declaring participation in that slave traffic to be piracy, and thus a capital offense. Adams's reaction to this scheme and these schemers in cabinet discussions—and even more candid reaction in his diary—was redolent of his suspicions of British antislavery pretensions. It also captured how constitutionally conservative he could be at this stage of his career.

10. French minister Jean-Guillaume Hyde de Neuville.

March 12, 1819—At the President's this morning he mentioned that he wished shortly to have a meeting of the members of the Administration to consider the effect of the Acts passed at the late session of Congress against piracy and the slave-trade, and he intimated that the Committee of the Colonization Society had applied to him to purchase a territory on the coast of Africa to which the slaves who may be taken under the late Act may be sent. The President said there had been only an appropriation of one hundred thousand dollars, which could not be sufficient for purchasing a territory, but perhaps Congress would appropriate more hereafter.

I told him I thought it impossible that Congress should have had any purchase of territory in contemplation of that Act, and that I had no opinion of the practicability or of the usefulness of the object proposed by the Colonization Society, which object professes to be to establish a colony in Africa, where all the free blacks and people of color of the United States may be sent and settled. This project is professed to be formed: 1, without intending to use any compulsion upon the free people of color to make them go; 2, to encourage the emancipation of slaves by their masters; 3, to promote the entire abolition of slavery; and yet, 4, without in the slightest degree affecting what they call a certain species of property that is, the property of slaves. There are men of all sorts and descriptions concerned in this Colonization Society: some exceedingly humane, weak-minded men, who have really no other than the professed objects in view, and who honestly believe them both useful and attainable; some, speculators in official profits and honors, which a colonial establishment would of course produce; some, specu-lators in political popularity, who think to please the abolitionists by their zeal for emancipation, and the slave-holders by the flattering hope of ridding them of the free colored people at the public expense; lastly, some cunning slave-holders, who see that the plan may be carried far enough to produce the effect of raising the market price of their slaves. But although the plan obviously imports the engrafting of a colonial establishment upon the Constitution of the United States, and thereby an accession of power to the National Government transcending all its other powers, and although this tremendous machinery would be introduced under an ostensible purpose comparatively so trivial, and in a captivating form which might bring it in unperceived, I do not believe that is the actuating motive of any one member of the Society. For it would only be the motive of a man whose magnificence of design and depravity of principle would both go beyond my opinions of any man belonging to the Institution. The President said this subject had been recommended by a resolution of the Virginia Legislature. And then he enlarged upon the great earnestness there was in Virginia for the gradual abolition of slavery, and upon the excellent and happy condition of the slaves in that State—upon the kindness with which they were treated, and the mutual attachment subsisting between them and their masters. He said that the feeling against slavery was so strong that shortly after the close of our Revolution many persons had voluntarily emancipated their slaves, but this had introduced a class of very dangerous people, the free blacks, who lived by pilfering, and corrupted the slaves, and produced such pernicious consequences that the Legislature were obliged to prohibit further emancipation by law. The important object now was to remove these free blacks, and provide a place to which the emancipated slaves might go: the legal obstacles to emancipation might then be withdrawn, and the black population in time be drawn off entirely from Virginia.

At the office, the Committee from the Society, General John Mason, Walter Jones, and Francis S. Key, came and renewed the subject. Jones argued that the late Slave-Trade Act contained a clear authority to settle a colony in Africa, and that the purchase of Louisiana, and the settlement at the mouth of Columbia River, placed beyond all question the right of acquiring territory as existing in the Government of the United States.

I treated these gentlemen with all possible civility, but gave them distinctly to understand that the late Slave-Trade Act had no reference to the settlement of a colony, and that the acquisition of Louisiana, and the establishment at the mouth of Columbia River, being in territory contiguous to and continuous with our own, could by no means warrant the purchase of countries beyond the seas, or the establishment of a colonial system of government subordinate to and dependent upon that of the United States. To derive powers competent to this from the Slave-Trade Act was an Indian cosmogony: it was mounting the world upon an elephant, and the elephant on a tortoise, with nothing for the tortoise to stand upon.

They took leave of me with good humor, but satisfied, I believe, that they will have no aid from me. A politician would have flattered them.

March 16, 1819—The meeting of the heads of Departments was held this day at the President's, from noon to four o'clock, to consider the Slave-Trade and Piracy Acts passed at the late session of Congress, and what instructions it would be proper to give to the commanders of the armed vessels of the United States for carrying them into execution. It was soon settled that the Slave-Trade Act gave no authority to the President to purchase a territory or establish a colony in Africa, though it does authorize him to take measures for removing beyond the limits of the United States the negroes who may be taken, as imported contrary to the law, and to appoint an agent to receive them in Africa. Mr. Walter Jones's argument is, that the negroes when received there cannot be left to starve; that something must be done with them there; that lands must be given them to cultivate, which lands must be first owned by the United States. Therefore the President must have the right to purchase land for the nation and to settle a colony. Calhoun and Thompson[11] scouted this construction of the Act, and I therefore said nothing about it. Crawford is one of the Vice-Presidents of the Colonization Society, but says he has no faith in the practicability of their projects. It is one of his traps for popularity.

April 2, 1819—Going to my office this morning, I met Mr. Wirt, the Attorney-General, who told me he was coming there to meet Crawford and me at one o'clock, and they accordingly came. We first examined a question which has arisen under the Slave-Trade Act of the last session of Congress. It authorizes the President to send to Africa the slaves that may be taken by our armed vessels and brought into the United States, captured in vessels attempting to introduce them in contravention to any of the slave Acts, and also to appoint an Agent or Agents in Africa to receive such slaves. Crawford had seen in the Augusta Chronicle, a Georgia newspaper, an advertisement of thirty or forty slaves, imported contrary to the laws, to be sold for the benefit of the State, according to the provisions of the Acts of Congress and of the State of Georgia before the law of Congress of the last session. Crawford thought that this last Act was retrospective, and that under it the President might

11. Secretary of the Navy Smith Thompson, of New York.

send to Africa the slaves thus advertised for sale, although they were imported before the passage of the Act. The President, before he left the city, directed me to write accordingly to the Governor and the District Attorney of Georgia; but being, upon examination of the Act myself, convinced that this course of proceeding would not be warranted by it, I postponed writing the letters, and this day submitted the Act and the question to joint consideration. Mr. Wirt had doubts whether the Act would operate retrospectively in this case or not. Mr. Crawford finally came to the conclusion that it would not, and chiefly upon the suggestion that it would conflict with a vested right of the State. And he finally determined to apply to the Colonization Society to take the affair into their own hands, as he thought they were authorized to do by a late law of the State of Georgia.

The British government's drive to secure the cooperation of the Americans and European powers to suppress the Atlantic slave trade was unabated by Congress's piracy act of 1819. Adams's ordering of priorities relative to this issue jumps off the pages of his account of two conversations in April 1819. The first was with the French minister, Baron Hyde de Neuville, the second with Richmond attorney George Hay, who was Monroe's son-in-law and one of his era's leading critics of abolitionism. That Adams would have agreed—if not in every particular—with Hay suggests just how strongly his suspicion of abolitionists, especially of the British stripe, shaped his sense of the proper relationship between slavery and politics. The following entries also recorded Adams's ongoing interaction with the ACS and further revealed the roots of his antagonism to that organization.

April 24, 1819—We had also some conversation respecting the new treaties of Great Britain with Spain, Portugal, and the Netherlands, allowing a mutual right of search to armed vessels, and joint Courts for trying slave-traders. I told him I was glad that France and Russia . . . had refused acceding to this principle of mutual search in time of peace. But he thought it would not be inadmissible for the purpose of abolishing effectually the slave-trade. He said he was sure there would be no slaves in the United States in forty years from this time. There would be, to be sure, in Louisiana, but then Louisiana would not form a part of the United States. I said that civil war would then be substituted instead of the Union.

April 29, 1819—At the office I found Mr. George Hay, who borrowed a Parliamentary pamphlet containing papers relating to the slave-trade, received with the last dispatches from R. Rush. Hay said he had a great avidity for all papers concerning the project for abolishing the slave-trade, a project which he believed would ultimately fail, which had already produced incomparably more mischief than good, and which he had no doubt would continue to be pernicious. For he had no doubt that the insurrection in Saint Domingo, and the total destruction of the white powers there, were the legitimate offspring of Mr. Wilberforce's first abolition plans; and our Colonization Society here, whatever pretences they may put forth, and whatever some enthusiastic people among them might believe and intend, could have no other ultimate object than a general emancipation. I said that the Colonization Society were pushing their objects with so much zeal and importunity that I very much wished their memorials might be taken up by Congress and fairly discussed; for, under the color of colonizing black people, I was afraid they would smuggle in upon us a system of establishing Colonies beyond sea, of the consequences of which the people of this country were little aware; while in England, under the mask of abolishing the slave-trade, they were introducing, and had already obtained the consent of Spain, Portugal, and the Netherlands to, a new principle of the law of nations more formidable to human liberty than the slave-trade itself—a right of the commanders of armed vessels of one nation to visit and search the merchant vessels of another in time of peace. I observed that the Colonization Society had derived great strength from the part which the Virginia Legislature had taken in their favor.

He said the Virginia Legislature had been tricked into that Resolution; that there was no such absurd reasoner in the world as humanity—it never looked but at one side of a question; that the Resolution of the Virginia Legislature had been obtained by Mr. Mercer,[12] who was the father of the Colonization Society and of all their projects; that he [Hay] himself had inconsiderately voted for it under the impulse of

12. Charles Fenton Mercer, a congressman from Virginia.

humanity, and three hours after, and ever since, had bitterly repented his vote. . . . and now, if a vote of the Virginia Legislature could be taken, it would be anything but in favor of the Colonization Society and its projects. Mr. Jefferson, he said, had favored them because it was he who many years since had introduced and carried through the law of the State for partial emancipation of the slaves, and after witnessing the pernicious consequences that had followed from it he was desirous of finding another remedy for it. But the friends of emancipation had a memorable example before them, of which it was surprising that they would not avail themselves as an admonition. The negro slave trade itself was the child of humanity—the contrivance of Las Casas to mitigate the condition of the American Indians.[13]

Mr. Hay's opinions upon the Colonization Society and its projects were unexpected to me. There are so many considerations of difficulty and of delicacy mingling with this subject that I would gladly keep aloof from it altogether. But I apprehend the Society, which, like all fanatical associations, is intolerant, will push and intrigue and worry till I shall be obliged to take a stand and appear publicly among their opponents. Their project of expurgating the United States from the free people of color at the public expense, by colonizing them in Africa, is, so far as it is sincere and honest, upon a par with John Cleves Symmes's project of going to the North Pole, and travelling within the nutshell of the earth.[14]

13. Bartolome de las Casas, a Dominican friar, proposed in 1516 that Africans be substituted for Indian slaves in the Spanish colonies of the New World. He railed against the forced labor and destruction of family life that Indian slavery involved, as well as the demographic catastrophe they were already witnessing. Las Casas later came "to revise his views on the acceptability of African slavery," but ironically enough "while the Dominican's representations on behalf of the Indian chimed in with royal concerns, his retraction concerning the Africans had no impact on imperial policy." Robin Blackburn, *The Making of New World Slavery: From the Baroque to the Modern, 1492-1800* (New York: Verso, 1997), 136.
14. Symmes, who served in the US Army from 1802 to 1816, first announced his theory in 1818 by distributing a circular "to every learned institution and . . . to numerous distinguished individuals, throughout the United States." It was probably in this way that Adams learned about Symmes. Symmes lectured in western cities of the United States beginning in 1820, and in 1822 and 1823 petitioned Congress to support an expedition to one or both of Earth's poles. He received endless ridicule, as Adams's entry suggests. See *The Symmes Theory of Concentric Spheres, Demonstrating That the Earth Is Hollow, Habitable within, and Widely Open about*

April 30, 1819—I had not a thought, when writing my journal of yesterday, that I should so soon be brought into direct collision with the Colonization Society. But this morning Mr. Laurie,[15] the Presbyterian, and Mr. Hawley,[16] the Episcopalian clergyman, came to my office, as deputies from the Society, with a subscription paper to raise money to send to Africa the slaves which have been advertised for sale for the benefit of the State of Georgia. The Legislature of Georgia authorized the Governor to deliver over those slaves to the Colonization Society if they would take upon themselves the whole expense of sending them to Africa or elsewhere, and pay back to the State all the charges and expenses occasioned to them by the smuggling in of these negroes. The Society have accepted this offer, and are now soliciting subscriptions to collect the money. They have been for some days addressing the public and soliciting in the newspapers; and now these clergymen are going round as their deputies with the subscription paper. Mr. Crawford's name was down for fifty dollars. I declined subscribing, and told Messrs. Laurie and Hawley that on full deliberation I had with regret made up my opinion that the object of the Society was impracticable to any considerable extent, and that as far as it would be practicable it would be productive of evil more than of good; that, without answering for the feelings or the fortunes of individuals, one or more, I believed that the mass of colored people who may be removed to Africa by the Colonization Society will suffer more and enjoy less than they would if they should remain in their actual condition in the United States; that their removal will do more harm than good to this country, by depriving it of the mass of their industry, and thus that the result of the whole, to both parties, will be evil and not good. Mr. Laurie argued the subject with me for more than an hour, but Mr. Hawley took no part in the conversation. Laurie observed that the Society would greatly regret not having the weight and countenance of my name, but would hope I should hereafter be convinced by the experience of their success.

the Poles. *Compiled by Americus Symmes, from the Writings of His Father, Capt. John Cleves Symmes* (Louisville, KY: Bradley and Gilbert, 1878), quotation on ix.

15. Dr. James Laurie, a longtime Presbyterian pastor in Washington.
16. William Dickinson Hawley, chaplain of the Senate from 1817 to 1818 and long-tenured rector at Washington's influential St. John's Episcopal Church.

I told them I would certainly not throw impediments in their way. I had the highest respect for the motives of the Society and for the characters and opinions of many of its members. My deference for those opinions made me distrustful of my own. Yet by my own I must necessarily abide. I wished not to appear or be thought an adversary to the Society, but I could not, with my present opinions, give it any countenance. I was willing their experiment should be fairly made; I had no faith in its success. So far as my refusal to subscribe might operate against the Society, I should wish what had passed between us might not be made known, but so far as it concerned only myself, I had no wish that it should be kept private. Their deportment was entirely proper, and Hawley looked assent to almost all that I said.

When the Missouri Territory applied for statehood in February 1819, New York Congressman James Tallmadge sparked a massive sectional conflict when he added an amendment to the statehood bill outlawing the importation of slaves into Missouri. The resultant debate dominated American politics for the next year, until Congress crafted the first Missouri Compromise in March 1820 admitting Missouri without the Tallmadge restriction. During this protracted and threatening conflict, Adams had much to say in cabinet discussions and much more to say in his diary, but said little to nothing in public. The changes over time in even his private statements illustrated the complexity of the questions involved, intermingling as they did with a wide variety of other current issues.

That complexity emerged in his first diary statement, which showed how presidential politics mixed in with the whole affair. Monroe's re-election was a foregone conclusion for 1820, so rival camps were already looking toward 1824.[17] The occasion that prompted the following entry was an Independence Day celebration at a Washington hotel.

July 5, 1819—There were twenty-one toasts, but the State of Alabama being now the twenty-second State, I gave it as a volunteer; upon which Crawford, who seems to have thought I was encroaching upon his territories, gave—"The admission of new States on the principles of the

17. For a good passage on how Adams expected little but presidential jockeying throughout the second Monroe term, see Diary, January 8, 1820.

SECRETARY OF STATE   63

Federal Constitution, that they should be *Republican*." This toast glanced
at the failure of the Territory of the Missouri to become a State at the
last session of Congress, owing to a restriction introduced by the House
of Representatives excluding slavery from the State, and declaring free
all persons to be born there after a certain period. The Senate struck out
the provision, and the bill failed by the disagreement between the two
Houses. The attempt to introduce the restriction produced a violent
agitation among the members from the slave-holding States, and it has
been communicated to the States themselves, and to the Territory of
Missouri. The slave-drivers, as usual, whenever this topic is brought up,
bluster and bully, talk of the white slaves of the Eastern States, and the
dissolution of the Union, and oceans of blood; and the Northern men,
as usual, pocket all this hectoring, sit down in quiet, and submit to the
slave-scourging republicanism of the planters. Crawford, who sees how
this affair will ultimately go, and who relies on the support of the slave-
drivers, is determined to show them that he is on their side, and gave this
toast to exhibit himself as their champion. On this particular question
I did not approve of the attempted restriction upon the State of Missouri,
because I believe it not compatible either with the Constitution of the
United States or with the Louisiana Treaty. But I think Crawford's toast
not remarkable for delicacy towards the Legislature, while the question
is pending before them, and he an officer of the Executive Government.
He also flatters himself with support from New York and Pennsylvania.
I doubted a little whether this toast was altogether judicious, in reference
to its possible effect upon them. It may, however, pass unnoticed in that
quarter. I was diverted at perceiving how it was brought out by my toast
of Alabama, the simplest thing in the world, originating in the oversight
of the managers in preparing, only twenty-one toasts. I withdrew immediately after these volunteers were given.

*Two entries in 1819 showed Adams still to be dismissive of both slave traders
and overzealous reformers. At the end of a passage on a "piratical privateer,"
Adams found it remarkable that the man "did not appear to be conscious
in the slightest degree that he had been doing anything wrong. Just so it is
with the slave-traders."*[18] *The following entry illuminates Adams's sense that a*

18. Diary, April 28, 1819.

distinctly American view of liberty was moderate in nature. This passage helps explain his cautious response to the ACS and the Missouri controversy, as well as his general political cast of mind heading into the 1820s.

November 22, 1819—Mr. B. Irvine[19] brought me a report upon Venezuela, of two or three folio volumes of manuscript. If labor deserves compensation, he has certainly earned his wages. He is one of the men with whom this age abounds—a fanatic of liberty for the whole human race—honest, but with a brain always in a snarl—with learning just enough to be pedantic, and temper just enough to be indiscreet; bitter in his dislikes, and unmeasured in his resentments—but withal indefatigably industrious and persevering. He is by birth an Irishman, and has no native American feelings. He, therefore, like all the European republicans whom I have known, habitually thinks of liberty as a blessing to be acquired, and never as a blessing to be enjoyed.

Along with all these other issues, in late 1819 the Monroe administration continued intensive discussions about whether the recent slave trade act authorized establishing an American colony in West Africa. Adams consistently took a more guarded stance toward this scheme than did Crawford or Monroe.[20] Adams most fully articulated his strict constructionist position in the meeting recorded next.

December 10, 1819—There was a Cabinet meeting at the President's at noon, Messrs. Crawford, Thompson, and Wirt present. The Act of Congress against the slave-trade of the last session, and the questions of construction arising from it, were under consideration. The Colonization Society are indefatigable in their efforts to get hold of the funds appropriated by that Act; and having got the ear of the President,

19. Baptiste (also spelled Baptist or Baptis) Irvine, a longtime Democratic-Republican editor in the Mid-Atlantic region. Adams had appointed him a special agent to Venezuela with instructions to protect American interests there during its revolution. See "Baptis Irvine" in the Archives of Maryland Biographical Series, at http://msa.maryland.gov/megafile/msa/speccol/sc3500/sc3520/013900/013915/html/13915bio.html.

20. See Diary, November 10, 16, 1819; January 6, 1820.

and Crawford for purposes of his own being one of them, they have already got their fingers into the purse; the Government is to pay fifteen hundred dollars for half the freight of a vessel they are about sending to Africa. Their Colony is to be formed at the island of Sherbro, on the Coast of Guinea, about five degrees north of the line, so perfect a desert that they are to send out even the timber to build the huts in which their colonists are to dwell. And with all the multitudes of their members, and auxiliary societies and newspaper puffs, they have no funds, and they are ravenous as panthers for the appropriation of a hundred thousand dollars of the last session. Crawford's construction of the law would deliver up to them the whole of it without reserve, though he professes to be very much upon his guard against them, and to have no belief in their success. This Agent, with a discretionary credit of twenty thousand dollars upon London, is a clear forecast of what is to follow. Wirt in the first instance construed the law much more strictly than I did. He was brought over by the arguments of Crawford, who is ready to make a Colony out of the law of the last session; and Mr. Thompson, who thinks the law very loosely worded, and that it ought to be explained, still thinks it will admit of a liberal construction to give effect to the President's power of spending the money. Crawford urges the most liberal construction, because the object of the Act is beneficent and affects no rights. I objected that there was no authority given by the law to spend money to maintain the blacks in Africa at all; that if the authority is to be assumed constructively, I see no limit to it but the amount of the appropriation, which will be soon expended if we are to maintain the Colony, and which will plunge us deep enough into the plan to bind the honor of the nation to further appropriations. The money is to be entrusted to the discretion of an Agent under little responsibility, and from the tendency of all such expenditures to swell, exemplified in the application of similar funds to the relief of distressed American seamen, and in the army pensioner law, this would soon become a drain upon the nation. Then would come complaints of extravagance and waste; then enquiries in Congress how the money has been spent, and then by what authority. Then, too, would come the temper, not so well disposed to construe the law liberally, or to regard it as exclusively beneficent. And the time for the Executive to think of all this is now.

The President finally concluded to pay half the freight of this ship now, and then to send a message to Congress informing them how the law has been understood and acted upon; and then if Congress do nothing to explain the law, it will give the sanction of their tacit assent to the liberal construction and the discretionary expenditure.

The ongoing Missouri crisis prompted Adams to contemplate the Declaration of Independence at greater depth, and moved his complex feelings toward its author Thomas Jefferson decidedly in a negative direction.

December 27, 1819—Mr. Mark Langdon Hill, a representative in Congress from Maine, ... showed me a letter from Mr. Jefferson to the late John Langdon, of New Hampshire, written in the year 1810, full of his political Shandyism,[21] a mixture of profound and sagacious observation, with strong prejudices and irritated passions. It is a sort of epitome of his political opinions and feelings. Jefferson is one of the great men whom this country has produced, one of the men who has contributed largely to the formation of our national character—to much that is good and to not a little that is evil in our sentiments and manners. His Declaration of Independence is an abridged Alcoran[22] of political doctrine, laying open the first foundations of civil society; but he does not appear to have been aware that it also laid open a precipice into which the slave-holding planters of his country sooner or later must fall. With the Declaration of Independence on their lips, and the merciless scourge of slavery in their hands, a more flagrant image of human inconsistency can scarcely be conceived than one of our Southern slave-holding republicans. Jefferson has been himself all his life a slave-holder, but he has published opinions so blasting to the very existence of slavery, that, however creditable they may be to his candor and humanity, they speak not much for his prudence or his forecast as a Virginian planter. The seeds of the Declaration of Independence are

21. The Free Dictionary defines Shandyism as "a tendency to whimsical conduct in accord with absurd theories from past ages. [Allusion to the actions of Walter, father of the hero in Sterne's *Tristram Shandy*.]" See http://www.thefreedictionary.com/Shandyism.
22. Alternate title for the holy book of Islam, the Koran.

yet maturing. The harvest will be what West, the painter, calls the terrible sublime.[23]

Adams's growing uneasiness about the Missouri imbroglio and its potential impact came into focus as he recorded his thoughts in early 1820. It is telling that it seemed self-evident to him that those thoughts must stay private. This larger context also helps us understand why Adams oscillated between wishing the whole crisis would just go away and fearing that a solution friendly to slavery would be what ended it.

January 2, 1820—There are several subjects upon which the public mind in this country is taking a turn which alarms me greatly for the continuance of this Union—the bank; the currency; the internal improvement question; the extension or repression of slavery; the conflicting ambition of the great States of New York and Virginia, and the workings of individual ambition, mingling with all these controversial topics. It seems to me that we are at the eve of a great crisis, of which scarcely any one is yet aware.

January 3, 1820—The question concerning our affairs with Spain appears to be much more agitated among the members of Congress. Wirt says they will do nothing; that the proposition in the message to carry the treaty[24] into execution, as if it had been ratified, is producing a very great fermentation in the House of Representatives, and is very much censured. The objection is, that there is no precedent for it. Wirt himself made that objection at the time when the message was preparing, and it is a natural County Court objection. The Barbours[25] are taking it up in both Houses, and, as it is apparently now the interest and the policy of all the intriguers that the treaty should not be ratified nor Florida taken possession of, it is quite apparent that nothing will be

---

23. American-born British painter Benjamin West (1738–1820), who was one of many in his generation dedicated to the aesthetic of "the sublime." See Christine Riding and Nigel Llewellyn, "British Art and the Sublime," at http://www.tate.org.uk/art/research-publications/the-sublime/christine-riding-and-nigel-llewellyn-british-art-and-the-sublime-r1109418.
24. The Adams-Onis Treaty.
25. The Virginia brothers Representative Philip P. Barbour and Senator James Barbour.

done. The real motives operating to produce this effect will be altogether different from those disclosed. There will be a difficulty in resuming the negotiation with Spain without disgracing the country in its own eyes and in those of other nations. But the real interests of the nation will not be otherwise much affected by it. For this, and deeper mortifications, it behooves me to have my mind prepared. I mentioned that Lowndes[26] had told me the Missouri question might ultimately affect the vote on Spanish concerns, and I found the observation worked not kindly. The Missouri question thrills in every Southern nerve. It is yet in a state of chaos in my mind.

January 8, 1820—[I told President Monroe that the] dark and unpropitious [prospect] abroad is far more gloomy and threatening when we turn our eyes homeward. The bank, the national currency, the stagnation of commerce, the depression of manufactures, the restless turbulence and jealousies and insubordination of the State Legislatures, the Missouri slave question, the deficiencies of the revenue to be supplied, the rankling passions and ambitious projects of individuals, mingling with everything, presented a prospect of the future which I freely acknowledged was to me appalling. I asked him whether these apprehensions were visionary, and, if not, whether he had contemplated any distinct system of measures to be in preparation for the embarrassments which it was obvious to foresee as inevitable at no distant day.

He said that, as to the Missouri question, he apprehended no great danger from that. He believed a compromise would be found and agreed to, which would be satisfactory to all parties.

I did not enquire further, though I was much surprised at this remark. All the public appearances are directly the reverse; and either there is an underplot in operation upon this subject, of which I had no suspicion, or the President has a very inadequate idea of the real state of that controversy, or he assumed an air of tranquillity concerning it in which there was more caution than candor, more reserve than sincerity.

January 10, 1820—The Missouri question has taken such hold of my feelings and imagination that, finding my ideas connected with it very numerous, but confused for want of arrangement, I have within these few days begun to commit them to paper loosely as they arise in my

26. Representative William Lowndes of South Carolina.

mind. There are views of the subject which have not yet been taken by any of the speakers or writers by whom it has been discussed—views which the time has not yet arrived for presenting to the public, but which in all probability it will be necessary to present hereafter. I take it for granted that the present question is a mere preamble—a title-page to a great tragic volume. I have hitherto reserved my opinions upon it, as it has been obviously proper for me to do. The time may, and I think will, come when it will be my duty equally clear to give my opinion, and it is even now proper for me to begin the preparation of myself for that emergency. The President thinks this question will be winked away by a compromise. But so do not I. Much am I mistaken if it is not destined to survive his political and individual life and mine.

January 15, 1820—After I returned to the office, the Russian Minister, Mr. Poletica,[27] called there with a packet of dispatches for the Russian Ambassador at Paris. He told me he had given a full account in that dispatch of the Missouri or slave question, which is beginning to shake this Union to its foundations. Poletica seems already to have taken his side, for he said he considered it a question whether this country should hereafter be a Colony or an independent power. I entered not, however, into conversation with him upon the subject.

January 16, 1820—In my walk for exercise before dinner, I paid several visits, and called upon Mr. Lowndes, with whom I had a long conversation upon public affairs. . . .

We had also much conversation upon the Missouri or slave question. Lowndes, who is from South Carolina, and a large slave-holder, is of course on the slavery side of the question, which there is now every appearance will be carried by the superior ability of the slavery party—for thus much is certain, that if institutions are to be judged by their results in the composition of the councils of this Union, the slave-holders are much more ably represented than the simple freemen. With the exception of Rufus King, there is not in either House of Congress a member from the free States able to cope in powers of the mind with William Pinkney or James Barbour. In the House of Representatives, the freemen have none to contend on equal terms either with John

27. Pyotor Ivanovich Poletika, Russian minister to the United States from 1817 to 1822.

Randolph or Clay. Another misfortune to the free party is, that some of their ablest men are either on this question with their adversaries or lukewarm in the cause. The slave men have indeed a deeper immediate stake in the issue than the partisans of freedom, their passions and interests are more profoundly agitated, and they have stronger impulses to active energy than their antagonists, whose only individual interest in this case arises from its bearing on the balance of political power between North and South.

February 4, 1820—Mr. R[ufus] King ... passed a couple of hours with me at my office. ... Shortly before the meeting of Congress, he published, at the request of a Missouri question meeting at New York, the substance of his two speeches last winter in the Senate on that bill, which was then lost by the disagreement between the two Houses on the restricting clause. This publication has largely contributed to kindle the flame now raging throughout the Union on that question, and which threatens its dissolution. King is strongly affected and agitated by it.[28] Whether he sees the consequences in their full extent, and has made up his mind to promote them, even to the separation of the Union, I am not sure; but my own opinion is, that no man ought to take an active part in that discussion without being first prepared for that and reconciled to it, because it must end in that.

As the Missouri conflict ground on, Adams spent more and more time in the hallways and legislative chambers of Congress seeking to discern the direction of events.[29] This only increased his admiration for—and perhaps his envy of—Rufus King as the great champion of the free states. His accounts of the Missouri issue's intrusion into social and even religious events illustrate how pervasive it had become. That pervasiveness kept it foremost in his mind but did not produce a consistency of response in Adams. His antislavery sentiments became more vehement and lofty, but he was neither any closer to expressing them publicly nor more certain about the merits of a compromise to settle the frightful controversy.

28. For the publication of these two radical antislavery speeches and King's uncertainty surrounding that publication, see Matthew Mason, *Slavery and Politics in the Early American Republic* (Chapel Hill: University of North Carolina Press, 2006), 208.
29. See also Diary, January 24, February 5, 1820.

February 11, 1820—I went up to the Capitol and heard Mr. King in the Senate, upon what is called the Missouri question. He had been speaking perhaps an hour before I went in, and I heard him about an hour. His manner is dignified, grave, earnest, but not rapid or vehement. There was nothing new in his argument, but he unravelled with ingenious and subtle analysis many of the sophistical tissues of the slave-holders. He laid down the position of the natural liberty of man, and its incompatibility with slavery in any shape. He also questioned the Constitutional right of the President and Senate to make the Louisiana Treaty; but he did not dwell upon those points, nor draw the consequences from them which I should think important in speaking to that subject. He spoke, however, with great power, and the great slave-holders in the House gnawed their lips and clenched their fists as they heard him. . . .

We attended an evening party at Mr. Calhoun's, and heard of nothing but the Missouri question and Mr. King's speeches. The slave-holders cannot hear of them without being seized with cramps. They call them seditious and inflammatory, when their greatest real defect is their timidity. Never since human sentiments and human conduct were influenced by human speech was there a theme for eloquence like the free side of this question now before the Congress of this Union. By what fatality does it happen that all the most eloquent orators of the body are on its slavish side? There is a great mass of cool judgment and plain sense on the side of freedom and humanity, but the ardent spirits and passions are on the side of oppression. Oh, if but one man could arise with a genius capable of comprehending, a heart capable of supporting, and an utterance capable of communicating those eternal truths that belong to this question, to lay bare in all its nakedness that outrage upon the goodness of God, human slavery, now is the time, and this is the occasion, upon which such a man would perform the duties of an angel upon earth!

February 13, 1820—Attended the divine service at the Capitol, and heard Mr. Edward Everett, the Professor of the Greek language at Harvard University, a young man of shining talents and of illustrious promise.[30] . . . The house was full, but not crowded. The New England

---

30. Everett had been one of Adams's pupils when Adams taught rhetoric at Harvard.

hearers were rapt in enthusiasm. Mr. King told me he had never heard anything like it. The Southern auditors approved more coolly. Mr. Clay, with whom I walked, after the service, to call upon Chief-Justice [John] Marshall, told me that although Everett had a fine fancy and a chaste style of composition, his manner was too theatrical. . . .

Clay started, however, immediately to the Missouri question, yet in debate before both Houses of Congress, and, alluding to a strange scene at Richmond, Virginia, last Wednesday evening, said it was a shocking thing to think of, but he had not a doubt that within five years from this time the Union would be divided into three distinct confederacies. I did not incline to discuss the subject with him. . . . Mr. Otis had invited me to go and dine with him at Crawford's [Hotel], in Georgetown, and I walked there. Mr. King, Judge Story, Mr. Everett, and Mr. Webster, of Boston, formed the party, with Mrs. Otis.[31] . . . The party was quite social, and the Missouri subject was very freely canvassed. King has made a desperate plunge into it, and has thrown his last stake upon the card. It agitates him accordingly with deep and vehement emotion. He has, however, great self-control, cool judgment, and spirit-breaking experience. There was difference enough of opinion between us to occasion much, though no angry, discussion.

February 20, 1820—I met . . . General Bloomfield,[32] who, with many others, is much alarmed at the dissensions which have arisen in the nation and in Congress from the Missouri or slave question. . . .

When the [Tallmadge] amendment was first presented, its importance and consequences were certainly foreseen by no one, not even by those who brought it forward. Its discussion disclosed a secret: it revealed the basis for a new organization of parties. Clay had been two years laboring, first upon South American patriotism and then upon the Seminole War,[33] first in defiance of Crawford and then as a subaltern

31. Rufus King of New York, US senator Harrison Gray Otis from Massachusetts and his wife Sally Foster Otis, associate US Supreme Court justice Joseph Story, Edward Everett, and Daniel Webster.
32. Representative Joseph Bloomfield of New Jersey.
33. Clay had grounded his opposition to the Monroe administration on his impatience for it to recognize the independence of the new republics in what had been Spanish America, and on his umbrage at the high-handed military actions of General Andrew Jackson in the First Seminole War.

to him, to get up a new party. In both instances he had failed. But here was a new party ready formed, but of no pleasing aspect to either Clay or Crawford, terrible to the whole Union, but portentously terrible to the South threatening in its progress the emancipation of all their slaves, threatening in its immediate effect that Southern domination which has swayed the Union for the last twenty years, and threatening that political ascendency of Virginia, upon which Clay and Crawford both had fastened their principal hopes of personal aggrandizement. The failure of the bill, and the attempt to exclude slavery from the future State of Missouri, produced great fermentation there and in the Southern States, but particularly in Virginia. North and East it excited less feeling, but Mr. King, who had taken a considerable part in the debate at the last session in Senate, in the course of the summer set on foot and organized a concert of measures which have resulted in the struggle which now shakes the Union to its centre. Bloomfield, though a member from New Jersey, took at the last session the Southern side of this question, and still adheres to it. But he says he received yesterday a letter from a very sober and respectable neighbor of his, who asks him whether a civil war would not be preferable to the extension of slavery beyond the Mississippi. This is a question between the rights of human nature and the Constitution of the United States. Probably both will suffer by the issue of the controversy.

February 23, 1820—A[rthur] Livermore and W[illiam] Plumer, Junr., members of the House of Representatives from New Hampshire, called upon me, and, conversing on the Missouri slave question, which at this time agitates Congress and the nation, asked my opinion of the propriety of agreeing to a compromise. The division in Congress and the nation is nearly equal on both sides. The argument on the free side is, the moral and political duty of preventing the extension of slavery in the immense country from the Mississippi River to the South Sea. The argument on the slave side is, that Congress have no power by the Constitution to prohibit slavery in any State, and, the zealots say, not in any Territory. The proposed compromise is to admit Missouri, and hereafter Arkansas, as States, without any restriction upon them regarding slavery, but to prohibit the future introduction of slaves in all Territories of the United States north of 36(o) 30' latitude. I told these gentlemen that my opinion was, the question could be settled no

otherwise than by a compromise. The regulation, exclusion, or abolition of slavery in the system of our Union is among the powers reserved
to the people of the several States by their separate Governments,
though I have no doubt that Congress have Constitutional powers to
prohibit any internal traffic in slaves between one State and another.
In the States where slavery does not exist, neither Congress, nor the
State Legislature, nor the people have any rightful power to establish it. For the admission into the Union of a State where no slavery
exists, Congress may prescribe as a condition that slavery shall never be
established in it, as they have done to the States of Ohio, Indiana, and
Illinois; but where it exists, and where there are already slaves in great
numbers, as in Missouri and Arkansas, the power of extirpating it is not
given to Congress by the Constitution. To proscribe slavery, therefore,
in Missouri or Arkansas, I believe to be impracticable. But if a provision can be obtained excluding the introduction of slaves into future
Territories, it will be a great and important point secured. I apprehend,
however, that Livermore and Plumer did not concur with me in my
opinion.

February 24, 1820—I had some conversation with Calhoun on the
slave question pending in Congress. He said he did not think it would
produce a dissolution of the Union, but, if it should, the South would
be from necessity compelled to form an alliance, offensive and defensive, with Great Britain.

I said that would be returning to the colonial state.

He said, yes, pretty much, but it would be forced upon them. I asked
him whether he thought, if by the effect of this alliance, offensive and
defensive, the population of the North should be cut off from its natural outlet upon the ocean, it would fall back upon its rocks bound
hand and foot, to starve, or whether it would not retain its powers of
locomotion to move southward by land. Then, he said, they would find
it necessary to make their communities all military. I pressed the conversation no further; but if the dissolution of the Union should result
from the slave question, it is as obvious as anything that can be foreseen
of futurity, that it must shortly afterwards be followed by the universal
emancipation of the slaves. A more remote but perhaps not less certain
consequence would be the extirpation of the African race on this continent, by the gradually bleaching process of intermixture, where the

white portion is already so predominant, and by the destructive progress of emancipation, which, like all great religious and political reformations, is terrible in its means, though happy and glorious in its end. Slavery is the great and foul stain upon the North American Union, and it is a contemplation worthy of the most exalted soul whether its total abolition is or is not practicable: if practicable, by what means it may be effected, and if a choice of means be within the scope of the object, what means would accomplish it at the smallest cost of human sufferance. A dissolution, at least temporary, of the Union, as now constituted, would be certainly necessary, and the dissolution must be upon a point involving the question of slavery, and no other. The Union might then be reorganized on the fundamental principle of emancipation. This object is vast in its compass, awful in its prospects, sublime and beautiful in its issue. A life devoted to it would be nobly spent or sacrificed. This conversation with Calhoun led me into a momentous train of reflection. It also engaged me so much that I detained him at his office, insensibly to myself, till near five o clock, an hour at least later than his dining-time.

February 27, 1820—Called upon Mr. R. King at his lodgings at Crawford's Hotel, Georgetown. Found him still absorbed in the Missouri slave question, upon which he has been the great champion of freedom and the Northern interest. The partisans of slavery have spread abroad the idea that he has been actuated in this affair by motives of personal ambition—that he is making an effort to get up a new division of parties and to put himself at the head of half the Union, despairing of ever being able to obtain the highest powers and honors of the whole. It is not easy to account for the course that King has pursued throughout this affair without allowing something for the instigations of personal expectancy. He has probably been pushed forward eagerly by his friends, and he has been spurred into more violent exertions, and has opened his heart to warmer hopes, on this occasion, than I think the event will justify. He reckons more upon the apparent ardor of the popular sentiment against slavery to the North than it is worth. The question to the North and in the free States is merely speculative. The people do not feel it in their persons or their purses. On the slave side it comes home to the feelings and interests of every man in the community. Hence, if this question is ultimately decided, as it will be, in favor of slavery in Missouri, the people in the free States will immediately acquiesce in the decision, and it will be impossible to keep the controversy alive. King, however, indulges hopes that it may survive the present question.

In late February 1820, Adams visited with Captain Richard O'Brien, who had been enslaved in North Africa and then an American consul in various Mediterranean ports. What this authoritative voice had to say about slavery reinforced the growing antislavery fervor discernible in Adams's first private reactions to the passage of the first Missouri Compromise. Those reactions were a complex stew of high moral principle and continuing uncertainty about how accommodating to the South Adams should be in practice. His stance on the constitutionality of the Tallmadge Amendment had clearly changed by the time of the cabinet debate on March 3, and during that same discussion he even advanced into ground that Rufus King had occupied. But while Adams edged toward a more public antislavery posture in cabinet meetings and in conversation with Calhoun, at other moments he still shrunk from the Union-menacing conflict this whole debate had produced. Still, the cabinet fray of March 3 better predicted who would take a strict or a broad construction of the Constitution in the 1820s, and why, than previous ones in which Adams had occupied strict constructionist ground. These extensive diary entries also feature telling passages on slavery and the Constitution and Union.

February 28, 1820—O'Brien has brought me again the whole budget of his documents, correspondence, accounts, and claims. But he talks more about the Missouri question and slavery than even about his own concerns. He is one of the most ardent opposers to the extension of Slavery and says it is because he knows by experience what it is having been nearly ten years himself a Slave in Algiers.

March 2, 1820—The compromise of the slave question was this day completed in Congress. The Senate have carried their whole point, barely consenting to the formality of separating the bill for the admission of the State of Maine into the Union from that for authorizing the people of the Territory of Missouri to form a State Government. The condition that slavery should be prohibited by their Constitution, which the House of Representatives had inserted, they have abandoned.

Missouri and Arkansas will be slave States, but to the Missouri bill a section is annexed, prohibiting slavery in the remaining part of the Louisiana cession north of latitude 36(o) 30'. This compromise, as it is called, was finally carried this evening by a vote of ninety to eighty-seven in the House of Representatives, after successive days and almost nights of stormy debate.

March 3, 1820—Went with Mrs. Adams to the Capitol Hill, and . . . [w]hile we were there, Jeremiah Nelson, a member of the House from Massachusetts, came in and told us of John Randolph's motion this morning to reconsider one of the votes of yesterday upon the Missouri bill, and of the trickery by which his motion was defeated by the Speaker's declaring it not in order when first made, the journal of yesterday's proceedings not having been then read; and while they were reading, the Clerk of the House carried the bills as passed by the House to the Senate, so that when Randolph, after the reading of the journals, renewed his motion, it was too late, the papers being no longer in the possession of the House.[34]

And so it is that a law for perpetuating slavery in Missouri, and perhaps in North America, has been smuggled through both Houses of Congress. I have been convinced from the first starting of this question that it could not end otherwise. The fault is in the Constitution of the United States, which has sanctioned a dishonorable compromise with slavery. There is henceforth no remedy for it but a new organization of the Union, to effect which a concert of all the white States is indispensable. Whether that can ever be accomplished is doubtful. It is a contemplation not very creditable to human nature that the cement of common interest produced by slavery is stronger and more solid than that of unmingled freedom. In this instance the slave States have clung together in one unbroken phalanx, and have been victorious by the means of accomplices and deserters from the ranks of freedom. Time only can show whether the contest may ever be with equal advantage renewed. But so polluted are all the streams of legislation in regions of slavery, that this bill has been obtained only by two as unprincipled

34. This was just the last of the parliamentary maneuvers Speaker Clay pursued to secure a compromise, including the original act of joining the Missouri and Maine statehood bills.

artifices as dishonesty ever devised: one, by coupling it as an append-age to the bill for admitting Maine; and the other, by this outrage perpetrated by the Speaker upon the rules of the House.

When I came this day to my office, I found there a note request-ing me to call at one o'clock at the President's house. It was then one, and I immediately went over. He expected that the two bills, for the admission of Maine, and to enable Missouri to make a Constitution, would have been brought to him for his signature, and he had sum-moned all the members of the Administration to ask their opinions in writing, to be deposited in the Department of State, upon two ques-tions: 1. Whether Congress had a Constitutional right to prohibit slav-ery in a Territory? and 2. Whether the 8th section of the Missouri bill (which interdicts slavery *forever* in the Territory north of 36½ Latitude) was applicable only to the Territorial State, or could extend to it after it should become a State.

As to the first question, it was unanimously agreed that Congress have the power to prohibit slavery in the Territories; and yet neither Crawford, Calhoun, nor Wirt could find any express power to that effect given in the Constitution; and Wirt declared himself very decid-edly against the admission of any implied powers. The progress of this discussion has so totally merged in passion all the reasoning faculties of the slave-holders, that these gentlemen, in the simplicity of their hearts, had come to a conclusion in direct opposition to their premises, without being aware or conscious of inconsistency. They insisted upon it that the clause in the Constitution, which gives Congress power to dispose of and make all *needful* rules and regulations respecting the territory and other property of the United States, had reference to it only as land, and conferred no authority to make rules binding upon its inhabitants; and Wirt added the notable Virginian objection, that Congress could make only *needful* rules and regulations, and that a pro-hibition of slavery was not *needful*. Their argument, as Randolph said of it in the House, covered the whole ground, and their compromise, measured by their own principles, is a sacrifice of what they hold to be the Constitution. I had no doubt of the right of Congress to interdict slavery in the Territories, and urged that the power contained in the term dispose of included the authority to do everything that could be done with it as mere property, and that the additional words, authorizing needful rules and regulations respecting it, must have reference to persons connected with it, or could have no meaning at all. As to the force of the term needful, I observed, it was relative, and must always be supposed to have reference to some end. Needful to what end? Needful in the Constitution of the United States to any of the ends for which that compact was formed. Those ends are declared in its preamble; to establish justice, for example. What can be more needful for the establishment of Justice than the interdiction of slavery where it does not exist?

As to the second question, my opinion was that the interdiction of slavery in the 8th section of the Bill *forever* would apply and be binding upon the State as well as the Territory, because, by its interdiction in the Territory, the people, when they come to form a Constitution, would have no right to sanction slavery.

Crawford said that in the new States which have been admitted into the Union upon the express condition that their Constitutions should consist with the perpetual interdiction of slavery, it might be sanctioned by an ordinary Act of their Legislatures.

I said that whatever a State Legislature might do in point of fact, they could not, by any rightful exercise of power, establish slavery. The Declaration of Independence not only asserts the natural equality of all men, and their inalienable right to liberty, but that the only just powers of government are derived from the consent of the governed. A power for one part of the people to make slaves of the other can never be derived from, consent, and is, therefore, not a just power.

Crawford said this was the opinion that had been *attributed* to Mr. King.

I said it was undoubtedly the opinion of Mr. King, and it was mine. I did not want to make a public display of it where it might excite irritation, but, if called upon officially for it, I should not withhold it. But the opinion was not peculiar to Mr. King and me. It was an opinion universal in the States where there are no slaves. It was the opinion of all those members of Congress who voted for the restriction upon Missouri, and of many of those who voted against it. As to the right of imposing the restriction upon a State, the President had signed a bill with precisely such a restriction upon the State of Illinois.[35] Why should the question be made now which was not made then?

Crawford said that was done in conformity to the compact of the Ordinance of 1787;[36] and, besides, the restriction was a nullity, not binding upon the Legislatures of those States.

I did not reply to the assertion that a solemn compact, announced before heaven and earth in the Ordinance of 1787, a compact laying the foundation of security to the most sacred rights of human nature against the most odious of oppressions, a compact solemnly renewed by the Acts of Congress enabling the States of Ohio, Indiana, and Illinois to form State Governments, and again by the acts for admitting those States into the Union, was a *nullity* which the Legislatures of either of those States may at any time disregard and trample under foot. It was sickening to my soul to hear the assertion; but to have discussed it there would have been useless, and only have kindled in the bosom of the Executive the same flame which had been raging in Congress and in the country. Its discussion was unnecessary to the decision of the question proposed by the President. I therefore only said that the Ordinance of 1787 had been passed by the old Congress of the Confederation without authority from the States, but had been tacitly confirmed by the adoption of the present Constitution, and the authority given to Congress in it to make needful rules and regulations for the Territory. I added that in one of the numbers of The Federalist[37] there was an admission that the old Congress had passed the ordinance without authority under an impulse of necessity, and that it was used as an argument in favor of the enlarged powers granted to Congress in the Constitution.

Crawford said it could therefore have little weight as authority.

35. Illinois's 1818 state constitution included Article VI of the Northwest Ordinance, so this was really a self-restriction. Adams was correct in spirit here, for keeping Article VI was contentious within Illinois statehood politics, but "Illinois politicians recognized that Congress would block admission if Illinois failed to include Article VI in its constitution"; see John Craig Hammond, *Slavery, Freedom, and Expansion in the Early American West* (Charlottesville: University Press of Virginia, 2007), 122.
36. The Northwest Ordinance, Article VI of which banned the growth of slavery in the territories north and west of the Ohio River.
37. The "Federalist Papers," the series of essays written by James Madison, Alexander Hamilton, and John Jay to advocate ratification of the Constitution.

I replied that it was not wanted as authority; that when the old Confederation was adopted the United States had no territory. Nor was there, in the Act of Confederation in which the powers of Congress under it were enumerated, a word about territory. But there was a clause interdicting to Congress the exercise of any powers not expressly given them. I alluded to the origin of the Confederation with our Revolution; to the revolutionary powers exercised by Congress before the Confederation was adopted; to the question whether the Northwestern Territory belonged to the United States or the separate States; to the delays occasioned by that question in the acceptance of the Confederation, and to the subsequent cessions of territory by several States to the Union, which gave occasion for the Ordinance of 1787; to all which Crawford said nothing.

Wirt said that he perfectly agreed with me, that there could be no rightful power to establish slavery where it was "res nova."[38] But he thought it would not be the force of the Act of Congress that would lead to this result; the principle itself being correct, though Congress might have no power to prescribe it to a sovereign State.

To this my reply was, that the power of establishing slavery not being a sovereign power, but a wrongful and despotic power, Congress had a right to say that no State undertaking to establish it "de novo"[39] should be admitted into the Union; and that a State which should undertake to establish it would put herself out of the pale of the Union, and forfeit all the rights and privileges of the connection.

The President said that it was impossible to exclude the principle of implied powers, being granted to Congress by the Constitution. The powers of sovereignty were distributed between the General and State Governments. Extensive powers were given in general terms; all detailed and incidental powers were implied in the general grant. . . . The material question was only when the power supposed to be implied came in conflict with rights reserved to the State Governments. He inclined also to think with me, that the rules and regulations which Congress were authorized to make for the Territories must be understood as

38. Latin for "a new thing," in legal principle an issue that had not been previously decided.
39. Latin for "of the new," or "afresh."

extending to their inhabitants. And he recurred to the history of the Northwestern Territory, the cessions by the several States to the Union, and the controversies concerning this subject during our Revolutionary War. He said he wished the written opinion of the members of the Cabinet, without discussion, in terms as short as it could be expressed, and merely that it might be deposited in the Department of State.

I told him that I should prefer a dispensation from answering the second question, especially as I should be alone here in the opinion which I entertained; for Mr. Thompson, the Secretary of the Navy, cautiously avoided giving any opinion upon the question of natural right, but assented to the slave-sided doctrine that the eighth section of the bill, the word *forever* and all, applied only to the time and condition of the Territorial Government. I said, therefore, that if required to give my opinion upon the second question, standing alone, it would be necessary for me to assign the reasons upon which I entertained it.

Crawford saw no necessity for any reasoning about it, but had no objection to my assigning my reasons.

Calhoun thought it exceedingly desirable that no such argument should be drawn up and deposited. He therefore suggested to the President the idea of changing the terms of the second question, so that it should be, whether the eighth section of the bill was consistent with the Constitution; which the other members of the Administration might answer affirmatively, assigning their reason, because they considered it applicable only to the Territorial States, while I could answer it also affirmatively, without annexing any qualification.

To this the President readily assented, and I as readily agreed. The questions are to be framed accordingly.

This occasion has remarkably manifested Crawford's feelings, and the continually kindling intenseness of his ambition. I have had information from the Governor of the State of Indiana that there is in that State a party countenanced and supported by Crawford, whose purpose it is to introduce slavery into that State, and there is reason to believe that the same project exists in Ohio and Illinois. This avowed opinion, that in defiance of the Ordinance of 1787, and of the laws admitting those States into the Union, slavery may be established in either of those States by an ordinary Act of its Legislature, strongly confirms the impressions of him communicated to me by the Governor of Indiana. It is apparent that Crawford is already aware how his canvass for the Presidency may be crossed by this slavery contest. The violence of its operation upon his temper is such that he could not suppress it.

After this meeting, I walked home with Calhoun, who said that the principles which I had avowed were just and noble; but that in the Southern country, whenever they were mentioned, they were always understood as applying only to white men. Domestic labor was confined to the blacks, and such was the prejudice, that if he, who was the most popular man in his district, were to keep a white servant in his house, his character and reputation would be irretrievably ruined.

I said that this confounding of the ideas of servitude and labor was one of the bad effects of slavery; but he thought it attended with many excellent consequences. It did not apply to all kinds of labor—not, for example, to farming. He himself had often held the plough; so had his father. Manufacturing and mechanical labor was not degrading. It was only manual labor—the proper work of slaves. No white person could descend to that. And it was the best guarantee to equality among the whites. It produced an unvarying level among them. It not only did not excite, but did not even admit of inequalities, by which one white man could domineer over another.

I told Calhoun I could not see things in the same light. It is, in truth, all perverted sentiment—mistaking labor for slavery, and dominion for freedom. The discussion of this Missouri question has betrayed the secret of their souls. In the abstract they admit that slavery is an evil, they disclaim all participation in the introduction of it, and cast it all upon the shoulders of our old Grandam Britain. But when probed to the quick upon it, they show at the bottom of their souls pride and vainglory in their condition of masterdom. They fancy themselves more generous and noble-hearted than the plain freemen who labor for subsistence. They look down upon the simplicity of a Yankee's manners, because he has no habits of overbearing like theirs and cannot treat negroes like dogs. It is among the evils of slavery that it taints the very sources of moral principle. It establishes false estimates of virtue and vice; for what can be more false and heartless than this doctrine which makes the first and holiest rights of humanity to depend upon the color of the skin? It perverts human reason, and reduces man endowed with logical powers[,] to maintain that slavery is sanctioned by the Christian religion, that slaves are happy and contented in their condition, that between master and slave there are ties of mutual attachment and affection, that the virtues of the master are refined and exalted by the degradation of the slave; while at the same time they vent execrations upon the slave-trade, curse Britain for having given them slaves, burn at the stake negroes convicted of crimes for the terror of the example, and writhe in agonies of fear at the very mention of human rights as applicable to men of color. The impression produced upon my mind by the progress of this discussion is, that the bargain between freedom and slavery contained in the Constitution of the United States is morally and politically vicious, inconsistent with the principles upon which alone our Revolution can be justified; cruel and oppressive, by riveting the chains of slavery, by pledging the faith of freedom to maintain and perpetuate the tyranny of the master; and grossly unequal and impolitic, by admitting that slaves are at once enemies to be kept in subjection, property to be secured or restored to their owners, and persons not to be represented themselves, but for whom their masters are privileged with nearly a double share of representation. The consequence has been that this slave representation has governed the Union. Benjamin portioned above his brethren has ravined as a wolf. In the morning he has devoured the prey, and at night he has divided the spoil.[40] It would be no difficult matter to prove, by reviewing the history of the Union under this Constitution, that almost everything which has contributed to the honor and welfare of the nation has been accomplished in despite of them or forced upon them, and that everything unpropitious and dishonorable, including the blunders and follies of their adversaries, may be traced to them. I have favored this Missouri compromise, believing it to be all that could be effected under the present Constitution, and from extreme unwillingness to put the Union at hazard. But perhaps it would have been a wiser as well as a bolder course to have persisted in the restriction upon Missouri, till it should have terminated in a convention of the States to revise and amend the Constitution. This would have produced a new Union of thirteen or fourteen States unpolluted with slavery, with a great and glorious object to effect, namely, that of

40. This is a political application of a prophecy of the ancient patriarch Jacob concerning his sons who became the tribes of Israel; see Genesis 49:27.

rallying to their standard the other States by the universal emancipation of their slaves. If the Union must be dissolved, slavery is precisely the question upon which it ought to break. For the present, however, this contest is laid asleep.

March 4, 1820—[Rufus] King apparently came to talk with me of the compromise and the Maine and Missouri bills. There were, however, so many persons present that he said but little. He is deeply mortified at the issue, and very naturally feels resentful at the imputations of the slave-holders, that his motives on this occasion have been merely of personal aggrandizement—"close ambition varnished o'er with zeal."[41] This imputation of bad motives is one of the most envenomed weapons of political and indeed of every sort of controversy. It came originally from the devil: "Doth Job fear God for nought?"[42] The selfish and the social passions are intermingled in the conduct of every man acting in a public capacity. It is right that they should be so, and it is no just cause of reproach to any man that in promoting to the utmost of his power the public good, he is desirous at the same time of promoting his own. There are, no doubt, hypocrites of humanity as well as of religion—men with cold hearts and warm professions, trading upon benevolence, and using justice and virtue as the stakes upon the turn of a card or the cast of a die. But this sort of profligacy belongs to a state of society more deeply corrupted than ours. Such characters are rare among us. Many of our public men have principles too pliable to popular impulse, but few are deliberately dishonest; and there is not a man in the Union of purer integrity than Rufus King.

March 5, 1820—The President sent me yesterday the two questions in writing upon which he desired to have answers in writing, to be deposited in the Department of State. He wrote me that it would be in time if he should have the answers tomorrow. The first question is in general terms, as it was stated at the meeting on Friday. The second was modified to an enquiry whether the eighth section of the Missouri bill is consistent with the Constitution. To this I can without hesitation answer by a simple affirmative, and so, after some reflection, I concluded to answer both. It was said that in the hottest

41. John Milton, *Paradise Lost*, 2nd book, line 485.
42. Job 1:9.

paroxysm of the Missouri question in the Senate, James Barbour, one of the Virginia Senators, was going round to all the free-State members and proposing to them to call a convention of the States to dissolve the Union, and agree upon the terms of separation and the mode of disposing of the public debt and of the lands, and make other necessary arrangements of disunion. Dana[43] said he told him that he was not for calling a convention to separate, but he had no objection to a convention to form a more perfect union. I observed that I thought a convention might, in the course of a few years, be found necessary to remedy the great imperfections of the present system, and that it might be called whenever a majority of the people should become convinced of its necessity. I added that there were three subjects, each of which might produce a state of things issuing in such a necessity. One was, the regulation of the currency, banks, and paper money; another, the impotence of the National Government to make internal improvements by roads and canals; and the third was slavery. The idea that a majority of the people might hold a convention appeared to startle some of the gentlemen, and particularly Mr. Thompson. It is nevertheless sound Constitutional doctrine.

March 7, 1820—Captain O'Brien came to the office to talk about his claims, and the final decision of the Missouri question, and the politics of Pennsylvania. The most remarkable circumstance in the history of this transaction is that it was ultimately carried against the opinions, wishes, and interests of the free States by the votes of their own members. They have a decided majority in both Houses of Congress, but lost the vote by disunion. The slave-holders clung together without losing one vote. Many of them, and almost all the Virginians, held out to the last even against the compromise. The cause of this closer union on the slavish side is, that the question affected the individual interest of every slave-holding member and of almost every one of his constituents. On the other side, individual interests were not implicated in the decision at all. The impulses were pure republican principle and the rights of human nature. The struggle for political power and geographical jealousy may fairly be supposed to have operated equally on both sides. The result affords an illustration of the remark, how much more keen

43. Senator Samuel W. Dana of Connecticut.

and powerful the impulse is of personal interest than is that of any general consideration of benevolence or humanity.

Adams encapsulated the swirl of competing imperatives that checked his growing antislavery principles in three especially perceptive and eloquent reflections on what the Missouri Crisis and Compromise meant for foreign relations and presidential politics. The occasion of the first entry was Adams's attendance at a Senate committee discussion of the long-running problem of Britain's prohibitions on American trade with her colonies. The occasion for the second was a conversation with Illinois senator Ninian Edwards. The latter entry revealed just how stubborn—if not uncontested—Adams's self-identification as a statesman for the whole Union was proving in the aftermath of Missouri. The third entry recorded Adams's reflections on a conversation with Representative Timothy Fuller from Massachusetts and provides strong evidence that Adams was almost willing to admit to himself that he was a viable and willing presidential candidate for 1824.

March 27, 1820—[Senator Nathaniel Macon of North Carolina argued] that Great Britain especially was not going to give up in this contest within one, two, or three years—Great Britain and the other European powers would wait to see how we should get along with our own concerns. During the whole discussion of the Missouri question, every one of the Ministers from all the European powers residing here was attending the debate as constantly as he himself did, and he was not absent from it an hour. They were not there for nothing. He had no doubt every one of them had reported to his Government what had passed; and the consequence would be that Great Britain, and France too, would be in no haste to yield to us upon any point of difference which we have with them.

March 31, 1820—Clay's affairs, private and public, have been growing desperate ever since the commencement of Mr. Monroe's Administration. He then refused the War Department and the mission to London; nothing would satisfy him but the Department of State; and, failing to obtain that, he projected a new opposition, of which he should be the head, and which should in the course of two Presidential terms run down Monroe, so that he might come in as the opposition successor. His engines the first session were South America and internal improvement. Both then failed. The next session he took up the Seminole War, but of that mighty controversy he was no longer the primary leader. He had ranged himself under the Crawford banners. That struggle was more stubborn, but also failed. The great majority of the people took the other side. The Missouri question then arose, and disconcerted Clay's projects by presenting party combinations and divisions very unsuitable to them. It looked to a dissolution of the Union upon principles which could not serve his purposes. But, that question having been for the present compromised, he recurs to South American and Spanish affairs for his main engine of opposition. . . . The Missouri question, too, has operated to indispose every part of the Union against the treaty [with Spain]: the North and East, because they do not wish even to have Florida as another slave State; and the South and West, because they wish to have all the territory to the Rio del Norte for more slave States. Clay seizes upon this state of things, and has brought forward these resolutions, which are to operate in every possible contingency against the Administration.[44] . . .

I told Edwards that I had very little attachment to the treaty . . ., and shall now be very ready to abandon the treaty if the opinion of an adequate portion of either House of Congress should be adverse to it; that, as a servant of the whole Union, the interests of every part of the Union were equally dear to me—there was neither East, West, North, or South to my duty or my feelings; but, as an Eastern man, I should be disinclined to have either Texas or Florida without a restriction excluding slavery from them, and if I were now a member of either House of Congress I would offer resolutions that the treaty ought not now to be accepted without an article prohibiting and excluding slavery from the territory to be acquired. I had been continually expecting that such resolutions would be offered by some one of the Northern or Eastern members.

May 2, 1820—Fuller said it was apparent that preparations were making for a violent canvass for the Presidential election of 1824. I said

44. On March 28, Clay introduced two resolutions to the House asserting congressional veto authority over treaties, and complaining that the territory taken by the Adams-Onis Treaty was "inadequate." See *Annals of Congress*, 16th Congress, 1st Session, 1691.

there had been scarcely anything but such canvassing since 1816. He said he hoped I did not intend to withhold myself from the contest. I told him the principle of my life had been never to ask the suffrage of my country, and never to shrink from its call. If life, and health, and private circumstances admitting of it, and a belief of competency to the station, not inferior to others who may be competitors for it, should be mine after the vicissitudes of the next four years, I shall adhere to the principle upon which I have always acted. Whether any portion of the country will think of calling for my services will certainly depend upon the series of future events. I know the disadvantages on which I now stand, and am conscious of my inability to make interest by caballing, bargaining, place-giving, or tampering with members of Congress. I have been here three sessions, with a colleague in the Executive Administration[45] who . . . considers himself . . . as quite entitled to the succession; who, as a Virginian born, is sure of the support of that State against any one not of the same origin; as a slave-holder, has the first pledge of votes from the South and Southwest; and possesses an immense patronage throughout the Union, which he exercises to promote his purposes without scruple and without restraint.

At the same time, the Speaker of the House of Representatives, a very popular man and speaker, a disappointed rival, openly avowed as a political opponent to me, and exercising against me both publicly and insidiously all his influence. . . . In the course of three sessions I have formed slight personal acquaintances with most of the members, but have had neither time nor opportunity to become intimate with any of them. My means of acquiring personal adherents, therefore, are nothing. Upon the foundation of public service alone must I stand; and when the nation shall be called to judge of that, by the result, whatever it may be, I must abide. Were it in my power, I would sink in oblivion the very idea of a Presidential election in 1824; but, forget it as I might, it would be ever present to the minds of my adversaries. The three sessions of Congress have been three wrestling-matches to bring me down by the ruin of Mr. Monroe's Administration. The first and second attempts failed. That of the present session has been favored by circumstances. The Missouri question is indeed a flaming sword that

45. Crawford.

waves round on all sides and cuts in every direction; but the baseness of the King of Spain has played the game into the hands of Clay, and that which at the close of the last session appeared to be the most fortunate of events to me, is now the most powerful engine wielded against me. In Congress, and in the nation, the most indefatigable efforts are made to represent me as singly and exclusively responsible for everything that can be exhibited as odious, unpopular, or unsuccessful in Mr. Monroe's Administration, and efforts not less laborious are made, whenever anything prosperous or popular occurs, to deprive me even of my portion of it. This cabalistic influence is of itself sufficient, eventually, to put me down. May the blessed Disposer of events shield me from the calamity of contributing to the same event by misconduct or incapacity of my own!

In the autumn of 1820, Adams had multiple, long, repetitive discussions with British ambassador Stratford Canning concerning cooperation against the slave trade. Adams's responses continued to stress American sovereignty above all else, no matter his private reflections on slavery in recent months (which included an entry during this same period that castigated American race prejudice).[46] The following entry rises above the others by capturing Adams's weariness with the issue.[47]

October 26, 1820—Mr. Canning called, and kept me two hours or more upon the subject of the slave-trade. He brought with him a long written paper, containing what he had understood as the substance of our former conversations, which he said he had informally drawn up, and wished to read to me to ascertain that he had correctly understood the purport of my observations. He read it accordingly. There were several very important variations in the paper from what I had actually said; all of which I successively noticed. The first was an inference of his own, which he had apparently written down as an experiment to see what I should say to it. The remark was almost at the beginning of the paper, and was an avowal of satisfaction that, in reviewing the conversation between us, he had perceived that none of the objections

46. See Diary, October 22, 1820.
47. See also Diary, October 2, 20, 1820.

which had been suggested by me to the project of Great Britain applied to the plan itself. I stopped him immediately, and said that was more than I thought could safely be said. I had told him there was one certain Constitutional difficulty which we saw no way of getting over. This of itself was decisive for the present. . . .

I then read to him the fifth article of amendment to the Constitution, which amounts to an express prohibition to subjecting any citizen of the United States to trial before such a tribunal as that proposed. I said, further, that the objection to the principle of admitting the right of search by foreign officers in time of peace, for its analogy to search for impressment in time of war, was an objection to the plan itself.

He then commenced a discussion upon this point, and said that I had been so long and so fully conversant with it that he was sure I knew and appreciated the merits of their side of the question. I knew that it was, on the part of Great Britain, a conviction of necessity which compelled her to adhere to what she considered as a right. When she is at war, the temptation and opportunity are so great for a portion of her seamen to come into the merchant service of the United States that, without some control over them, the damage to her was vital; and he went through the usual topics of the British doctrine on this controversy.

I told him that it was not my wish to debate the point. We had more than once exhausted the argument with his Government; we had endeavored to adjust it at Ghent; we had renewed the effort twice since the war, and by various Ministers; we greatly regretted that the differences of opinion and of principle between the parties were so radical that they had found all compromise of it impracticable. But, such having been the issue, we were in no wise disposed to renew the subject at present; we acquiesced in the result so far as to have concluded to say no more about it. The question had no immediate practical interest connected with it, and our hopes were that if Great Britain should again be engaged in a naval war she would of her own accord give such instructions to her naval officers as would prevent the question from arising. We knew it depended entirely upon her, and we were willing to hope her Government would not be disposed to seek a contest with us. But we knew also that it depended upon the temper of her Administration, and that every change of that would endanger our peace. We went over the whole ground of impressment, and, as usual, to no purpose. His paper concluded with the remark, that if our objections to the mode of co-operation proposed by Great Britain were insuperable, she had reason to expect we should bring forward some propositions on our part.

I told him I should submit the whole subject to the consideration of the President, and if anything should occur to him as suitable to be proposed, I should advise him (Canning) of it.

Adams greeted the revival of the Missouri controversy in late fall 1820 with alarm. He was incredulous that given the trouble Missouri had in getting its statehood through Congress with slavery intact, the Missouri state constitutional convention chose to include in its handiwork provocative clauses guaranteeing the future of slavery in the state and barring free people of color from entering Missouri. That second provision, which struck Adams and many other observers as unconstitutional, threatened to reopen the explosive question of whether Missouri would be admitted as a state. Its potential to paralyze the government was on full display when the House of Representatives' election of a Speaker became deadlocked along sectional lines.[48] Despite this sense of dread about renewing that conflict, Adams articulated an uncompromising position on Missouri statehood in a consultation with Representative William Eustis of Massachusetts. A conversation with Rufus King the next day must have given Adams pause, but he still articulated advanced antislavery opinions in his record of a colloquy that same week with Representative Henry Baldwin of Pennsylvania.

November 24, 1820—[Eustis] came to consult me upon the Missouri question. The clause in their Constitution was directly repugnant to the article in the Constitution of the United States. He had no doubt of that, nor had I; but what was to be done? I said the course appeared to me very obvious. Pass a resolution declaring the State to be admitted from and after the time when they shall have expunged from their Constitution the article repugnant to the Constitution of the United States. He said that was precisely what he intended to propose; but he intimated a distrust of many of those who are on the free side of the question.

48. See Diary, November 12, 13, 1820.

November 25, 1820—Upon the Missouri question he [King] has much cooled down since last winter. The question is now not the same as it was then, and is much more clear against Missouri. But he has discovered that the people of the North, like many of their Representatives in Congress, flinch from the consequences of this question, and will not bear their leaders out. Personal and ambitious motives have also been imputed to Mr. King for the part he has taken in this affair. The old party feelings have been revived against him. . . . He says that, as a statesman of the Union, he has lost rather than gained ground by his ardent pursuit of this slavery question, and seems now disposed to say little more about it.

November 29, 1820—I returned Mr. Baldwin's visit, and had a long conversation with him on the subject of the Missouri question of the present session, which he agreed was a totally different question from that of the last. He said, however, that those who now objected to the admission of Missouri, on the ground of the exceptionable article in her Constitution, connected the restriction question of the last session with it, and wished to reopen the whole controversy.

I told him I believed there would be a very small portion of the House for that, and I thought it would be quite unjustifiable; but the article in the Missouri Constitution was directly repugnant to the rights reserved to every citizen of the Union in the Constitution of the United States. Its purport went to disfranchise all the people of color who were citizens of the free States. The Legislatures of those States were bound in duty to protect the rights of their own citizens; and if Congress, by the admission of Missouri with that clause in her Constitution, should sanction this outrage upon those rights, the States, a portion of whose citizens should be thus cast out from the pale of the Union, would be bound to vindicate them by retaliation. And if I were a member of the Legislature of one of these States, I would move for a declaratory act, that so long as the article in the Constitution of Missouri depriving the colored citizens of the State, say of Massachusetts, of their rights as citizens of the United States within the State of Missouri, should subsist, so long the white citizens of the State of Missouri should be held as aliens within the Commonwealth of Massachusetts, not entitled to claim or enjoy within the same any right or privilege of a citizen of the United States. And I would go further, and declare that Congress having, by their sanction of the Missouri Constitution, by admitting that State into the Union without excepting against that article which disfranchised a portion of the citizens of Massachusetts, had violated the Constitution of the United States; wherefore, until that portion of the citizens of Massachusetts whose rights are violated by the article in the Missouri Constitution should be reintegrated in the full enjoyment and possession of those rights, no clause or article of the Constitution of the United States should, within the Commonwealth of Massachusetts, be so construed as to authorize any person whomsoever to claim the property or possession of a human being as a slave. And I would prohibit by law the delivery of any fugitive slave upon the claim of his master. All which I would do, not to violate, but to redeem from violation, the Constitution of the United States. It was indeed to be expected that such laws would again be met by retaliatory laws of Missouri and the other slave-holding States, and the consequence would be the dissolution de facto of the Union, but that dissolution would have commenced by the article in the Missouri Constitution. That article was in itself a dissolution of the Union. If acquiesced in, it would change the terms of the federal compact—change its terms by robbing thousands of citizens of their rights—and what citizens, the poor, the unfortunate, the helpless, already cursed by the mere color of their skin, already doomed by their complexion to drudge in the lowest offices of society, excluded by their color from all the refined enjoyments of life accessible to others, excluded from the benefits of a liberal education, from the bed, from the table, and from all the social comforts of domestic life, this barbarous article deprives them of the little remnant of right yet left them—their rights as citizens and as men. Weak and defenceless as they are, so much the more sacred is the obligation of the Legislatures of the States to which they belong to defend their lawful rights; and I would defend them should the dissolution of the Union be the consequence. For it would not be the defence, it would be the violation of their rights, to which all the consequences would be imputable; and if the dissolution of the Union must come, let it come from no other cause but this. If slavery be the destined sword in the hand of the destroying angel which is to sever the ties of this Union, the same sword will cut in sunder the bonds of slavery itself. A dissolution of the Union for the cause of slavery would be followed by a servile war in the slave-holding States, combined with a war between the two severed portions of the Union. It seems to me that its result must be the extirpation of slavery from this whole continent; and, calamitous and desolating as this course of events in its progress must be, so glorious would be its final issue, that, as God shall judge me, I dare not say that it is not to be desired.

As the Missouri Crisis resurfaced, Adams's image of Southerners continued to deteriorate. This vision of Southern politicians as hypersensitive obstructionists would only grow stronger through the rest of this decade.[49]

February 16, 1821—William A. Burwell, a member of the House of Representatives from Virginia, died this morning. He had been once for a short time private Secretary to Mr. Jefferson during his Presidency, and soon after was elected member of Congress, when little beyond the age necessary for qualification. He was always re-elected, and has been fourteen years a member. He was a man of moderate talents and respectable private character, full of Virginian principles and prejudices, a mixture of wisdom and Quixotism, which has done some good and much mischief to the Union. Burwell took no lead in anything. He scarcely ever spoke; never originated a measure of any public utility, but fancied himself a guardian of the liberties of the people against Executive encroachments. His delight was the consciousness of his own independence, and he thought it heroic virtue to ask no favors. He therefore never associated with any members of the Executive, and would have shuddered at the thought of going to the drawing-room. Jealousy of State rights and jealousy of the Executive were the two pillars of Burwell's political fabric, because they are the prevailing popular doctrines in Virginia. He floated down the stream of time with the current, and always had the satisfaction of being in his own eyes a pure and incorruptible patriot. Virginia teems with this brood more than any other State in the Union, and they are far from being the worst men among us. Such men occasionally render service to the nation by

49. For more on how the confluence of Missouri and presidential politics affected his reading of both past and present Virginia leaders, see Diary, October 20, November 17, 1821; October 1, 1822.

preventing harm; but they are quite as apt to prevent good and they never do any.

In his inextricably linked roles as presidential contender and statesman of the Union, Adams carefully scrutinized the congressional maneuverings that brought the second Missouri Crisis to an end. For all his tough antislavery talk in recent months (including in this entry), in the final analysis he evinced no wish that the controversy continue.

February 28, 1821—The Senate this day, by a vote of twenty-eight to fourteen, adopted the resolution for the conditional admission of the State of Missouri into the Union, reported by the large joint committee, and which had yesterday passed the House of Representatives; and thus this second Missouri question has been compromised, like the first. The greatest results of this conflict of three sessions have been to make John W. Taylor[50] Speaker of the House of Representatives, and to bring into full display the talents and resources of influence of Mr. Clay. By a singular piece of good fortune for him, just at the moment of his arrival here, Mr. Lowndes, in whose management it had been, was confined by severe illness to his chamber, and is so still. The majority against the unconditional admission was small, but very decided. The problem for the slave representation to solve was the precise extent of concession necessary for them to detach from the opposite party a sufficient number of anti-servile votes just to turn the majority. Mr. Clay found at last this expedient, which the slave voters would not have accepted from any one not of their own party, and to which his greatest difficulty was to obtain the acquiescence of his own friends. The timid and weak-minded dropped off one by one from the free side of the question, until a majority was found for the compromise, of which the serviles have the substance and the liberals the shadow. In the progress of this affair the distinctive character of the inhabitants of the several great divisions of the Union has been shown more in relief than perhaps in any national transaction since the establishment of the Constitution. It is perhaps accidental that the combination of talent

50. A leading restrictionist from New York.

and influence has been greatest on the slave side. The importance of the question has been much greater to them than to the other side. Their union of exertion has been consequently closer; and more unshakable. They have threatened and entreated, bullied and wheedled, until their more simple adversaries have been half coaxed, half frightened into a surrender of their principles for a bauble of insignificant promises. The champions of the North did not, however, judiciously select their position for this contest. There must be at some time a conflict upon this very question between slave and free representation, but this is not the time, nor was this the proper occasion, for contesting it.

Adams's October 26, 1820, declaration that the US government was through discussing abolition cooperation with Britain proved inefficacious in the extreme; indeed, this issue would drag on for another four decades. In the shorter term, Canning initiated discussion in early 1821.[51] The following entry captured both Adams's inflexibility and the pressure Canning was receiving from home that impelled his continued agitation of this question.

March 7, 1821—[Canning's] object [in seeking out another meeting] was to enquire if I had any further propositions to make to him in relation to the co-operation for the suppression of the slave-trade. I had none . . ., and I told Mr. Canning that the views of the President upon the subject had not changed. Mr. Canning indulged himself in invectives against the slave-trade—a topic upon which I had neither inclination nor motive to contradict him. He finally said that he could only justify himself to his own Government by satisfying them that he had done everything in *his* power to prevail upon that of the United States to join in the concert of measures in which several other nations had agreed to concur with Great Britain. And he asked if there had been any omission on his part of any exertion which might have contributed to its success. I told him, by no means; that he had with great earnestness and perseverance urged every argument which would have operated as persuasion to us; that the answer on our part having been in the first instance altogether explicit, and having been given repeatedly both to

51. See Diary, January 2, 9, 10, 1821.

Lord Castlereagh and himself, as well as the insuperable reasons upon which it was founded, it would henceforth be as agreeable to us not to be further urged upon it. He made no further reply, but rose and took leave.

As he contemplated the 1824 election soon after Monroe's second inauguration, Adams took note of how voting against the restriction of slavery in Missouri had killed the career of a New York congressman, Henry R. Storrs.[52] *The lesson Adams derived from Storrs and Rufus King combined was likely that taking any sort of extreme position on the Northern political spectrum on slavery could blast individual political prospects. That he believed national statesmen should avoid sectional extremes also emerged in yet another critical reading of Henry Clay's presidential machinations and the kind of administration he would run.*

March 9, 1821—Clay is an eloquent man, with very popular manners and great political management. He is, like almost all the eminent men of this country, only half educated. His school has been the world, and in that he is a proficient. His morals, public and private, are loose, but he has all the virtues indispensable to a popular man. As he is the first very distinguished man that the Western country has presented as a statesman to the Union, they are proportionably proud of him, and, being a native of Virginia, he has all the benefit of that clannish preference which Virginia has always given to her sons. Clay's temper is impetuous, and his ambition impatient. He has long since marked me as the principal rival in his way, and has taken no more pains to disguise his hostility than was necessary for decorum and to avoid shocking the public opinion. His future fortune, and mine, are in wiser hands than ours; I have never, even defensively, repelled his attacks. Clay has large and liberal views of public affairs, and that sort of generosity which attaches individuals to his person. As President of the Union, his administration would be a perpetual succession of intrigue and management with the legislature. It would also be sectional in its spirit, and sacrifice all other interests to those of the Western country and

52. See Diary, March 3, 1821.

the slave-holders. But his principles relative to internal improvements would produce results honorable and useful to the nation.

Adams's high-flying antislavery statements in his diary and private conversations would have no greater impact on American foreign policy in his second term than they had in his first. In neither did he think or act in abolitionist terms. He did not hesitate, for instance, to complain of British officials in Canada sheltering American fugitive slaves, in order to score points in a debate with Canning over extradition of criminals.[53] Adams likewise entertained no squeamishness about treating American slaves as property in relation to Georgia citizens seeking compensation for African Americans lost to the British and the Creek Indians during the War of 1812.[54] In a cabinet debate over how to approach a French vessel seized on suspicion of slave trading, Adams framed the essential question as being the right of boarding a foreign vessel in time of peace. And legal and diplomatic issues took precedence over humanity in Adams's considerations of how to deal with a fugitive slave from the Danish West Indies that had reached American soil.[55]

Meanwhile, the leading citizens of Washington, DC, had invited Adams to address the city's official July 4 celebration in 1821. He used the occasion to contrast the glorious American tradition of liberty embodied in the Declaration of Independence with Britain's much more checkered history of liberty alternating with and compromised by tyranny. The American Union, then, embodied the pinnacle of the history of human liberty, and its prospects in a too-often-hostile world thus had global stakes. He called on its critics abroad to refrain from their abuses and respect American sovereignty.[56] In a letter to a Pennsylvania politician who had praised the speech, Adams submitted that "there never was a moment in our history, when there was a more urgent want of some one who should speak out, to and for this nation; and in a voice which would be heard by the whole race of civilized men." He took as his task to vindicate "the Cause of Man and the Cause of our Country" against leading Britons' "unrelenting war of

53. See Diary, October 13, 1821.
54. Diary, October 16, 1821; May 24–25, June 3, 1822.
55. See Diary, November 6–8, 1821; September 16–17, 1822.
56. John Quincy Adams, *Address, Delivered at the Request of the Committee of Arrangements for Celebrating the Anniversary of Independence, At the City of Washington on the Fourth of July, 1821* (Cambridge, MA: Hilliard and Metcalf, 1821).

*slander and invective" against the United States.[57] Thus, for all his engage-
ment with the question of American slavery during the Missouri controversy,
what he thought the world most needed was a defense of the United States
against Britons.*

*In a late 1821 parley with Canning on abolition cooperation, Adams
asserted the good faith of American efforts to suppress the Atlantic slave trade.
But Canning's irritating confidence that the United States "should ultimately
be convinced on the necessity" of ceding the right of search elicited a statement
from Adams that showed just how little had changed.*

December 4, 1821—I said that was impossible. There were objections
of the most serious nature against the thing itself in any shape; but
unless Britain would bind herself by an article, as strong and explicit as
language can make it, never again in time of war to take a man from an
American vessel, we never for a moment could listen to a proposal for
allowing a right of search in time of peace.

He asked me, in a half-bantering tone, whether I had not intended
last winter to make some such proposal to him. I told him no. We had
exhausted negotiation in endeavoring to make an arrangement with
Great Britain on the subject of impressment. We had failed, and were
not desirous of obtaining the object by indirect means. The proposal
must come from them, if they were prepared for it. We merely refused
to admit a right of search in time of peace.

*Although Adams felt that he and Canning were on an endless loop, the Anglo-
American politics of abolition cooperation were not changeless. By 1822, there
was momentum in Congress—aided in complex ways by domestic politics—
behind working out a formula for cooperation that would involve both countries granting the other a limited right to search the other's vessels. This seemed
like a way to put Americans on the right side of this powerful international
moral issue while tamping down concerns about sovereignty. Two exchanges
between Canning and Adams showed what had and had not changed in
their discussions of the issues. One essential thing that had never changed was*

57. John Quincy Adams to Charles Jared Ingersoll, July 23, 1821, Charles Jared Ingersoll
Collection, Historical Society of Pennsylvania, Philadelphia.

Adams's determination, as he put it in another diary entry, to preserve "the
nation" from assuming "an attitude of inferiority and humiliation."[58]

June 7, 1822—Mr. Canning paid me one of his long two or three hour
visits. . . . He asked me if I had been informed by Mr. Rush that it was
the intention of the British Government to renew the application for
admitting the mutual right of search and capture. I said I had, and
should be ready to receive any new proposals that he might make,
adding, by way of a joke in earnest, that I hoped he would not press
them much in hot weather. He spoke of the report of the committee
of the House of Representatives in Congress in favor of the right of
search, and intimated that there were other members of the administration, less averse to it than I was. I assured him that he was mistaken
as there was no diversity of opinion in the Administration concerning
it. He hinted that some or one of them had spoken otherwise of it to
himself—which is not impossible; but I told him, if they had, it was
only by the complaisance of conversation, avoiding to come to a direct
issue, of opinion.

He said he had understood me to say that I never would sign a treaty
agreeing to the principle of a mutual search; but, as he had considered it
merely as a strong expression of my individual opinion, he had not communicated it to his Government in a dispatch, which might have been
laid before Parliament. I told him that I had no doubt I did say so—not
with an expectation that it would be communicated in a dispatch, but
merely to make known to him in the most explicit manner my impressions on the subject. I had no objection, however, on my own account to
its being known to Parliament. My individual opinion was of very little
consequence, as, by the course of events, in less than three years there
will be a total change of the Administration of this country; but I did
not think there was one member of the present Administration more
willing than I was to agree to the principle of search.

June 29, 1822—Mr. Canning had written me a note yesterday requesting to see me. I appointed this day at one, and he came. It was to take
up the subject of the slave-trade. He said from the communications of

58. Diary, October 26, 1822.

Lord Londonderry[59] to Mr. Rush it appeared that his Lordship believed that one main difficulty which had been made on our part to the arrangements proposed by Great Britain might be removed—that is, the trial by the mixed Courts; and he hoped, therefore, that we should be willing to yield the other point, the limited and reciprocal right of search.

I told him that any proposition that he had to make upon that subject would be received with the most respectful and friendly consideration. He gave me, however, to understand that he had no proposition to make, and he evaded answering the question which I put, what was Lord Londonderry's proposed substitute for the mixed Courts. With some circumlocution he came finally to the statement that he expected a new proposition from us. This had so much the appearance of a trick, that it heated me. I said to him—

> Mr. Canning, there is nothing I like so well as a straightforward course. We have seen no cause to change our opinions upon any of the points which have been so fully discussed between us. We have no new proposition, therefore, to make. It is one thing to make a proposition, and another to ask that a proposition should be made. When the Marquis of Londonderry, therefore, gave notice to Mr. Rush that it was proposed to resume the correspondence upon the slave-trade, we certainly expected that the British Government was prepared to make some new proposition to us. We are not prepared to make any to them. I could make none without authority from the President, and the President, I was persuaded, would authorize none without consulting all the members of the Administration.

He asked me then whether I declined discussing the matter further with him. I said, no; I was willing to hear, and would faithfully report to the President, anything that he wished to say to me.

He took from his pocket some printed documents laid before Parliament—correspondence from British officers at Sierra Leone, containing lists of slave vessels examined on the coast of Africa, under

---

59. One of British foreign minister Castlereagh's titles was Marquis of Londonderry.

French and Portuguese colors, and actively engaged in the slave-trade—
and he launched into a strong and general invective against the trade.

I observed that in the lists contained in the papers there was not a
single vessel under American colors, and alleged this circumstance as a
proof of the efficacy of the measures adopted by us to suppress the use
of our flag in the trade, which is all that could be accomplished by our
agreeing to the right of search and the mixed Courts. I remarked that it
was evident from these papers that if we had, two years ago, signed treaties with Great Britain like those which she had obtained from Spain,
Portugal, and the Netherlands, there would not have been one slave
vessel the less upon these lists. Search and the mixed Courts, therefore,
would have effected nothing for the suppression of the trade, which has
not been effected without them.

He said that a main purpose for which they wished to obtain our
assent to the principle of search was, that it might be urged as an example to France. I said that we should rather wish France to adhere to her
principles in this respect than to give them up. He asked if I could conceive of a greater and more atrocious evil than this slave-trade. I said,
Yes: admitting the right of search by foreign officers of our vessels upon
the seas in time of peace; for that would be making slaves of ourselves.
We went over this ground again, as we had often done before, repeating
on both sides the same arguments as before; he particularly repeated
that many persons in this country were in favor of conceding this right
of search, and alleged the two successive reports of committees of the
House of Representatives in its favor. I merely said that there were other
views upon which those reports could be accounted for. I finally desired
him to leave with me his Parliamentary printed paper, which I wished
to take to the President, to whom I promised him to make a full report
of this conference.

We conversed also upon the report of the Commissioners under
the fifth article of the Treaty of Ghent; upon the Convention recently
signed by me and the French Minister; upon the question of arbitration depending before the Emperor of Russia. . . . He observed . . . that
he believed one of the most difficult things in the world was to draw
up the articles of a treaty, and particularly to avoid stipulating more
than is intended. And he cited the article which we have in arbitration
before the Emperor of Russia as a memorable example of this; for the

British Plenipotentiaries never would have agreed to the article if they had been aware that it was susceptible of the construction upon which we now insist. I said it was certainly then the fault of Dr. Adams and Mr. Goulburn, who were intelligent men, and who were bound to see the purport of our proposed amendment. I added that we should not have signed the Peace without it; which he seemed inclined to doubt. I told him they had no right to carry away private property or to emancipate slaves. He said, banteringly, that if he were at war he would emancipate every slave he could find. "Then," said I, "I would never make peace with you till you paid for them. But who are you, to talk of emancipating slaves?" He said they had none. "And what are your West India islands? What would you say if we should land in Jamaica and emancipate your slaves?" "Ay, but," said he, "we do not mean to let you land in Jamaica." "Not if you can help it," said I. "Do no right and take no wrong, I have heard was the English sailor's motto."

This conversation lasted about three hours.

The weak impact antislavery moral principle had on Adams's foreign policy decisions in his second term became even clearer when he aligned his views with Calhoun's. He seems to have calmly joined Calhoun and others in discussing in cold-cash terms the value to be assigned to runaway slaves from the War of 1812.[60] On the growing question of the future of empire, slavery and freedom in the Caribbean, Adams espoused more diplomatic and constitutional caution than Calhoun did. But he expressed no qualms about annexing Cuba on grounds of it becoming a slave state, and his reference to "moral duty" in a conversation with Calhoun did not mean antislavery moral duty.

September 27, 1822—Mr. Calhoun has a most ardent desire that the island of Cuba should become a part of the United States, and says that Mr. Jefferson has the same. There are two dangers to be averted by that event: one, that the island should fall into the hands of Great Britain; the other, that it should be revolutionized by the negroes. Calhoun says Mr. Jefferson told him two years ago that we ought, at the first possible opportunity, to take Cuba, though at the cost of a war with England;

60. See Diary, September 24, October 8, and November 2, 1822.

but as we are not now prepared for this, and as our great object must be to gain time, he thought we should answer this overture by dissuading them from their present purpose, and urging them to adhere at present to their connection with Spain.

I thought it advisable to take a different course; to give them no advice whatever; to say that the Executive of the United States is not competent to promise them admission as a State into the Union; and that if it were, the proposal is of a nature which our relations of amity with Spain would not permit us to countenance.

Mr. Calhoun suggested that it would be proper for the President to make it a subject of a confidential communication to Congress at their next session. . . .

I replied that there would be no possibility of proceeding in the business by confidential communication to Congress: first, because there has not been one message with closed doors during the present Administration, nor, I believe, since the peace—the very notice of a secret session would raise an insatiate curiosity throughout the nation to know what could be its object; and, secondly, the proposal was of a nature which would not admit of secrecy. The power of Congress itself to act upon it was questionable. It involved external war and internal revolution in its essential and inevitable consequences. It would neither be possible nor proper that such business should be transacted by secret sessions of Congress. The whole affair would be divulged in a week—perhaps in a day. All Europe, as well as America, would have notice of it, and the very communication of the proposal to Congress as a subject for their deliberations, by the President, might be taken by Spain as hostility to her, and give warning to Great Britain to take an immediate and determined stand against it. As to taking Cuba at the cost of a war with Great Britain, it would be well to enquire, before undertaking such a war, how it would be likely to terminate; and for the present, and for a long time to come, I held it for certain that a war with Great Britain for Cuba would result in her possession of that island, and not ours. In the present relative situation of our maritime forces, we could not maintain a war against Great Britain for Cuba. Nor did I think that a plain, distinct answer, that our relations with Spain forbid our encouragement of a proposal to annex one of her Colonies to our own Union, could be construed into an instigation to revolt. It was a reference to a plain principle of moral duty, expressly applicable to the case, suitable to be acted upon as a motive, and honorable to the good faith of the nation. I would give them at the same time to understand that the Government of the United States entertain the most friendly sentiments towards the inhabitants of Cuba, and are fully aware of the common interests which point to a most intimate connection between them and the United States. . . .

Mr. Calhoun said he inclined to think there would be no immediate danger of a transfer of the island to Great Britain.

September 30, 1822—I attended the Cabinet meeting at the President's. . . . The proposition [under discussion] is, that the people of Cuba should immediately declare themselves independent of Spain without any co-operation of the United States, and then ask admission to the Confederation as one of the States of the Union. . . . I doubted the authority not only of the Executive, but of Congress, to perform this. Mr. Calhoun thought the case of [the] Louisiana [Purchase] had settled the Constitutional question. But a transaction which should make an island separated from this continent by the ocean at once a member of the Union, with a representation in both Houses of Congress, would certainly be an act of more transcendent power than a mere purchase of territory contiguous to our own.

The degree to which opposition to the illegal slave trade could serve to unite the Monroe administration was evident in the following entry. This episode may have reinforced Adams's growing sense that malevolent slaveholders like the marshal in question could impede the enforcement of humane laws—and indeed it is significant that he expressed mild surprise that humane sentiment on this question could have emanated from a Crawford supporter. But he may also have been impressed at other slaveholders' effective banding together to see those laws enforced.

October 26, 1822—Mr. Calhoun asked me if Mr. Early, of Georgia,[61] had called upon me. He had not. He had upon Calhoun, and upon the

---

61. We have not been able to identify this man. Presumably he was a relative of prominent Georgia politician Peter Early (1773–1817).

President. His object was to represent that the Marshal for the District of Georgia was now accumulating a fortune of at least thirty thousand dollars a year by working a number of African negroes who are in his possession as Marshal of the District, while at the same time he is making the most enormous charges against the public for the maintenance of the very same negroes; that he makes it his open boast that he holds the office of Marshal for no other purpose, and that he intends to *swamp* the negroes—that is, to work them to death—before they shall be finally adjudicated out of his possession. Mr. Early adds that his cruelty to negroes is universally notorious, and that it is equally well known that he did commit the murder of the black man for which he was tried and acquitted. The principal witnesses against him were *spirited* away. Early declares himself to be of the same political party with the Marshal (Crawford's), but is so horror-struck at the character and conduct of the man that he feels it to be his duty to denounce him. Yet he does not incline to support his charges with his name, the Marshal being a man of such desperation that everybody fears him. Early wished that the District Attorney and Judge might be authorized to investigate the circumstances of the custody of these negroes, but I thought it very doubtful whether that would avail. The District Attorney had shown in a former case that he was not the man to grapple with deep and deadly villainy supported by wealth and standing in society. The President inclined to send a person to Savannah specially charged with the investigation. Mr. Calhoun intimated the propriety of dismissing the Marshal immediately from office, but the President said that could not be done while there was no avowed accuser against him. I received last year two *anonymous* letters charging him with the murder of the negro, but Mr. Tatnall and Mr. Cuthbert,[62] both highly-respectable members of the Georgia delegation in Congress, took so deep an interest in his favor that he was re-appointed to the Marshal's office, though I did believe that the ineffaceable stain of blood was upon his hands. The President determined for the present only to direct that the accounts for keeping the negroes should not be paid at the Navy Department, and that further examination should be made hereafter.

62. Representatives Edward Fenwick Tattnall and Alfred Cuthbert.

That presidential politics was never far from the Monroe cabinet's minds, and sectionalism and the legacy of the Missouri Crisis were never far from the politics of the early 1820s, was confirmed by Adams's notes of a palaver with John Taylor of New York.[63]

November 30, 1822—As to the next Presidential election, I had no concert or understanding with any one.

He said he had been for some time convinced that there would be but one candidate from the North, for although the Vice-President was coming to take the chair of the Senate, and proclaimed his health restored, he would not be restored as a candidate.[64] Now, on the score of qualifications and services, if the South in the present case could not be induced to vote for the Northern candidate, he considered that their acquiescence in the choice of such a candidate would be postponed indefinitely. There was no reason to believe it would *ever* be obtained; because there was no reason for expecting that the claims of the North would ever stand upon more unequivocal ground. But at the last session of Congress there were numbers of the Northern men, and particularly Holmes, of Maine,[65] who professed a very high opinion of the Northern candidate, but always insisting that there was no chance in his favor, no possibility of his being elected. He [Taylor] had heard during the recess of Congress frequent conversations to the same effect, and had constantly maintained the opposite opinion.

I observed that he had never before spoken to me in a manner so explicit on this subject; that I had not known what his opinions concerning it were, but that intimations had been given to me that they were favorable to Mr. Crawford, which I had not credited.

He said that his own wishes were in favor of a Northern candidate. Should it ultimately appear that the chance of election in his favor is

---

63. For a pithy summary of how Adams expected slavery issues foreign and domestic would mingle with a variety of others in the presidential election, see Diary, June 5, 1823.

64. Vice President Daniel D. Tompkins, of New York, had been incapacitated for much of the early 1820s, and died in 1825.

65. Senator John Holmes, who had become notorious as an ardent sectional compromiser, or doughface, during the Missouri Crisis.

desperate, he should perhaps incline to favor that of Mr. Crawford. . . .
I believed Mr. Calhoun was now sensible he had been misadvised in
preventing the election of Taylor as Speaker; but it was the prejudice
raised by the Missouri slave question that had been the cause of it.

*Adams's last official interview with the outgoing minister, Canning, predict-
ably turned in large part on stubborn Anglo-American slavery-related issues.
The year before the British government had accepted the Russian mediator's
declaration that it must compensate American masters for fugitive slaves, but
the exact value to be assigned remained to be haggled over. Propelled largely
by a March 1823 House of Representatives resolution urging the administration to increase diplomatic efforts to cooperate with Britain against the slave
trade if Britain would join the United States in declaring the traffic piracy,
Adams proposed a convention that would establish a mutual right of search
strictly limited to the purposes of abolition. Adams also wanted the British to
foreswear impressment as part of this formula; Canning's response underscored
how politically dangerous it would be to abandon a practice that most Britons
thought of as necessary to the survival of their empire.[66] But Adams believed
mutual compromise was part and parcel of Britain recognizing the United
States as "a great nation."[67] When Adams presented his scheme to the cabinet,
the slight differences of opinion on practical matters were less significant than
the collective will to demonstrate the United States' good faith in the abolition
cause. This would protect not only the United States on the world stage, but
also the administration (and Adams himself) in the domestic arena.*

June 17, 1823—[I] gave [Canning] the general outlines of my plan.
He appeared to be uneasy at the idea that in my reply the subject of
impressment would be discussed, and said he hoped, in the disposition between the two Governments so strongly tending towards con-
ciliation, whatever was of an irritating character might be avoided. He
intimated, as in candor, that the proposition to Great Britain to pass

66. Bradford Perkins, *Castlereagh and Adams: England and the United States, 1812-1823*
    (Berkeley: University of California Press, 1964), 276–77; Denver Brunsman, *The
    Evil Necessity: British Naval Impressment in the Eighteenth-Century Atlantic World*
    (Charlottesville: University of Virginia Press, 2013).
67. Diary, June 20, 1823.

a law would excite some feeling, and that, in proposing to treat on the subjects of maritime law, the form of suggestion that Great Britain might have changed her principles would be less acceptable than if it were made in general terms.

I observed that in all her negotiations for the suppression of the slave-trade Great Britain not only asked the powers with whom she treated to pass laws, but made it a matter of express stipulation in the treaties; and in supposing that she might now view more favorably than heretofore the interests of neutrality, I had no thought of asking her to change her principles, but supposed that the difference of her position would necessarily produce different views.

June 19, 1823—There was a Cabinet meeting at the President's at one o'clock. Messrs. Crawford, Calhoun, and Thompson present; Mr. Wirt absent. My project of a Convention for the suppression of the slave-trade, answer to Mr. Canning, and instruction to R. Rush were first considered. Mr. Crawford and Mr. Calhoun started objections on various grounds—Crawford to the argument in the letter to Canning against the right of search, which, he said, was completely given up in the project of Convention, and therefore the argument might be represented by the British as a mere declamation against a practice which the project essentially conceded. This objection had weight, and I had been fully aware of it in drawing up the papers. But two objects were to be aimed at in them: one, fully to justify the repugnance which we have heretofore manifested against the right of search as practised by Great Britain in war; the other, to carry into effect the resolution of the House of Representatives recommending negotiation to obtain the recognition of the slave-trade to be piracy by the law of nations. To piracy, by the law of nations, search is incident of course, since wherever there is a right to capture there must be a right to search. The end desired by the resolution of the House of Representatives cannot be obtained without conceding the right so far of search, and all that is left us is to keep it still inflexibly within the class of belligerent rights, as exercised only against pirates, the enemies of all mankind. It was therefore that in my project of Convention the first article assumes as a fact that both parties have declared the slave-trade piracy, and my instructions to Mr. Rush are not to offer it but after an Act of Parliament declaring the slave-trade to be piracy.

Mr. Calhoun's objection was to the admission of the right of capture by foreign officers at all, as weakening us upon the general objection to conceding the right of search. Mr. Thompson did not think the right of search conceded in the project at all. The search for pirates had, he said, absolutely nothing in common with the search of neutral vessels. . . .

Mr. Calhoun thought we should at once say we will never concede the right of search for slaves unless Britain will renounce search for her seamen in our vessels in war. I said I was willing to make one the condition of the other.

It was finally understood by the President that the project, much as drafted, should be proposed, provided the British make the offence capital by Act of Parliament, and not be communicated in detail to the British Government without that.

Crawford hinted at an additional guard: that lists of the vessels authorized to capture the slave-traders should be mutually furnished. But it would be very inconvenient to us, as instructions of capture are issued to all our cruisers.

The project is to go, but the letter to Mr. Canning is to be modified.

June 20, 1823—Note from the President to call at his house. He read over the part of the draft of my reply to Mr. Canning, which he thinks should be sent, and suggested the substance of a substitute for what he would omit.

I told him all my motives for writing the draft as it was, and, among the rest, that of exhibiting to the people of this country and to the world the real grounds of objection to the right of search. I reminded him particularly of the appearance that in Congress a combination of parties was endeavoring to turn this into a party question. They had twice reported against the opinion of the Executive; and . . . I was satisfied that views unfriendly to his Administration, and personally so to me, were mingling themselves with this subject. It had appeared to me that an exhibition of the grounds upon which the aversion of this Government to conceding the right of search was founded would at once serve for its justification, and guard against the prevalence of a disposition in Congress to counteract the views of the Executive.

The President said he was aware of this tendency to an opposition in the House, and that he wished the whole of that part of my draft to Mr. Canning which he proposed to omit should be inserted in the

instructions to Mr. Rush. It would all be fully justified in the sentiments of this country; but in urging upon Great Britain her adoption
of our plan instead of her own, he wished to avoid everything which,
by irritating them, might give the British Ministers the opportunity
of imputing insincerity or ill will to us. He wished to gain over to our
views Mr. Wilberforce and his party, and to discard for that purpose
all that, by touching their national pride, would turn them against us.
By addressing to Mr. Rush that part of my reply to Mr. Canning, the
whole will in proper time be communicated to Congress, and it will
there have all its effect, without giving any cause of complaint to the
British Ministry.

I requested him to mark with a pencil the part of my draft which
he would wish to have transferred, and to sketch what he would
have substituted in the reply to Mr. Canning; which he promised he
would. I told him that my whole project had been merely formed
for his consideration, to carry into effect the resolution of the House
of Representatives, and to meet the urgent pressure of the British
Government concerning the slave-trade. My object was to give all the
aid in my power to *his* measures, and I wished not one line of my writing to go forth that should not have his hearty approbation.

*In the aftermath of the uncovering of Denmark Vesey's major slave insurrec-
tion plot in Charleston, southeastern states passed laws detaining all black
sailors while their ships were in their docks. Adams, like many Northerners,
found these draconian laws, known as the Negro Seaman Acts, unsettling.
But his record of what he and others found most disturbing in a conversation
about them was telling.*

September 4, 1823—Dined at General H. A. S. Dearborn's, at Brinley
Place, Roxbury [Massachusetts]. There was a company of about thirty
men. ... There was at table a conversation, chiefly between Colonel
Hayne[68] and George Blake, upon a decision of Judge Johnson's, of the
United States Supreme Court,[69] pronouncing an Act of the Legislature

68. Freshman senator Robert Y. Hayne of South Carolina, an ardent champion of
    slavery and Southern power.
69. Associate Justice William Johnson, a Jefferson appointee.

of South Carolina unconstitutional, in which Hayne discovered so much excitement and temper that it became painful, and necessary to change the topic. It was the Act prohibiting free persons of color from coming or being brought into the State as sailors, upon penalties, among which are their being sold as slaves.

Adams's response to a request for a donation foreshadowed his reactions to similar requests in future years in Washington. Such requests never raised a straightforward antislavery or even philanthropic question in Adams's mind; here, philanthropy mingled with presidential politics.

January 13, 1824—A Black woman and boy, Slaves, came to ask contributions to purchase their freedom. The boy belonged to Mr. Crawford. It seemed to me that asking a contribution for such a purchase, was craving alms for the Master; and not for the Slave.

4

The Making and Unmaking
of a President (1824–29)

In the context of US politics, the year 1824 has been called a moment of transition or flux; from the perspective of the two-party system that solidified later, partly in reaction to the year's events, it can appear downright dysfunctional. There was only one national party, a second-term president, and at least five potential successors. Adams seemed as viable as any of them, not least because every previous president after the first, George Washington, had served as vice president or secretary of state beforehand. This time, however, the very ill vice president, Daniel D. Tompkins, was not in the running.

Precisely because of this uncertainty, the jockeying had started early. Adams's wife Louisa and other friends urged him to commit to a candidacy and start lobbying congressmen and other influential people. In response, on January 18, 1823, he wrote a memo (really an extended diary entry) titled "The Macbeth Policy." Here he agonized at length over what sort of electioneering he could consider appropriate—for instance, he weighed the difference between seeking to "parry the daggers of" his political enemies and actually "canvass[ing] votes for the Presidency." One thing of which he was more certain was that while "sectional sympathies" had become an inescapable part of American political life in the early 1820s, he would not cater to them. "Let us distrust" even the most apparently innocuous of those sympathies, he exhorted himself and by extension his fellow Americans, "and let us indulge no sectional antipathies."[1] Sectional considerations remained a reason the National Republicans could not easily cohere around one ticket, but as candidate and as president, Adams would do his best to be a statesman for the Union.

The diary played an important role in the development of Adams's strategic thinking and politicking, just as it had during his earlier years as secretary of state. The January 30 entry shows the negotiating and strategizing well under way in early 1824. Members of Congress anticipated that, with multiple candidates, the election might well be thrown into the House of Representatives in the increasingly likely event that no one received more than half of the electoral college vote. Representatives already had a special role to play early on because the National Republicans had previously nominated candidates in an informal congressional caucus. With one party so dominant, the stakes were raised: If they met in caucus, they would seem to claim for themselves the privilege of naming the next president, not merely a preferred candidate to be submitted to a popular election. If they did not caucus, it would increase the likelihood of there being more than two candidates and, if none received a majority in the electoral college, throwing the election right back into the House, where deal making could be even less transparent. The table was set for intrigue, as well as for accusations of corruption and undemocratic procedure. Complicating things further, the front runner for the congressional caucus nomination was William H. Crawford—who, as one senator noted to Adams, was in bad health and unlikely to survive one term. This made the nomination of a vice president equally weighty.[2]

January 30, 1824—Colonel R. M. Johnson, Mr. R. King, and Mr. Fuller had long conversations with me concerning the movements of the parties here for the Presidential succession.[3] Johnson says that Calhoun proposed to him an arrangement by which I should be supported as

1. "The Macbeth Policy," in Charles Francis Adams, ed., *Memoirs of John Quincy Adams* (Philadelphia: J. D. Lippincott, 1874–77), 6: 132–37, quotations on 135.
2. See Diary, December 4, 1824.
3. Richard Mentor Johnson was a senator from Kentucky. Timothy Fuller was a member of the House of Representatives from Massachusetts.

President, General Jackson as Vice-President, Clay to be Secretary of State, and he himself Secretary of the Treasury; not as a bargain or coalition, but by the common understanding of our mutual friends.

I made no remark upon this, but it discloses the forlorn-hope of Calhoun, which is to secure a step of advancement to himself, and the total exclusion of Crawford, even from his present office at the head of the Treasury.

Johnson said that Governor Barbour, Senator from Virginia, after a conversation with him, in which he had insisted, and Barbour had agreed, that upon an election in the House, should it come there, the vote would be at least two thirds for me against Crawford, said he had thoughts of giving in his adhesion to me, which Johnson advised him by all means to do. Mr. King spoke of the state of affairs in New York. His own views are in some respect biassed by his situation. He has been heretofore himself a candidate for the Presidency. He had at one time during the present Administration hopes of being the next in succession. There is a spice of disappointment in all his opinions, and his grounds of preference now are too much sectional. There is something peculiar in the state of his mind, for it is transparent in his conduct and discourse that although strenuous for the Northern man, he would, in the event of his failure, not be without consolation. King is one of the wisest and best men among us. But his own ambition was inflamed by splendid success in early life, followed by vicissitudes of popular favor and hopes deferred, till he has arrived nearly at the close of his public career. He has one session of Congress to sit in Senate, but talks even now of resigning. Fuller mentioned the meetings which have been held, and are holding, to ascertain the number of the members of Congress who deem it inexpedient at this time to make a caucus nomination for the next Presidency.

Treasury Secretary William H. Crawford was a former Virginian, popular in Georgia, and experienced in Washington. He had been maneuvering in the cabinet to position himself for the presidential nomination for years, much to the disgust of Adams and Calhoun, both of whom came to distrust his judgment and to despise his seeming lack of principles. But this was not just Washington intrigue: newspapers around the country trumpeted and downgraded possible candidates for a variety of reasons, and Adams and his supporters paid close attention to the prospects for alliance, as it became clear that any successful bid for the presidency would have to be a sectional coalition of some sort. In Adams's eyes, he himself was the best hope for a coalition truly devoted to "the whole union." Not only was he the only Northern candidate: he had demonstrated his willingness and ability to work with Southerners like Madison and Monroe.

On January 8, he and Louisa had hosted a huge party in honor of General Andrew Jackson of Tennessee.[4] *This was part of an effort to advance Adams's candidacy and possibly a sectionally balanced Adams–Jackson ticket. Adams had supported Jackson against other members of the cabinet in the controversy over Jackson's unauthorized actions in Florida during the Seminole War. Jackson did not himself enter the race for president until the spring.*

February 4, 1824—I attended in the evening the drawing-room at the President's. On returning home, I found J. W. Taylor at my house, and had a long conversation with him. He told me that Jesse B. Thomas, a Senator from Illinois, had strongly urged upon him the expediency of my acquiescing in the nomination as Vice-President, with Mr. Crawford for the Presidency. He said that Mr. Crawford would certainly be elected, and he spoke of certain members of Congress as ultimately to vote for him who appear to be far otherwise disposed at this time; that it was, however, very desirable that he should carry with him the strength which he would derive from the co-operation of my friends; that from the state of Mr. Crawford's health it was highly probable the duties of the Presidency would devolve upon the Vice-President, which had made it necessary to select with peculiar anxiety a person qualified for the contingency which was to be anticipated; that a compliance with the views of Mr. Crawford's friends on this occasion would be rendering them a service which would recommend me to their future favor, and would doubtless secure my election hereafter to the Presidency. Taylor said he had answered that admitting even the

4. For the party honoring the anniversary of the Battle of New Orleans, see Diary, January 8, 1824; Louisa Catherine Adams Diary, January 8, 1824, in Margaret A. Hogan and C. James Taylor, eds., *A Traveled First Lady: Writings of Louisa Catherine Adams* (Cambridge, MA: Harvard University Press, 2014), 324–25; Catherine Allgor, *Parlor Politics* (Charlottesville, VA: University Press of Virginia, 2000), ch. 5.

certainty that Mr. Crawford should be elected, that was no sufficient reason for the acquiescence of my friends in the proposed arrangement. If the election should be carried against them, they will at least have followed their own sense of what was right and fit. They could not place me in subordination to Mr. Crawford without inverting the natural order of things and placing the North in a position of inferiority to the South. Should they be so placed by the Constitutional voice of the people, they must undoubtedly submit; but they could not consent to be so placed by their own act. Taylor said Thomas had asked him to see him again after thinking on the subject. I said he might tell him then, if he thought fit, that he had seen me, and I had told him that I was so satisfied of the inexpediency of a Congressional caucus nomination at this time that I should decline accepting it, were it even for the Presidency. He said he thought it would be better that, without referring to me or to my determination, he should simply state the perseverance of my friends in the sentiments he had already expressed as being theirs.

May 1, 1824—John Reed, a member of the House from Massachusetts . . . said he was soon going home, and spoke of the Presidential election. He is a federalist, but he says that two thirds of his constituents are Republicans. He professed to be very friendly to me, but intimated an opinion that it would ultimately be necessary for my friends to unite with those of Mr. Crawford. I told him there was nothing to be expected from that, but he said the assurances from the friends of Mr. Crawford were very strongly otherwise. I said that I had understood that a systematic effort was making to unite the federal party in Massachusetts in favor of Mr. Crawford, and that the great struggle of the federalists at the recent State election for Governor was connected with that purpose. He said it was not a general feeling, but that some of the federalists favored Mr. Crawford from an apprehension that my prejudices against them were so strong, that in the event of my election they would be altogether proscribed.

I asked him if he thought there was a doubt of my election by a large majority of the electoral votes but for an opposition from the Republican party on the very ground of my being suspected of too much federalism. He said there was not. I told him I had originally been a federalist, just such as President Washington had been. But of the course that had been pursued by the federalists during and preceding the late war my opinion was well known, and had been fully manifested by my conduct. Personally, the federalists had done me wrong, and I expected no favor from them. But during the whole of the present Administration it had been at least as much supported by the federalists as by the Republicans. If it should be the pleasure of the people of the United States that I should serve them as their President, I should be the President not of a section, nor of a faction, but of the whole Union. If the federalists chose, as a body, to array themselves against me, I should not complain, and very probably they might prevent my election. Possibly their opposition, however, might strengthen me in the opposite party, and if, after a combined and continued movement against me, I should still be elected, they must be aware how much the difficulty would be increased of favoring them with appointments without disgusting those of the opposite party claiming the merit of friendly support against them.

It was in large part pressure from Congress that had initiated the 1823 Anglo-American slave trade convention venturing a limited mutual right of search. But this convention's prospects for ratification ran into trouble in the spring of 1824 in the Senate.[5]

May 14, 1824—Mr. R. King called this morning on me, and said he was apprehensive it would be absolutely necessary for the Senate to annex in some form a limitation to the Slave-Trade Convention now before them. He was much averse to it himself, and thought it very absurd. But there was no reasoning with fear. The members from some of the Southern States had taken a panic at the late speeches in the British Parliament looking to the abolition of slavery, and were exceedingly adverse to forming any concert with the British Government whatever in reference to the subject of slavery. The question was, whether the limitation should be for a term of years, or that the Convention may at any time be annulled on either side by giving a notice of days or months.

I said, of the two evils the limitation for a term of years would be the least; but either would be highly pernicious; that it would defeat the

5. See also Diary, May, 19, 20, and 23, 1824.

joint attempt to influence other nations to make the slave-trade piracy. For how absurd that we should try to prevail upon all other nations to declare it piracy, when they might retort upon us that we have shrunk from our own obligations, and made it a piracy for a term of years, reserving ourselves the right of repealing our own law! I said, also, that *any* limitation would be peculiarly ungracious from us, the whole project being our own, and adopted at our instance by Great Britain; of all which Mr. King himself is fully sensible. . . .

Mr. Addington, the British Chargé d'Affaires, came to speak of the Slave-Trade Convention, and of the duties upon iron. He was much disconcerted at the unexpected opposition to the Convention in the Senate; at which I am not less mortified.

Adams's stance on the Missouri question became of great interest to prospective supporters. William Plumer Jr., a senator from New Hampshire, asked how he should handle the issue of Adams's stance in 1819–21. This entry exemplified the dance Adams was prepared to perform to avoid having Missouri turned against him in either the North or the South. In a letter to supporter Edward Everett in 1827, Adams would similarly finesse this issue especially for Southern consumption by emphasizing his early statements against the Tallmadge Amendment's constitutionality, at the expense of later statements.[6]

May 20, 1824—Mr. Plumer was here, and we had a long conversation upon political topics generally. He showed me a letter from General Cocke, of Tennessee, to him, not signed, enquiring concerning conversations at the boarding-house at which they both lodged in 1821—concerning my opinions the year before upon the restriction of slavery in Missouri. Cocke intimates that he had understood Plumer to have said I was in favor of the restriction. And Plumer said he had a letter from Hill, the editor of the New Hampshire Patriot, now a thorough Crawfordite, saying he had formerly understood Plumer to, have told

6. John Quincy Adams to Edward Everett, April 11, 1827, Edward Everett Papers, 1675–1910, Microfilm Edition, MHS; Diary, July 5, 1819; February 23; and March 3, 1820.

him that I was in favor of the restriction, and now it was published that I had been against it.

Plumer said he very indistinctly recollected both the conversations to which Cocke referred and anything that had passed between him and me on the subject. The object of Cocke was to get an electioneering weapon against me for the Southern country, and that of Hill, to get one against me for the North, and also one against Plumer himself. Plumer said Barton, one of the Missouri Senators, told him that Cocke had been all this session at him to get a certificate from him about those conversations, but that Barton, considering the whole controversy as past and gone by, had refused to give him any. He had written to Judge Archer, who had also been present at the boarding-house conversations, to enquire of his recollections concerning them; and he asked me for mine, of what my opinions had been. I told him that the only conversation I recollected to have had with him on the first Missouri question, that of the restriction, was on the 23d of February, 1820, and I read to him the account of it given at the time in my diary of that date. He said he particularly recollected the distinction I had drawn between a restriction upon Illinois and one upon Missouri, and wished me to give him a copy of the extract from my diary—which I promised. Both Houses of Congress have agreed to adjourn this day week, and Plumer still thinks the investigating committee will report in favor of Crawford upon Edwards's charges, avoiding all research into the attack of Crawford upon him. Walter Forward, member of the House from Pittsburgh, Pennsylvania, came, he said, by the advice of some of my friends, to ask me what were my opinions upon the subject of the tariff and the protection of manufactures. He said it was a subject of great interest among his constituents, and he knew he should be enquired of by many of them concerning my opinions with reference to it. I told him I had no desire either to obtrude or to withhold them. I was glad the Tariff bill had passed, though I had no other knowledge of its details than had been elicited in the debate, and had formed no decisive opinion upon them. I hoped its operation would be satisfactory to those whose interests it was particularly adapted to promote, without being oppressive upon the agricultural and commercial interests, as had been apprehended. I was cautioned to distrust Forward by my Pittsburgh correspondents two years ago. He attended the caucus last February, and voted there for Crawford. Since then my correspondents themselves have come out, held a public meeting, and nominated Crawford; and now Forward comes and asks me these questions. For what? N'importe.[7]

After a May 18 meeting Adams described the cabinet's discussion of the "ostensible pretences of this unexpected opposition" to the slave trade convention in the Senate: "the concession of the right of search, and the panic of the South at the measures taking in England for the abolition of slavery, and with which this Convention was there associated." He wrote more ambiguously that "the real, or at least more operating, causes were only glanced at." Five days later, with the help of Rufus King, he was willing to name this other cause of opposition: the desire of his rivals and their supporters to sink his presidential prospects.

May 23, 1824—Mr. D. Brent came, to mention the issue in the Senate on the Convention; of which he had heard, and thought I was not informed. Mr. Rufus King came, and in a long conversation gave, me all the particulars of the proceedings in the Senate; showed me the parts of the Convention which have been stricken out, and the yeas and nays upon every question that was taken. He said that in the management of the opposition there had been great disingenuousness and rancor, and it had been clearly and plainly disclosed to the observation of every one that the main object of it was an electioneering engine against me. He said that after making the crime piracy, and inviting all others to do the same, to cavil at the right of searching for the pirates was an absurdity; and, without meaning to compliment me, he would say he thought the abuses to which the exercise of the right were liable had been guarded against with the utmost care in the Convention. He knew not how they could have been better guarded. The message of the President had been very properly sent in; but all that it contained had already been said in the Senate before it came in. He did not know whether now the Convention would be worth accepting, or would be accepted, by Great Britain. I told him I thought it would. The essential

7. A French phrase for, literally, "unimportant."

bases of the Convention were untouched. The three great principles— that the trade shall be piracy, the mutual right of search and capture, and the trial of the captured party by his own country—are secured. The two articles eliminated were no part of our project. The exception of the coast of America from the searchable seas has operation only with regard to the coast of Brazil; and may hereafter be removed, so far as may be necessary, by further negotiation. The only material injury done to the Convention is the reservation of the power in either party to renounce it with six months' notice—a power leaving an impor- tant question, what authority in the organization of *our* Government is competent to give that notice? I presume it must be by authority of an Act of Congress. . . .

The British Chargé d'Affaires, Addington, called likewise, to speak upon the subject of the Convention. He had been informed of the manner in which it passed, and said he hoped it would be accepted as it has been ratified here. He said it had been explained by him in letters already dispatched to his Government. He understood the opposition to have arisen purely from party spirit and to be in a great measure occasional. He asked me if I could let him have confidentially a copy of the President's last message to the Senate urging the ratification of the Convention to send to his Government. It would undoubtedly have the effect of reconciling them to the modifications annexed to the ratification here.

I said I would propose it to the President, and thought he would probably not object. But, as there was a motion pending before the Senate for taking off the injunction of secrecy from all their proceed- ings on the subject, the message would perhaps in that manner be made public.

On the very next day, Adams went out of his way to tell South Carolina sen- ator George McDuffie, who had been one of the senators who spoke against the slave trade convention, that he had opposed the Tallmadge Amendment.

May 24, 1824—Hayden, of New York, and McDuffie, of South Carolina, members of the House, came to take leave. McDuffie, hav- ing reference to the Presidential election, said he was returning to

Carolina, and, as there might be in the Legislature of that State a con-tested support of Mr. Crawford and of me, he should be glad, if I had no objection to stating them, to know my sentiments upon the tariff policy. I told them freely. That it was one of those subjects in which great opposing interests were to be conciliated by a spirit of mutual accommodation and concession. I was satisfied with the Tariff bill as it has passed, because it appeared to me to have been elaborated pre-cisely to that point. I thought I had seen in it an admirable illustra-tion of the practical operation of our national Government. The two parties had contested every inch of the ground between them, with great ardor and ability, and the details of the bill had finally brought them to questions decided by the casting vote of the presiding officer in each House, and an adjustment by conference between the two Houses. With the result it was reasonable to expect that both parties would be satisfied.

McDuffie appeared to be well satisfied with it himself, and he said that the final vote upon it in the House gave a majority of fifty votes in its favor.

I told him that there was another subject upon which my opinions had been greatly misrepresented in the Southern country, with a view to excite local prejudices against me. It was upon the slave question generally, and the Missouri restriction particularly. My opinion had been against the proposed restriction in Missouri, as contravening both the Constitution and the Louisiana Treaty. This was the first Missouri question. The second was upon an article introduced into the Constitution of the State of Missouri, which I thought contrary to the Constitution of the United States. I then stated explicitly what my opinions had been upon both questions, and noticed the artifice of the misrepresentation, which, from my opposition to the article in the Missouri Constitution, inferred my having favored the restric-tion. I added that the article of the Missouri Constitution required the Legislature of that State to do precisely what the Legislature of his own State of South Carolina had since done; and which Judge William Johnson, a native and citizen of the State itself, had pro-nounced to be contrary to the Constitution of the United States. McDuffie said he had no doubt it was so, and was very glad I had given him this explanation.

Representative Charles Fenton Mercer and Secretary of the Navy Samuel Southard reinforced Adams's sense that senators opposed to his presidential prospects were playing politics with the slave trade convention.

May 27, 1824—With Mercer I had a long conversation upon the Slave-Trade Convention, and the proceedings of the Senate upon it. He said that when the National Intelligencer announced that no copy of those proceedings could be obtained, he himself had gone to the presiding officer and insisted upon having copies, and had obtained them, and they would be published in the Intelligencer.

I had observed to Mercer that after what had taken place in the Senate upon this Convention, and the subsequent effort, obviously intended to follow it up, to make it unpopular, the power of the President to negotiate further under the resolution of the House would be much checked until there should be some further manifestation of opinion by Congress in its favor.

He now expressed to me some doubt whether this could be done at the next session of Congress. He said it was apparent and known to everyone that the opposition now started against the Convention was merely personal, pointed against me with reference to the Presidential election, and but for that would not have existed; that it was barely temporary and occasional; but that probably the excitement from which it arose would be at its height at the next session of Congress, and that then would be a moment peculiarly unfavorable for a calm discussion of the subject in the House.

I told him I had no doubt it would be so at the beginning of the session, but that my project was this. If the British government should ratify the Convention as modified, the President will of course notice it in his annual message at the commencement of the session, and it will be among the documents communicated with the message. That part of the message will, in the ordinary course of business, be referred to a select committee, which may take the whole subject under consideration, including what is further to be done. They may keep it before them until the Presidential election shall have been decided, after which there will be no motive for persisting in the factious opposition to the principles of the Convention, which has now so suddenly and unexpectedly gotten up to benefit Mr. Crawford by fastening odium upon me. But Mr. Crawford had favored the concession of the right of search even while I resisted it, and without the preliminary condition of making the slave-trade piracy. He had encouraged Mr. Canning in pressing for its concession. The project of Convention, which I sent to Mr. Rush, had been submitted to his inspection; he had been present at the Cabinet meeting when it was determined to propose it, and fully assented to that measure—though he now denied that fact.

Mercer asked me upon what authority I made that statement.

I said, from the lips of the President.

Mercer appeared surprised, and said that he had mentioned to the President that he had heard this stated concerning Crawford, but the President, instead of confirming it, had spoken as if he doubted it. He said he wondered why the President should have used this reserve with him while consulting him confidentially on the subject, and after having had frequent communications with him upon subjects of a still more confidential nature. He had always considered me as opposed to his views in relation to the suppression of the slave-trade, and Mr. Crawford as favoring them; that I thought the Colonization Society wild and visionary in their plans, while Mr. Crawford was one of their Vice-Presidents, and last summer had spent a day in presiding at one of their meetings. He further said that while Baron Hyde de Neuville was here he had proposed a Convention between the United States and France for the suppression of the slave-trade, granting a mutual right of search and capture, and stipulating to send on board of every cruiser against the slave-traders a joint commission of judges to try the persons captured of either nation; that the President authorized him (Mercer) to make such a Convention with De Neuville, but afterwards withdrew the authority. Mercer spoke also of Alexander Smyth's attacks upon me as being a favorer of the slave-trade; of his handbill detailing their private conversations and mine with Mercer, and of his own relations with Crawford, which, he said, had not been intimate. He approved the idea of acting in Congress upon the slave-trade at the next session, after the decision upon the Presidential election; and, on his parting from me, I assured him I should be happy to co-operate with him in the further support of the cause—at which he expressed his satisfaction.

May 29, 1824—Southard told me he was going upon business next week to Norfolk. He said, too, that Van Buren and Dickerson were gone to Richmond, whence they were to proceed on visits to Mr. Jefferson and Mr. Madison, and there was much speculation as to the object of their journey.

I said I had little doubt it was to prepare and concert the movement of Mr. Crawford's partisans in the event of his being withdrawn or declining as a candidate for the Presidential election, and my belief was they meant to take up Mr. Clay for their substituted candidate.

Southard said Clay had expectations of that sort himself, and had also been much elated by three meetings lately gotten up in his favor in New Jersey, about which he had yesterday asked him several questions. The truth was that if those meetings had been convened by those whom he suspected, there was nothing that would so effectually secure against him the vote of New Jersey, unless it was his being supported by Mr. Dickerson. I told him that my main reason for believing that Clay was the man they intended to push for was the profligate opposition they had got up and pressed in Senate against the Convention for the suppression of the slave-trade, the only object of which was to use it as a weapon to raise a popular clamor against me. This they would have avoided under the high probability of Crawford's withdrawing from the field, if they had not determined, at all events, to keep me out.

For the remainder of the year Adams tried to make sure that the slave trade convention did not get pinned on him alone. He also worked hard not to get maneuvered into making what might be seen as antislavery policy statements, even with the support of the rest of the cabinet. South Carolina's Negro Seamen Act, which required free black sailors at port to be held in jail, presented a similar challenge.

April 24, 1824—I took the President's several despatches . . . and a new remonstrance against the South Carolina Law, prohibiting colored people from coming into the State. I urged upon the President the necessity of doing something in this case. I said I saw nothing that could be done, except to lay the subject before Congress; but, as a last resource for avoiding that appeal, I left the letter with him, to see if Mr. [Joel]

Poinsett of the South Carolina delegation could devise any other way of getting rid of that law.

July 2, 1824—At the President's, who sent for Calhoun. Read my draft of an article in answer to that of the Intelligencer; discussed. Question whether any reference should be in it to the President. Statement that the negotiation of the Slave-Trade Convention was with the unanimous assent of the members of the Administration. Draft approved as written. . . .

A. B. Woodward.[8] His projected meeting for to-morrow evening. Resolutions for abolition of slavery. Advised him to countermand the meeting, and talk with P[resident]. U. S. about the resolutions. Note from P. U. S. with Mercer's statement.

November 10, 1824—Cabinet meeting. Present W. H. Crawford, J. C. Calhoun. Samuel L. Southard, and J. Q. Adams. Subject of consideration, the Slave-Trade Convention with G. B. I read the dispatches, No. 11 and 12 of the separate series, from R. Rush, and my drafts of a public and of a secret and confidential dispatch to him; also a note from Mr. Addington, the British Charge d'Affaires, announcing his receipt of a full power to conclude a new Convention, with the single addition of the words "of America" to that sanctioned by the Senate. The opinion was unanimous against acceding to the proposal for concluding a new Convention—at least for the present. Both my drafts were unanimously approved; the President objecting slightly to the word "unseemliness," and suggesting the use of *impropriety* in its stead. I altered the draft accordingly, having used the term unseemliness only with reference to its having been used by Mr. Canning himself, though afterwards withdrawn.

Mr. Crawford told twice over the story of President Washington's having at an early period of his Administration gone to the Senate with a project of a treaty to be negotiated, and been present at their deliberations upon it. They debated it and proposed alterations, so that when Washington left the Senate-chamber he said he would be damned if he

8. Augustus B. Woodward, former chief justice of the Michigan territory, scientist, and founder of the University of Michigan. Woodward's biographer does not mention this proposal. Frank B. Woodford, *Mr. Jefferson's Disciple: A Life of Justice Woodward* (East Lansing: Michigan State University Press, 1953).

ever went there again. And ever since that time treaties have been nego-tiated by the Executive *before* submitting them to the consideration of the Senate.

The President said he had come into the Senate about eighteen months after the first organization of the present Government, and then heard that something like this had occurred. Crawford then repeated the story, varying the words, so as to say that Washington *swore* he would never go to the Senate again.

Mr. Crawford and Mr. Calhoun both expressed themselves strongly upon the absurdity of Canning's two official notes, the second of which retains the argument, while it retracts as erroneous the allegation of facts upon which it was maintained in the first.

Calhoun noticed the tone of both the original and substituted note of Canning as offensive. In the original note there were three gross blunders. One of them remains in the substitute, besides the absurdity of an argument retained, with the facts upon which it was founded withdrawn. Rush says Canning had been ill with a fever, and Southard observed he had not recovered from it when he wrote the notes.

Mr. Crawford now for the first time spoke against the concession of the right of search, and said the very proposal of it was an insult, because it implied an admission that we were not competent or not trustworthy to execute our own laws. This reasoning is not sound in its application to the Slave-Trade Convention. The object is to capture *pirates*; and, without any distrust of our own Executive officers, we may give our aid and accept that of another for the more effectual execution of a law common to both. But the remarkable fact in this case is the change of Mr. Crawford's opinion. When I stood almost alone in resist-ing the concession of the right of search, even before we had required as an indispensable preliminary that Britain should make the slave-trade piracy, Mr. Crawford, with two successive committees of the House of Representatives, was bearing down my resistance, and his partisans were using it as evidence that I was a friend to the slave trade. And now that his supporters in the Senate have taken ground against yield-ing the right of search, even for pirates, he joins in the cry with them, and discovers that the very proposal is an insult. To the argument in Addington's note urging that Great Britain, upon the faith of our ratify-ing the Convention, had, at our requisition, passed an Act declaring the slave-trade piracy, he said they might, if they pleased, repeal their Act. This is true, but it is not of itself a sufficient answer to their argument. I must have stronger ground.

The popular election in November 1824 failed to deliver any of the candidates a majority in the Electoral College, which threw the decision to the House of Representatives. Although he did not campaign publicly in the modern sense, at this stage Adams discreetly lobbied congressmen for the presidency. Historians and biographers now portray him as managing the peculiar election of 1824 with great political skill, appropriate to both the Washington intrigue and the press firestorms of the extended electoral season.[9] Adams tried to assure potential House supporters from Maryland that his administration would be neither partisan nor sectional.

February 7, 1825—Mr. Warfield[10] came, upon the notice given him, as I had yesterday requested, by Mr. [Daniel] Webster. He said that he had not expressed his determination for whom he should vote in the House on Wednesday. His friends, Mr. Charles Carroll, of Carrollton, and Mr. [Roger Brooke] Taney, of Baltimore, had urged him to vote for General Jackson, under an impression that if I should be elected, the Administration would be conducted on the principle of proscribing the federal party.

I said I regretted much that Mr. Carroll, for whose character I entertained a profound veneration, and Mr. Taney, of whose talents I had heard high encomium, should harbor such opinions of me. I could assure him that I never would be at the head of any Administration of proscription to any party—political or geographical. I had differed from the federal party on many important occasions, but I had always done justice to the talents and services of the individuals composing it,

9. David Callahan, "The Election of 1824," and Catherine Allgor and Margery M. Heffron, "A Monarch in a Republic: Louisa Catherine Johnson Adams and Court Culture in Early Washington City," in David Waldstreicher, ed., *A Companion to John Adams and John Quincy Adams* (Oxford, and Malden, MA: Wiley-Blackwell, 2013), 305–27, 466; James Traub, *John Quincy Adams: Militant Spirit* (New York: Basic Books, 2016), 292–94.
10. Representative Henry R. Warfield of Maryland.

and to their merits as members of this Union. I had been discarded by the federal party upon differences of principle, and I had not separated from one party to make myself the slave of another. I referred, in proof of my adherence to principle against party, to various acts of my public life, and Mr. Warfield declared himself perfectly satisfied with my exposition of my sentiments.

Historians have long lamented that the diary does not make clear the precise nature of the "bargain" that led Henry Clay to urge the Kentucky delegation to switch to Adams in the state-by-state House voting, assuring him the presidency and Clay, apparently, the position of secretary of state. Partisans of Adams stress their agreements on policy matters and Clay's ample qualifications for the cabinet and State Department: thus, there was no deal, and the alliance was natural and obvious. Critics are more likely to follow the Jacksonian opposition and accuse Adams, if not of smarmy deal making, at least of political tone-deafness. Some have attributed the gaps in the diary for that meeting to the secret nature of what became known as "the corrupt bargain."

From early in his presidency, Adams's nation-building agenda came under direct fire from Southerners who explicitly raised the threat that slavery faced from a stronger federal government. Partisans of Andrew Jackson sought to combine that critique of big government with assertions that Adams remained a closet Federalist: aloof, professorial, undemocratic, and so cosmopolitan and Anglophilic as to be un-American. Adams's wife, Louisa, expressed great frustration at this image problem: in light of her Southern and European experience, Adams's manners struck her as relatively democratic and unassuming. Considering his everyday behavior as president, she had a point. Much of his time as president was spent conversing with any citizens who wanted to talk with him, including political opponents. While he was at great pains during his presidency to try to prevent his Northern outlook on slavery from becoming an issue, he occasionally used the diary to vent his frustration with proslavery visitors. He continued to tread carefully, aware that any chance he had to pursue his program of "improvement" depended on Southern votes in Congress.

November 18, 1825—Casey of Tennessee, a young man, who came he said to see me, merely, from curiosity; being a near neighbor of General Jackson, residing near Nashville, said he had been with him in the late

War. Conversed with him about Tennessean members of Congress. He came here to buy Negroes.

November 21, 1825—Barbour, James, S. W.,[11] who took back his papers relating to Indian concerns particularly the draft of his report urging the necessity of incorporating the Indians within our own system. He mentioned having had a conversation with Mr. [John] Gaillard, a Senator from South Carolina, who wished that something conciliatory to the South might be said in the message, to calm their inquietudes concerning their slaves. He wished something to sustain the friends of the Administration against the overwhelming influence of the Calhoun party, which they had been unable to resist, and by which they were oppressed.

I said I should be glad to do anything in my power to gratify Mr. Gaillard, but the Legislature of South Carolina itself had put it out of my power to say anything soothing to the South on that subject by persisting in a law which a Judge of the Supreme Court of the United States, himself a native and in habitant of South Carolina, had declared to be in direct violation of the Constitution of the United States; which the Attorney-General of the United States had declared to infringe the rights of foreign nations, against which the British Government had repeatedly remonstrated, and upon which we had promised them that the cause of complaint should be removed a proviso which the obstinate adherence of the Government of South Carolina to their law had disenabled us from fulfilling.[12] The Governor of South Carolina had not even answered the letter from the Department of State transmitting to him the complaint of the British Government against this law. In this state of things, for me to say anything gratifying to the feelings of the South Carolinians on this subject would be to abandon the ground taken by the Administration of Mr. Monroe, and disable us from taking hereafter measures concerning the law, which we may be compelled to take. To be silent, is not to interfere with any State rights; and not to interfere, renounces no right of ourselves or others.

January 11, 1826—The Speaker, J. W. Taylor,[13] stayed an hour after the rest of the company were gone, and spoke of Hamilton of South

11. Secretary of war.
12. The Negro Seamen Act of 1823. See entry for June 24, 1824.
13. Speaker of the House of Representatives John W. Taylor.

Carolina's sally at him for presenting to the House a memorial from a crazy man in France, who invited Congress to destroy all the States which should refuse the emancipation of slaves. Hamilton was not countenanced in his fit of chivalry, but Taylor said he had notice that a more formal attack upon him was intended, and by more formidable adversaries. He was told that a person of far more consideration and talents than Hamilton, and of the South Carolina delegation, had spoken of this incident as proof of a fixed determination of the present Administration to emancipate the Southern slaves. He spoke also of Hamilton's resolution to call for the papers relating to the Panama mission.[14]

I said I believed it would be best to keep it alive; but, if he called it up soon, to put it off, and bring him out in his Hotspur vein, till he shall disclose more of the secret views of his party. I told Taylor I believed the message concerning the Panama mission must be a confidential one; to which he assented.

September 11, 1826—Mount Wollaston Farm. ... Mr. B. J. Hunt was introduced to me by J. Greenleaf—Hunt is a native of this Region, the vicinity of Boston. Has been settled here since the year 1810 at Charleston, South Carolina has been a member of the Legislature of that State, and is a very active politician. He cautioned me to beware of Cleary the Sheriff who has written me several Letters; to all which I have returned one short answer. He said there was no reliance to be placed upon Cleary, who was honest in his intentions, sincere in the expression of his feelings, but flighty and changeable. Mr. Hunt's friends one Mr. Bennett and Judge Gaillard. He advises against removals from Office, and wishes something may be done [to] conciliate the Southern Planters with regard to the security of their Negro-property.

The very paucity of entries concerning slavery during his presidency suggests Adams's desire to keep aloof from the issue, but antislavery advocates, especially Quakers, continued to try to sound him out.[15] There are hints, including a poem he wrote on his father's birthday, that he was thinking about the issue, but mainly in the abstract and long term, not in terms of current policy.

14. The delegation to an international meeting of American states, including the newly independent South American nations such as Mexico.
15. See also Diary, May 25, 1827.

September 13, 1826—Elizabeth Robson, the female Quaker preacher, with two other women and two men, came upon their morning visit. Wistar and one of the women are from Philadelphia. The other woman came from England with Elizabeth, and Bassett is of Lynn. They are returning from a tour to Nantucket, and Elizabeth is now going to Montreal and Quebec.

After the usual salutations, Elizabeth sat some time with her hand covering her face as in deep meditation, and then addressed me in a formal religious exhortation of about a quarter of an hour concerning the cares and duties of the ruler of a nation; but particularly upon the condition of the poor oppressed colored people in this country. After finishing her address, and a short pause, she rose from the sofa, turned, and kneeled before it, and made a short prayer to God in my behalf. A short time after she had finished, the woman from Philadelphia made also a formal brief address; but in general terms, and without reference to the slaves.

My wife and my brother, with his family, were present. We heard them with respectful attention, and when they rose to withdraw, I thanked them for their exhortations and their prayers, observing that in the public trust with which I am charged I had great need of the prayers of all worthy persons and as to what Elizabeth had said concerning the condition of the poor colored people in this country, I should lay it seriously to heart, and should act with a view to promote the glory of God and the best interests of this great people. They then took leave.

October 30, 1826—This is my father's birthday, and the sonnet here enclosed is the meditation of my morning's walk. I record it thus that it may be legible only to myself, or to a reader who will take the trouble to pick it out of the short-hand. If it were better poetry I would have written it at full length.

> Day of my father's birth, I hail thee yet.
> What though his body moulders in the grave,
> Yet shall not Death th' immortal soul enslave;
> The sun is not extinct his orb has set.
>
> And where on earth's wide ball shall man be met,
> While time shall run, but from thy spirit brave
> Shall learn to grasp the boon his Maker gave,
> And spurn the terror of a tyrant's threat?

Who but shall learn that freedom is the prize
Man still is bound to rescue or maintain;
That nature's God commands the slave to rise,
And on the oppressor's head to break his chain.
Roll, years of promise, rapidly roll round,
Till not a slave shall on this earth be found!

Another way in which the problem of slavery continued to cross Adams's presidential desk lay in the efforts to police the illegal slave trade through the new convention with Great Britain, as well as in the presidential power of pardon.[16] For political reasons, it may have been easier for the Virginian James Monroe, himself a slaveholder, to forgive the death sentence for slave rebels than it was for Adams.

December 8, 1826—Mr. Cheves, Commissioner for Slave Indemnities, comes to attend a meeting of the Commission; at which nothing will be done, as nothing has been done for many months. Colonel Tallmadge, one Senator, and eleven members of the House of Representatives came to pay morning visits. John Edwards is the man who obtained from Mr. Monroe the pardon of a man convicted of piracy, but of whose guilt there was great doubt. He now came to implore of me the pardon of a slave convicted of having, with others, mutinied on board of a ship, murdered the master and mate, and thrown them overboard. This man is sentenced to be executed this day week at New York, and Edwards solicits his pardon. I heard what he had to say, and told him I should consider it, and act as I should think my duty required. He considered the crime in this case as the mere natural impulse of the slave to recover his freedom.

December 11, 1826—The members of Congress were only morning visitors, excepting Mr. [Gulian] Verplanck, who brought a letter from several respectable persons in the city of New York, some of them clergymen, addressed to [Churchill C.] Cambreleng, Verplanck, and Jeromus Johnson, the three city members [of Congress], requesting

16. See also Diary, January 31, February 2, 6, July 23, 1828; February 27, 1829.

them to solicit of me a reprieve for a month of the colored man named Hill, sentenced to death for throwing overboard the captain and mate of a vessel in which they were bound from Baltimore to Charleston. This is the same case in which John Edwards applied to me for a pardon. The only reason assigned in the letter for asking the reprieve was the allegation that Judge Thompson had said the man had been convicted upon the testimony of a single witness.

I said to Mr. Verplanck that it was very painful to me to refuse an application for a reprieve for a man under sentence of death. But this was only a mode of preparing for a petition to pardon. I had made up my mind in this case not to grant a pardon. It was, in all its particulars, one of the most atrocious murders ever perpetrated. I could grant a pardon upon no other principle than that of formally determining that I would in no case whatever permit a capital execution during my Administration. This I did not feel myself justified in doing; but if I should grant a pardon or a reprieve in this case, my imagination could not form an idea of any other in which I could consistently refuse it. But, averse as I was to granting a reprieve, if he, with Mr. Cambreleng and Mr. Johnson, his colleagues, would write me a letter requesting it, I would, in deference to them, do that which I could not yield to the petitioners of the letter, who I had no doubt were respectable persons, but whom I did not know.

He left me, saying that he did not think they would write me the letter. The man is to be executed next Friday.

Later in 1827, the fate of House Speaker John W. Taylor spurred the president to vent about the effects of the Missouri debates and about Southern planters' hypocrisy in seizing upon a sex scandal to depose him.

December 4, 1827—General Van Rensselaer spoke of the failure of Taylor's election as Speaker, and said that he had made himself odious to all parties in New York by his selfishness.[17] The General himself is prejudiced against him. I have seen in the political conduct and

17. Stephen Van Rensselaer, member of the House of Representatives from New York and the owner of vast tracts in New York State.

character of Taylor no peculiar marks of selfishness, and he certainly has been one of the most popular men in the State of New York a State, however, the most fickle in the dispensation of its popular suffrages of any one in the Union. But Taylor's manners are not attractive, and are sometimes repulsive. The members from the South will never forgive the part that he took in the Missouri question, and they have recently assailed his private life with charges of dissolute conduct here, which have deeply affected his reputation. It is a remarkable circumstance that these charges proceed from men of the most abandoned immorality themselves men who, having neither reputation to lose nor principle to restrain them, are invulnerable to the poisoned shafts which they hurl against others. On a slender foundation of truth they raised a fabric of falsehood against Taylor, and widely circulated reports affecting his personal courage, as well as his chastity. The difficulty of his situation was, that the falsehood could not be refuted without bringing the truth to more conspicuous light, and there was of truth enough to sully his fair fame. I deeply lament it; for Taylor has been one of the few men in whom I have hoped to find a friend of whom I could be proud, as well as a virtuous politician.

Adams displayed a desire to free individual slaves when he could while still following protocols to the letter, as in the case of the "prince" Abdul Rahman. This did not prevent the Jacksonians from using the case against Adams in the 1828 election.[18]

July 10, 1827—Mr. Brent came for papers relating to an African, who appears to be a subject of the Emperor of Morocco, but is a slave in Georgia. He procured a letter to be written for him to the Emperor of Morocco, by whom it was communicated to Mr. Mullowny, the Consul of the United States at Tangier. He has sent a translation of it here, with an earnest recommendation that the Government of the United States should purchase the man and send him home as a complimentary

18. Terry Alford, *Prince among Slaves: The True Story of an African Prince Sold into Slavery in the American South*, rev. ed. (New York: Oxford University Press, 2007), 118–20, 128–29, 146–48.

donation to the Emperor. I requested Mr. Brent to write to Georgia and ascertain the price for which he could be purchased, and, if practicable, to carry into effect the wish of Mr. Mullowny.

Slave trade prize cases sometimes ran afoul of Southern officials, and had the potential to become test cases not only of jurisdiction but also of the administration's commitment to the protection of slave property in various forms. Later in 1828 the administration proposed an act of Congress that would require illegally imported and shipwrecked slaves to be taken to Liberia, as advocates of African recolonization advocated.[19]

January 31, 1828—Mr. Clay brought a note from the British Minister, Mr. Vaughan, with several enclosures, relating to the capture of a Spanish slave-trading vessel, named the Guerrero, by a British armed schooner from the Bahamas, called the Nimble, Captain Holland. The captor and prize-vessel both grounded on the Florida Reef, within our jurisdiction. The captor was got off; the prize was wrecked, some of the slaves retaken by the prize-crews and carried off to Cuba, a hundred and twenty-one sent by Captain Holland to Key West and there seized by the Collector, Mr. Pinckney, who also demanded of Captain Holland payment of duties upon the cargo saved from the wreck of the prize. Captain Holland refused payment of the duties; demanded the delivery of the slaves to him, which was denied; and he complains of the Collector. Copies of their correspondence have also been transmitted by the Collector to the Secretary of the Treasury, with a request for instructions. I desired a Cabinet meeting on the subject, Saturday at one.

February 2, 1828—There was a Cabinet meeting at one o'clock, attended by the heads of the Departments of State, Treasury, War, and Navy. The Attorney-General was absent. The seizure of the prize-slaves by the Collector at Key West, and the note of the British Minister, Vaughan, were discussed, and the case has become yet more complicated by claims for salvage, this day received by Mr. Clay, from citizens of the United States, for having saved the British schooner herself when she had struck upon the reef, and the cargo of her prize, which

19. See Diary, April 11, 16, 1828.

was wrecked. In the correspondence forwarded with the claim, Captain Holland admits that salvage was due; but he went away without allowing anything. The whole transaction presents five or six different questions, involving 1, the fact of capture; 2, the right of capture, not by the law of nations, but by virtue of a treaty between Spain and Great Britain; 3, the laws against the slave-trade, of Spain, Great Britain, and the United States; 4, the territorial jurisdiction of the United States; 5, the revenue laws of the United States; 6, the Act of Congress of 3d March, 1825, concerning wrecks on the coast of Florida; 7, the right of salvage according to the laws of nations; 8, the privileges and exemptions of the public ships of one nation within the territorial jurisdiction of another; and, very probably, 9, a claim of protection and indemnity of the Spanish owners of the prize-ship stranded within the jurisdiction of the United States. Some of these questions are exclusively of judicial cognizance, others altogether Executive; but, even of those triable at law, some appear to be beyond the jurisdiction of our tribunals, and others of their cognizance alone. We had much conversation upon all these points, without coming to any definite result. Finally, Mr. Southard took the papers, with promise to put them into the hands of the Attorney-General to-morrow, and we are to have another meeting on Monday.

February 6, 1828—The other, and proper object of the present meeting, was the answer to be given to Mr. Vaughan's note, upon the complaint of Lieutenant Holland, for the seizure of the Africans by the Collector at Key West; the instructions to be given to the Collector; the course to be pursued with regard to the claim for the salvage, and the probable contingency that a Spanish claimant may hereafter appear of the wrecked slave-trader.

I never knew a transaction entangled with so many controvertible questions. After long discussion, which terminated more in passing from one difficulty to another than in settling any one of them, I concluded[:] I. That the answer to Mr. Vaughan should explicitly deny all right of complaint by Lieutenant Holland for the seizure of the negroes, and rather waive the claim of the Collector to payment of duties on the goods; but the claim to salvage to be explicitly stated to him. An offer of time to be made within which Lieutenant Holland may bring the question of his right to the negroes before the competent judicial tribunal within the United States, but with information that the men, being emancipated by our laws, must within a reasonable time be sent to the Colony of Liberia, in Africa. Corresponding instructions are to be given to the Collector at Key West, and Mr. Southard is to be making all necessary preparations to provide, without unnecessary delay, for the transportation of these people from Key West to the Colony.

The Adamses rented slaves during their years in Washington, DC, and appear to have held at least one, Holzey, the property of Louisa Catherine's nephew, at the White House.[20]

February 23, 1828—Holzey, the black boy belonging to Johnson Hellen and who has been several years with us, died about five o'clock this afternoon. He has been sinking several months in a consumption.

February 24, 1828—My nephew's black boy was buried.

> Pallida mors sequo pulsat pede pauperum tabernas
> Regumque turres.
> Viiae summa brevis spem nos vetat inchoare longam.[21]

As the 1828 campaign heated up, some of Adams's supporters tried to find direct and indirect ways to make the point that Jackson was a slaveholder and sometime slave trader who had their interests at heart. They also dug up stories about Jackson's alleged African heritage. Adams expressed interest (he had a very low opinion of Jackson by 1828) but kept his distance.

20. For rented slaves, Jack Shepard, *Cannibals of the Heart: A Personal Biography of Louisa Catherine and John Quincy Adams* (New York: McGraw-Hill, 1980), 337, 408, and Alison T. Mann, "Slavery Exacts an Impossible Price: John Quincy Adams and the Dorcas Allen Case, Washington, D.C." (PhD diss., University of New Hampshire, 2010), ch. 3, who finds that around 1820 the Adamses had a slave who belonged to one of their young Hellen nieces or nephews who lived with them. Mann also discovered that on the day after Holzey's funeral, the same day that John Quincy Adams II married Mary Catherine Hellen, she signed manumission papers for "her Negro woman, Rachel Clark."
21. Horace, Odes I.4: "Pale death kicks with impartial foot at the hovels of the poor and the towers of kings." *Horace, The Complete Odes and Epodes*, trans. David West (Oxford: Oxford University Press, 1997), 29.

March 20, 1828—Governor Barbour brought also with him an original letter dated October, 1812, from General Jackson to George
W. Campbell, then a Senator from Tennessee, demanding the removal
of Silas Dinsmoor, then an Indian Agent, because he had stopped a
negro-trader who was passing through the Indian country, he not having
a passport. Jackson was so highly incensed at this that he wrote to G. W.
Campbell, requiring him to call upon the Secretary of War and give him
warning that if Dinsmoor should not be immediately removed the people of West Tennessee would burn him up in his Agency. This letter, and
several others relating to the same subject, have lately been found at the
War Department, in the searches for the correspondence concerning the
execution of the Tennessee militia-men at Mobile. Another motive, too,
has spurred the search for some of his original letters. In the Legislature
of Louisiana, last spring, some of his partisans got up a resolution inviting him to attend in person the anniversary celebration of the 8th of
January at New Orleans. He caught eagerly at this bait, and went with
a numerous train of attendants from Nashville to New Orleans, in the
dead of winter, to exhibit himself in pompous pageantry. His reception
was equivocal, with a laborious effort of magnificence, and mortifying
indications of ill will and disgust among the people. Deputations were
sent from various other States, from meetings of his devotees, to meet
him at the celebration, and five or six addresses of fulsome adulation
were delivered to him, to which he returned answers of cold and high-
wrought rhetorician eloquence. These answers were all written by Harry
Lee, who has become an inmate in his family and attended him to New
Orleans. As they were in an ambitious and court-dress style, some of his
impudent jackals fell into ecstasies in the newspapers at his eloquence
and fine literary composition, and they were boldly claiming for him
the reputation of an elegant writer. But the General, in one of his raving
fits, had sent one of his Nashville whitewashing committee's pamphlets
on his matrimonial adventures to Peter Force, editor of the National
Journal, and had written with his own hand, though without signing his
name, on the title-page, about four lines, insulting to Force and grossly
insolent to the Administration. Coarse, vulgar, and false in its invective,
it was couched in language worthy of ancient Pistol, and set all grammar
and spelling alike at defiance. When the panegyrics upon the composition of the answers to the New Orleans addresses began to thicken, and

the peal of parasitical applause to swell, Force published literatim the manuscript note sent him, with the Nashville Committee Report, and in a very short commentary marked the contrast between the wording of the note and the tawdry elegance of the answers to the addresses. On the day of Force's publication, White, the Senator, and Polk, a member of the House from Tennessee, called at his office and asked to see the pamphlet with the note. It was shown them, and to the enquiry whether they recognized the handwriting of the note they answered with equivocation and evasion. The liars of the newspapers were more bold: they denied that the manuscript note was written by Jackson, and treated as infamous calumny the assertion that it was. This has stimulated to the discovery of more of Jackson's autograph letters, and among the rest is this one to G. W. Campbell. It is still more ferocious than barbarous in style and composition. It has got wind among the friends of the Administration, and some of them are struggling to get it into light. It is evidently from the same hand as the note on the pamphlet sent to Force.

July 14, 1828—Dr. Watkins shewed me a Letter from C. Hammond, with one enclosed from him to Mr. Gaston of North Carolina giving a narrative attested by a man whom he represents to be of a fair and unimpeachable character and asserting of his own knowledge that Andrew Jackson, is the illegitimate son of a Campwoman who came from England with a Corps of troops in 1759 or 1760. That her name was Fanny Jenkins, and that his father was a semi mulatto named Jack, which was the origin of his name Jackson—That in September 1767 he was bound out by the magistrates of the County; and the next Stage of this history finds him reading Law and the next a judge in Tennessee. I told Watkins that this story however attested was fabulous on the face of it—but that if proved, it would do the General more good than harm.

African Americans were not shy about visiting Adams in the White House; it seems that the old stories that Abraham Lincoln or Theodore Roosevelt were the first presidents to formally receive blacks in the White House are a mere Republican Party legend. The Reverend Richard Allen, a longtime leader of the Philadelphia black community, came to see the president with his grandson, also a clergyman.

April 28, 1828—The Revd. Richard Allen is a black man, and a preacher from Philadelphia. He came with two persons of his own colour, one named Nathaniel Adams and the other Trout, belonging to Georgetown.

The redeemed African prince Abdul Rahman also stopped in to the White House, on his way back to Africa.

May 15, 1828—Abdel Rahman is a Moor, otherwise called Prince or Ibrahim, who has been forty years a slave in this country. He wrote, two or three years since, a letter to the Emperor of Morocco, in Arabic, in consequence of which the Emperor expressed to our Consul a wish that this man might be emancipated and sent home. His owner, residing at Natchez, Mississippi, offered to emancipate him on condition that he should be sent home by the Government of the United States; which we accordingly determined to do. He has now come on from Natchez, with his wife, and met Mr. Clay at Baltimore. He came in while Mr. Southard was with me, and we had some consultation how and when he should be dispatched to his home, which, he says, is Timbuctoo. He says he has left at Natchez five sons and eight grand-children, one of them only four days old when he came away all in slavery; and he wishes that they might all be emancipated, and be sent with or to him. He says he is sixty-six years of age, and assumes to have been the lawful prince of his country.

May 22, 1828—Abdul Rahaman the emancipated moor brought me a subscription book to raise a fund for purchasing the freedom of his five sons and his eight grand-children, to which I declined subscribing.

Adams noted the growth of nullification sentiment and opposition to his re-election in Southern states but saw nullification not as a sign of irreparable sectional antagonisms but more as part of a partisan cycle, identical to New England Federalist dissent between 1803 and 1815.

July 11, 1828—Mr. [Joseph] Gales . . . spoke of the recent movements in South Carolina, tending to civil war and a dissolution of the Union, and to a call in Kentucky upon John Rowan, one of the Senators from that State, to account for opinions openly avowed by him since his return from this city, that in the event of the re-election of the present President of the United States the next Congress would be the last that would ever assemble. These blusterings of the South Carolina politicians about the dissolution of the Union are used for the purpose of carrying the election by intimidation, or, if they fail in that, of laying the foundation for forcible resistance to the laws to break down or overawe the Administration after the event. It is the counterpart of the New England dissolution project, which began with the purchase of Louisiana and ended by the Hartford Convention.

5

The Making of an Antislavery Congressman (1829–36)

Adams continued to identify against sectionalism and with the Virginian-led National Republican establishment. But during the lead-up to the election of 1828, the alliance of some former New England Federalists with Virginians who supported Andrew Jackson led to a full-scale newspaper war over whom Jefferson would have approved—Adams or Jackson—and how the Federalists had behaved during the War of 1812. The sitting president had to endure the publication of a private Jefferson letter, one that criticized President Adams's first Annual Message of 1825 and then an earlier one that seemed to describe him, as a Massachusetts senator twenty years before, branding some of his own constituents as disloyal. After losing the election, President Adams spent even more of the first months of 1829 writing a book-length "Reply to the Appeal of the Massachusetts Federalists," which he did not publish. He began for the first time to lay the blame for his political difficulties on a proslavery political coalition.[1]

Having finished this treatise and placed it in the proverbial desk drawer, in the spring of 1829 the newly retired ex-president attempted to write a political

1. Samuel Flagg Bemis, *John Quincy Adams and the Foundations of American Foreign Policy* (New York, 1949), 575–76; Henry Adams, ed., *Documents Relating to New England Federalism, 1808-1815* (1877. Repr. Boston, 1905).

history of the United States. At the outset of this unfinished treatise Adams theorizes slavery as one of the six causes of the rise of parties. His definition of the other five causes makes it clear that the workings of slavery in politics had exacerbated other party-making engines, including differences of property, ethnicity, religion, and preexisting local structures of government. Sectional differences over slavery reinforced the original, material, and cultural bases of partisan differences but also complicated national politics by creating yet another cross-cutting basis for national parties: the politics of slavery itself, and the striking tendency for the resulting parties to champion or attack the federal government depending on who controlled it.

Perhaps feeling betrayed by the revelation that Jefferson had written critically about his presidency, Adams now depicted Jefferson as the source of current, Jacksonian woes. He had breathed life into New England sectionalism when he eviscerated the federal government through budget cuts while approving the Louisiana Purchase. He gave "immense preponderance" to the South, aggravated the "slave representation," and ultimately upended the federal Constitution, which had been formed to protect international and interstate commerce. In Adams's view, the third president's seeming concession to commerce as the "handmaid" of agriculture in his inaugural address "exhibited two great and equal interests in the community in the relative position of master and slave. It could have originated only on a tobacco plantation."[2]

Adams's narrative broke down, however, when he tried to come to terms with the National Republicans and what had happened to them. He did not have a useful story to tell about the Missouri Crisis itself, much less his election and the frustrations of his presidency. He put aside the manuscript. Yet these and other writing projects, along with the diary, helped him begin to rethink the relationship between his nationalism, his antislavery, and the current political scene.

---

2. John Quincy Adams, *Parties in the United States* (New York, 1941), 2–4, 6, 9, 25, 32, 39, 45. The Adams Papers project dates the manuscript at 1829. In the Diary he first mentions it on May 14, 1829; on December 29 mentions resuming it for the first time since the spring; and on May 26, 1830, calls it "yet unfinished" upon lending it out. The version published in 1941, as well as the manuscript of the "Reply to the Massachusetts Federalists" published by Henry Adams in 1877, appear to derive from copies made and bound in one volume, probably by Charles Francis Adams Jr. or by Henry Adams. Adams Family Papers, Reel 229, MHS; Adams Family Papers Collection Guide, http://www.masshist.org/collection-guides/view/fa0279.

A visit from Philadelphia Quaker philanthropist Elliott Cresson reveals that during 1829, Adams was far from willing to take a public antislavery, much less abolitionist, position. If anything, he was more hostile to colonization than he had been earlier in the 1820s.

April 27, 1829—Elliott Cresson called upon me again. He has been these three or four months in Virginia, and is now on his way returning to Philadelphia—He has asked me again to write something in his Album, which I promised to do. I had not had Time when he sent it to me before, in January. He is of the Society of Friends and spoke much of the Colonization Society: of the success of which he has a very favourable opinion—with which in this respect mine does not agree. He has a profound horror of the condition of the Slaves in the Southern States—There is I believe in this respect some misapprehension and much prejudice—There are no doubt cases of extreme oppression and cruelty and the impunity for them is complete; but I believe them to be very rare and that the general treatment of slaves is mild and moderate—Elliott spoke of some things relating to the present state of public affairs, with great severity, and especially of some scandals in great circulation.

Adams remained in Washington after his presidency ended and continued to receive many visitors, including politicians, lobbyists, and claim seekers he disdained for changing their "opinions to the doctrines of the times." The course of the Jackson administration alarmed Adams, not least in the realm of foreign policy. He told one visitor that "our present administration would take [Mexico] by War; and if so I believed the result of it would be to break up our Union." Other visitors told him about the sectional brinksmanship of the Webster–Hayne debate and of encounters "with some persons from South Carolina who were very inquisitive about the consequences of a state's seceding from the Union."[3] Older and retired acquaintances sometimes put him more at ease, as did Oliver Wolcott, the former governor of Connecticut and a leading Federalist.

3. Diary, November 16, 1829, and January 20, 21, 1830.

June 1, 1830—I received several visitors; Oliver Wolcott, a man whose condition somewhat resembles my own. Having survived the age of active life, he has no fixed abode, but resides chiefly with his children. He is nearly or quite fourscore years of age, and until about three years past was Governor of Connecticut. They then quietly dropped him, and elected Gideon Tomlinson in his place. Mr. Wolcott appears to retain possession of his faculties, and was much disposed to conversation upon the prevailing politics of the time. But we were very soon interrupted—against my inclination, for I should have been glad to listen long to Mr. Wolcott. He views the prospects of the Union with great sagacity, and with hopes more sanguine than mine. He thinks the continuance of the Union will depend upon the heavy population of Pennsylvania, and that its gravitation will preserve the Union. He holds the South Carolina turbulence rather too much in contempt. The domineering spirit naturally springs from the institution of slavery; and when, as in South Carolina, the slaves are more numerous than their masters, the domineering spirit is wrought up to its highest pitch of intenseness. The South Carolinians are attempting to govern the Union as they govern their slaves; and there are too many indications that, abetted as they are by all the slave-driving interest of the Union, the free portion of the population will cower before them and truckle to their insolence. This is my apprehension. Mr. Wolcott considers their bullying only according to its own character, and supposes it will be harmless, because it is impotent.

Soon after, when Jackson's internal improvement politics became clearer, Adams was more willing to be categorical about the state of national politics and the role of slavery in it. Jackson's reliance on executive privilege, and use of the pocket veto, signaled a constitutional crisis in the making.

June 6, 1830—The first session of the Twenty-First Congress was closed last Monday. Of the four bills of internal improvement which passed both Houses of Congress on Saturday, the President approved only one, and with that he sent a message announcing that he signed it with the understanding that it should receive a particular construction. As it was an appropriation for a road, the construction of the laws will depend entirely upon himself; but the explanatory message qualifying the signature of the President to an Act of Congress is unexampled in this country, and contrary to the spirit of the Constitution—a usurpation of the judiciary power, and susceptible of great abuse as a precedent. The appropriation for the road from Washington to Frederick he returned to the Senate with his objections, and the subsequent vote upon it there was twenty-two for and sixteen against it. His negative thus controls decided majorities in both Houses of Congress. He defeated the appropriation for the continuation of the Cumberland Road, and the bill authorizing the erection of several new light-houses and directing many new surveys, in a different manner. When the joint committee of the two Houses went to inform him that they were ready to adjourn, and to enquire if he had any further communication to make to them, he said he had nothing further, except that he retained those two bills for further consideration. The provision of the Constitution is that a bill presented to him shall become a law without his signature, if not returned by him within ten days, Sundays excepted—unless the Congress by their adjournment *prevent* its return. His remark to the committee, doubtless, was to give warning that Congress by their adjournment would prevent his returning those bills. These are remarkable events, as bringing into operation constitutional principles. The Presidential veto has hitherto been exercised with great reserve. Not more than four or five Acts of Congress have been thus arrested by six Presidents, and in forty years. He has rejected four in three days. The overseer ascendency is complete.

Conversations with his longtime protégé Alexander Hill Everett (who had been his secretary in Russia and later minister to Spain) and his old friend Judge John B. Davis about whether friendly congressmen should proceed to nominate Henry Clay for the presidency in 1832 encouraged Adams to place recent developments in geopolitical perspective. His tarnished reputation, he seemed certain, made it impossible for him to play a constructive role in national politics.

June 22, 1830—The whole strength of the present Administration rests upon [President Jackson's] personal popularity, founded upon his

military services. He has surrendered the Indians to the States within
the bounds of which they are located. This will strengthen and confirm his popularity in those States, especially as he has burdened the
Union with the expense of removing and indemnifying the Indians. He
has taken practical ground against internal improvements and domestic industry, which will strengthen him in all the Southern States. He
has, as might have been expected, thrown his whole weight into the
slave-holding scale; and that interest is so compact, so cemented, and
so fervent in action, that there is every prospect it will overpower the
discordant and loosely-patched policy of the free. The cause of internal
improvement will sink, and that of domestic industry will fall with
or after it. There is at present a great probability that this system will
be supported by a majority of the people. If the Presidential election
should be connected with this question, and turn upon it, Mr. Clay will
be the candidate of internal improvement and of the manufactures. But
it will be a minority. The Anti-Masonic spirit will operate against him
in New York, and perhaps elsewhere.

June 25, 1830—I suppose that the sacrifice of the Indians and of the
interest of internal improvement and domestic industry will strengthen,
rather than weaken, the popularity of the present Administration.
I have cherished the principle and the system of internal improvement, under a conviction that it was for this nation the only path to
increasing comforts and well-being, to honor, to glory, and finally to
the general improvement of the condition of mankind. This system
has had its fluctuations from the time of the establishment of the present Constitution of the United States. During the Administration of
Mr. Monroe it was constantly acquiring strength in Congress and in
the public opinion. It was then favored by [John C.] Calhoun and
[William C.] Lowndes, both of whom had hopes of rising upon it, and
with them the State of South Carolina was devoted to it. The combination in Congress became by their means so strong that it overpowered
the resistance of Mr. Monroe and produced the Act of Congress of
April, 1824. The slave-holders of the South have since discovered that it
will operate against their interests. Calhoun has turned his back upon
it, and Jackson, who to promote his election and obtain Western votes
truckled to it for a time, has now taken his decided stand against it. My
devotion to it has sharpened all the fangs of envy and malice against it,

and multitudes oppose it only because its success would contribute to my reputation. The cause will no doubt survive me, and, if the Union is destined to continue, will no doubt ultimately triumph. At present it is desperate.

The July revolutions in Europe and reform battles in England spurred Adams to record some of his thoughts on how European events might reverberate in the United States.

January 10, 1831—I answered Mr. Monroe's letter, and made some observations upon the present state of Europe. Perhaps the most important point of view in which we should consider it is the influence which it will exercise over this country. Its first effect will be, or rather has been, to strengthen the principle of democracy over all Europe and America, and it will proportionably diminish the securities of property. In England, the reform in Parliament cannot be effected without intrenching upon very extensive rights of property. The reduction of taxes will necessarily require at least a partial spunging of the national debt. It is scarcely possible to foresee the extent to which this will stagger the rights of property and shatter the confidence of credit. The abolition of tithes must overthrow the Established Church, and dissolve the connection between Church and State, and shake the pillars of the Christian religion. That it will only shake its pillars, I hope and believe. If the gates of hell shall not prevail against it, neither will the revolutions of empires nor the convulsions of the people. In France, the alliance between political reform and religious infidelity is closer than in England. It is everywhere formidable. The fall of the Church in England will exclude the Bishops from the House of Peers, and the hereditary rights of the temporal peerage will not much longer withstand the consuming blaze of public opinion. An hereditary crown has no support in popular sentiment, and none in reason, but as forming part of one system with an hereditary peerage. All are equally obnoxious to democracy. The abolition of slavery will pass like a pestilence over all the British Colonies in the West Indies; it may prove an earthquake upon this continent. The present English Ministry are nearly as much pledged to it as to the reform in Parliament. They will flinch from it, and forfeit their pledge, but they will probably not last long; a more democratic Ministry will succeed, and reform will not, cannot, stop short till it makes an effective attempt for the abolition of slavery. This is, perhaps, the only part of the doctrine of European democracy which will find no favor here. It may aggravate the condition of the slaves in our Southern States; but the result of the Missouri question, and the attitude of parties, have silenced all the declaimers for the abolition of slavery in the Union. This state of things, however, is not to continue forever. It is possible that the danger of the abolition doctrines, when brought home to the Southern States, may teach them the value of the Union—the only thing that can maintain their system of slavery.

However this may be, I apprehend that the inevitable predominance of democracy, which is impending over Europe, will not end without producing bitter fruits in our own country.

Thomas Jefferson's memoir and selected writings, edited by his grandson, appeared in early 1831. The autobiography included the first publication of Jefferson's draft of the Declaration of Independence, including the passage excised by Congress condemning the slave trade. Adams still admired the Declaration and many aspects of Jefferson's politics, but he objected strongly to the self-congratulatory tone of Jefferson's writings and to his pretensions to having been a great reformer.

January 17, 1831—There is in the memoir of Mr. Jefferson's life a copy of the Declaration of Independence as finally adopted by Congress, with marginal notes, italics in brackets, and of the final declaratory paragraph a concurrent column, showing the paper as reported by the committee. ... The parts struck out by Congress sound to my ear like effusions of frenzy—the paragraph against slavery indiscreet beyond measure, and not a little unjust. ... There is a very remarkable passage in pages 39 and 40 of the memoir, showing that although Jefferson was not inclined in his last days to avow his perseverance in his opinions upon negro slavery, he was willing to let them loose after his death—the motive for which appears to be to secure to himself posthumous fame as a prophet.

January 18, 1831—I answered a letter received last August from R. H. Lee, and had time left to read only a few pages of the correspondence of Jefferson. ... In the revision of the old system of laws [in Virginia after the Revolution], Mr. Jefferson took an active and leading part. He presented bills for the establishment of courts of justice; for converting tenancies in tail into fee-simple; for prohibiting the importation of negro slaves; for abolishing the Establishment of the Episcopal Church; and for asserting the natural right of expatriation, and prescribing the mode of exercising it. He also proposed and carried through a bill for a general revision of the whole code of laws by which the Colony had been governed, and he was appointed with four others to execute the work. One of the committee soon resigned, and one died. The three others divided the work between them: Jefferson had the common law and statutes till 4 James I, when the Virginia Legislature was first established; Wythe, the British statutes from that time to *the present day* (1776); and Pendleton, the Virginia laws. Now, if Mr. Jefferson's pretension that the British Parliament had *never* possessed the right of enacting laws for Virginia had been well founded, what would Mr. Wythe have had to do? Every British statute affecting Virginia, from 1607 to 1776, was a flagrant usurpation, which by the Declaration of Independence alone would have been swept away. This thought, however, never occurred to the committee. The first question they settled was, not to abolish the whole existing system of laws and prepare a new and complete institute, but to preserve the general system, and only modify it to the present order of things. Pendleton was for the former, and Lee; Jefferson, with Mason and Wythe, for the latter. Mr. Jefferson and Pendleton on this occasion both changed sides—Pendleton assuming the character of the bold innovator, and Jefferson that of the special pleader and defender of ancient things. He gives the reasons of his own opinion, but not those of Mr. Pendleton. But there were far other reasons than those assigned by Mr. Jefferson for not reconstructing the edifice of legislation in Virginia de novo, which he felt and understood, though he has had the prudence not to disclose them. 1. Mr. Jefferson was not a legislator—his genius was *destructive*, but not *constructive*: he could demolish, deface, and cast down; he could not build up or preserve. 2. The principle of setting aside the whole code of their legislation would of itself have emancipated all their slaves. In renovating their code, they must have restored slavery after having abolished it; they must have assumed to themselves all the odium of establishing it as a positive institution, directly in the face of all the principles they had proclaimed; they must have abandoned their laws privileging lands from responsibility for debts; and they must have enlarged their elective franchise, confined as it was almost exclusively to freeholders. For all this Mr. Jefferson was not prepared. It was easier to abolish the law of primogeniture, the Establishment of the Episcopal Church, capital punishment, except for treason and murder, and the professorships of divinity and the Oriental languages in William and Mary College. All this was accordingly done. But the lands of the planters retained their exemption from liability for the debts of their owners; the freeholders retained their exclusive right of voting at elections; and the bill on the subject of slaves was a mere digest of the existing laws respecting them, without any intimation of a plan for a future and general emancipation. This was, however, agreed upon by the committee to be proposed, by way of amendment, in the passage of the bill; but it was found that the public mind would not bear the proposition. The amendment was never offered, and Mr. Jefferson contents himself with a posthumous prophecy that it must soon come, or that worse will follow.

When Elliott Cresson visited again, Adams reiterated his stand against the ACS on pragmatic grounds, but also for the first time recorded his agreement with another set of arguments against the ACS: that the idea of removing free African Americans insulted them, implied that they were not citizens, and if anything played into the hands of slaveholders. These criticisms had gained increasing prominence between 1829 and 1831 as leading black and white abolitionists denounced colonization.

January 20, 1831—Visitors engrossed the morning. Elliott Cresson is here as a delegate from the Pennsylvania Colonization Society. The general Society have last evening had their annual meeting, which I received from the managers a written invitation to attend. Cresson, who is of the Society of Friends, is a member and ardent supporter of the Colonization Society—which I never have been, believing their principal objects impracticable, and entertaining great doubts of the usefulness of their measures which have been successful. I therefore did not attend their meeting, and had in like manner abstained from attending that of the last year. I told Cresson candidly what had been and were my impressions on the subject. I said that I did not believe it would diminish the number of slaves in the United States by a single individual; and that so far as it did effect the emigration of people of color, it was rather a public injury than a public benefit. This Society, however, is yearly increasing in numbers and power; and my opinions found no sympathy in those of Mr. Cresson.

Two weeks later, Cresson returned, having been angrily rebuffed by President Jackson, who saw federal patronage of the ACS's project in Liberia as a hold-over from the Adams administration—a contention Adams denied. Much of this was partisan politics, and a sign of the proslavery cast of Jackson's administration: Jackson himself had attended the inaugural meeting of the ACS held after hours in the Capitol building in 1819.

February 2, 1831—Elliott Cresson paid me a morning visit; just from President Jackson, who had been treating him roughly. Elliott is a member and delegate of the Colonization Society, who wish to have a public vessel stationed to cruise on the coast of Liberia, to protect our commerce with that flourishing settlement, and look out for slavers. But the Colonization Society is out of favor with Jackson, as it always has been with me. Cresson says that his language was almost abusive; that he charged me with having squandered the public money upon this establishment without law; that he said there were not three hundred colonists at the place; that almost all who went out there died of pestilence, and that every word that Mr. [Amos] Kendall had said was true. Cresson was in amazement at his ignorance.

The public expenditures with which Jackson reproached me were made under a construction of an Act of Congress passed during Mr. Monroe's Administration, sanctioned by him, by the Secretary of the Navy, Smith Thompson, and by W. H. Crawford, Secretary of the Treasury, a member and Vice-President of the Colonization Society. The language of the Act was ambiguous, and the construction given to it was against my opinion. At the ensuing session of Congress, however, Mr. Monroe gave notice to that body, by a message, of his construction of the Act, that they might control it if they thought proper.

They never did control it; and the expenditures under it continued during my Administration, because I did not feel myself at liberty to reverse the decision of Mr. Monroe and two or three eminent lawyers, his Secretaries, tacitly supported by Congress itself.

Adams's sense of Jefferson as a tragic and troubling figure deepened when he read his correspondence from the early and mid-1780s. Jefferson's Notes on the State of Virginia *had greatly impressed the younger Adams when he had read it in 1787.*

January 27, 1831—In his correspondence at the time when he first printed the book, he appears to have been under some alarm lest the freedom and severity of his remarks upon slavery, and upon the Constitution of Virginia then existing, would occasion irritation, and retard the reformation which he wished to promote. Mr. Jefferson's love of liberty was sincere and ardent—not confined to himself, like that of most of his fellow-slaveholders. He was above that execrable sophistry of the South Carolinian nullifiers, which would make of slavery the cornerstone to the temple of liberty. He saw the gross inconsistency between the principles of the Declaration of Independence and the fact of negro slavery, and he could not, or would not, prostitute the faculties of his mind to the vindication of that slavery which from his soul he abhorred. Mr. Jefferson had not the spirit of martyrdom. He would have introduced a flaming denunciation of slavery into the Declaration of Independence, but the discretion of his colleagues struck it out. He did insert a most eloquent and impassioned argument against it in his Notes upon Virginia; but on that very account the book was published almost against his will. He projected a plan of general emancipation in his revision of the Virginian laws, but finally presented a plan of leaving slavery precisely where it was. And in his memoirs he leaves a posthumous warning to the planters, that they must at no distant day emancipate their slaves, or that worse will follow; but he withheld the publication of his prophecy till he should himself be in the grave.

Adams devoted a widely read Fourth of July oration in Boston in 1831 to demolition of "the South Carolina doctrine of nullification." The occasion allowed him to go public with his reading of political history without having to attack the administration, or slavery, head on. Union, he insisted, preceded American independence; the states were not preexisting entities, as "the colonies are not named" in the Declaration. The "hallucination of State sovereignty" was based on the same error of undivided sovereignty that had misled the British parliamentarians into declaring their power to legislate for Americans "in all cases whatsoever." There was no such thing as complete sovereignty or power. American history proved it: the powers of the national government had been expanded by either party when in power. "Our collisions of principle," then, "have been little, very little more than conflicts for place." But worst of all, nullification "strips us of that peculiar and unimitated characteristic of all our legislation—free debate. It makes the bayonet the arbiter of law," and could only lead to civil war.[4]

At the same time, Adams was quite aware that antislavery arguments were being taken to lengths he considered extreme: to immediate abolition even at the price of disunion. Antislavery movements had begun to transform into more activist and more popular organizations, ones that simultaneously sought ideological purity and convergences with other causes. Abolitionists eyed him as a possible supporter. But he continued to keep his distance. When he met Benjamin Lundy, a colonizationist turned abolitionist with whom he would later work closely, Adams expressed surprise at how "freely" he expressed his antislavery. That spring he also took note of how the charismatic speaker and reformer Frances Wright's feminism, atheism, and links to the working-men's movement all pivoted on a professed hatred of slavery.

February 13, 1831—On returning home, I found the young Quaker to whom Gales and Seaton[5] had given a letter of introduction, Lindley, and another by the name of Benjamin Lundy, editor of a weekly paper called *The Genius of Universal Emancipation*. It was first published in Tennessee, afterwards in Baltimore, and now comes out in this city. Its object is to promote the abolition of slavery—of which Lundy freely expressed his confidence and hopes.

4. Diary, January 18, 27, June 29, 1831; Adams, *An Oration Addressed to the Citizens of the Town of Quincy, on the Fourth of July, 1831* (Boston, 1831), 6–7, 14, 23, 29, 36; Bemis, *John Quincy Adams and the Union*, 233.

5. Joseph Gales and William Seaton, editors of the Washington *National Intelligencer*.

June 26, 1831—Heard Mr. Whitney in the Morning from John 18:38, "Pilate saith unto him, what is truth." And in the afternoon, from Job 14:14, "If a man die shall he live again?" In both these discourses, Mr. Whitney gave some of his own peculiar opinions, and in that of the afternoon inveighed vehemently against Fanny Wright an English female Atheist who has been delivering Lectures in the principal cities of the United States, against slavery, marriage, and Christianity. She has every where gained numerous Proselytes, and there is a party scattered all over the Country who call themselves the working man's Party; but who are generally called by others Fanny Wright's Party—Fanny makes no pretension to believe in a future State; nor even in the existence of a God; but she has an inveterate aversion to Slavery of all kinds. To African Slavery—Matrimonial Slavery—Religious Slavery. She declaims against them all, and never wants an Auditory.

Adams was elected to the House of Representatives from his home district of Plymouth, which included Quincy, Massachusetts, in the fall of 1831. He had no plans to make slavery an issue in Congress. He even distanced himself from the first constituent petition he presented, for abolition in the District of Columbia—considering it his duty to present it but suggesting it merely be referred to a committee. He was aware that the arrival of an ex-president was unprecedented and much more worried about his own committee assignments and the impression he would make in his first speeches.

December 12, 1831—Attended the House of Representatives. The appointment of the standing committees was announced, and I am Chairman of the Committee of Manufactures—a station of high responsibility, and, perhaps, of labor more burdensome than any other in the House; far from the line of occupation in which all my life has been passed, and for which I feel myself not to be well qualified. I know not even enough of it to form an estimate of its difficulties. I only know that it is not the place suited to my acquirements and capacities, such as they are; yet, as little as I esteem the Speaker,[6] I have no fault to find with him for the appointment.

6. Speaker of the House Andrew Stevenson, Democrat of Virginia.

The petitions were called for by States, commencing with Maine and proceeding southward. I presented fifteen petitions, signed numerously by citizens of Pennsylvania, praying for the abolition of slavery and the slave-trade in the District of Columbia. I moved that they should be referred to the Committee on the District of Columbia.

The practice is for the member presenting the petition to move that the reading of it be dispensed with, and that it be referred to the appropriate, or to a select, committee; but I moved that one of the petitions presented by me should be read, they being all of the same tenor and very short. It was accordingly read. I made a very few remarks, chiefly to declare that I should not support that part of the petition which prayed for the abolition of slavery in the District of Columbia. It is so long since I was in the habit of speaking to a popular assembly, the assemblies in which I had ever spoken extemporaneously have been, comparatively speaking, so little popular, and I am so little qualified by nature for an extemporaneous orator, that I was at this time not a little agitated by the sound of my own voice. I was not more than five minutes upon my feet; but I was listened to with great attention, and, when I sat down, it seemed to myself as if I had performed an achievement.

So small and trivial are the things which often hang like burdens upon the soul. I am grateful that this one has been removed. After the petitions were gone through, the resolutions to be offered were called for, again by States; after which Mr. [James Moore] Wayne, of Georgia, moved that the House should resolve itself into a committee of the whole upon the state of the Union. The speaker requested General [John] Adair [of Kentucky] to take the chair. Mr. Wayne then offered a series of resolutions, distributing the President's message into paragraphs and referring each subject to a distinct committee. Most of them were adopted as proposed; but the one to be referred to the Committee of Ways and Means made no mention of the Bank of the United States.

Even though antislavery was clearly not his agenda in Congress, Adams could hardly avoid the issue, and it seems as if those concerned with slavery deliberately sought him out.

December 16, 1831—Major [William] Duval is a remnant of the Revolutionary Army of the Virginia Line—84 years of age as he informed me. He brought me an introductory Letter from Chief Justice [John] Marshall and is here to support before Congress a military claim on behalf of his old military associates—But his conversation with me was to bewail the existence of Slavery and the condition of the holders of Slaves in Virginia.

January 2, 1832—I had received this morning Letters from Nathaniel Curtis, my co-executor of Ward N. Boylston's Will, with an enclosure . . . from Isaac Candler enclosing an English pamphlet—a periodical called the Anti-Slavery Reporter. This Gentleman is scandalized at my remark on presenting the Anti-Slavery Petitions.[7]

January 10, 1832—Mr. [Evan] Lewis is a member of the Society of Friends, and taken much part for the last twenty years in the measures leading to the abolition of slavery. He came to have some conversation with me upon the subject of slavery in the District of Columbia. I asked him if he had seen the remarks that I made on presenting the petitions from Pennsylvania.

He said he had—but wished to know my sentiments upon slavery. I told him I thought they did not materially differ from his own; I abhorred slavery, did not suffer it in my family, and felt proud of belonging to the only State in the Union which at the very first census of population in 1790 had returned in the column of slaves—none; that in presenting the petition I had expressed the wish that the subject might not be discussed in the House, because I believed discussion would lead to ill will, to heart-burnings, to mutual hatred, where the first of wants was harmony; and without accomplishing anything else. I asked him what he should think of the inhabitants of the District of Columbia if they should petition the Legislature of Pennsylvania to enact a law to compel all the citizens of that State to bear arms in defence of their country. He said he should think they were meddling with what did not concern them. I said the people of the District of Columbia might say the same of citizens of Pennsylvanian petitioning for the abolition of slavery, not in that State itself, but in the District of Columbia. He said there were many persons of that opinion, and he

7. Isaac Candler was the author of *A Summary View of America* (London, 1824).

had been very desirous of distinctly knowing what my sentiments upon the subject were.

The petitioning process began to catch his imagination later in his first term—so much so that he described it as a fit subject for poetry. Adams was an occasional poet himself who at the time was writing an epic poem about a deeply flawed Irish liberator who bore more than a passing resemblance to Andrew Jackson. More than once he remarked in the Diary that if he could have chosen any vocation it would have been literature. This statement suggests a dawning realization of the possibility that his highest ambitions could be met in Congress after all.[8]

February 20, 1832—I rode to the Capitol. Being Monday, the States were successively called for presentation of petitions; a most tedious operation in the practice, though to a reflecting mind a very striking exemplification of the magnificent grandeur of this nation and of the sublime principles upon which our Government is founded. The forms and proceedings of the House, this calling over of States for petitions, the colossal emblem of the Union over the Speaker's chair, the historic Muse at the clock, the echoing pillars of the hall, the tripping Mercuries who bear the resolutions and amendments between the members and the chair, the calls of ayes and noes, with the different intonations of the answers from the different voices, the gobbling manner of the Clerk in reading over the names, the tone of the Speaker in announcing the vote, and the varied shades of pleasure and pain in the countenances of the members on hearing it, would form a fine subject for a descriptive poem.

The tariff and nullification controversies continued to spur predictions of the Union's dissolution.

February 22, 1832—Centennial birthday of Washington. The solemnities intended for this day at this place lost all their interest for me by the refusal of John A. Washington to permit the remains of George

8. John Quincy Adams, *Dermot MacMorrogh or the Conquest of Ireland: An Historical Tale of the Twelfth Century in Four Cantos* (Boston, 1832).

Washington to be transferred to be entombed under the Capitol—a refusal to which I believe he was not competent, and into the real operative motives to which I wish not to enquire. I did wish that this resolution might have been carried into execution, but this wish was connected with an imagination that this federative Union was to last for ages. I now disbelieve its duration for twenty years, and doubt its continuance for five. It is falling into the sere and yellow leaf. For this, among other reasons, I determined that my celebration of this day should only be by sharing in its devotions.

The first controversy around a petition presented by Adams revealingly turned on Indian removal. Georgia had imprisoned missionaries among the Cherokee, formerly federal employees, who had defied a new state law barring their presence. The issue had profound national political significance because Georgia (and the president) had ignored Chief Justice Marshall's recent ruling in favor of the Reverend Samuel Austin Worcester and the Cherokee Nation, Worcester v. Georgia, *during the same period when the president effectively opposed South Carolina's threats to nullify the federal tariff.*

March 5, 1832—At the House it was the day for calling petitions, and at the call of Massachusetts I presented the memorial from New York concerning the Cherokees and the missionaries imprisoned in Georgia. It was read at my request, and I moved that it should be printed and referred to a select committee.

This immediately gave rise to a debate, which consumed the day. [Jesse] Speight [of North Carolina] moved its reference to the Committee on Indian Affairs. [John] Bell, Chairman of that committee, made one of those speeches common in the House when a subject comes upon them unexpectedly—arguing against the reception of the memorial, but closing with a repetition of Speight's motion. The Georgia members were variously affected—[Augustin] Clayton raved, and said that before the decree of the Supreme Court should be carried into execution Georgia should be made a wilderness. [Wiley] Thompson, of Georgia, finally moved that the memorial be laid on the table. The question was taken by yeas and nays—ninety-one for, ninety-two against laying on the table.

The vote was first thought to be carried, for [Andrew] Stewart, of Pennsylvania, had voted in the affirmative by mistake. He corrected it before the decision was announced. Wayne then attempted to move a postponement of consideration for a fortnight. [William] Drayton [of South Carolina] actually moved a postponement. John Davis moved a reference to the committee of the whole on the state of the Union. Everett had proposed this to me, and said it was an understanding between the parties that the subject should be discussed in committee of the whole on the Union. This was personally satisfactory to me, but did not discharge my duty to the memorialists. Stewart moved the previous question, but withdrew it at my request to give me the opportunity to give my reasons for not assenting to Davis's proposition. [Samuel] Beardsley, of New York, followed with an argument that the memorial should be laid on the table. He said he thought I should have moved that myself.

[Churchill C.] Cambreleng [of New York] noticed that the memorial, though from New York, was not presented by any of the Representatives from that city.

I said I had reason to believe that it was from no disrespect to the members from New York that the memorial had been sent to me, but from a belief that it would be an unpleasing task to them. It was no pleasing one to me. I had wished to decline it, but, after examining the contents of the memorial, had deemed it my duty to present it. The House was now in possession of it, and would dispose of it as they thought best.

Stewart renewed his call for the previous question, which was seconded and taken. Wickliffe moved that the vote should be taken upon the simple question of commitment. I asked for the yeas and nays, and they were taken. The commitment was carried—ninety-six to ninety-three; and then it was referred to the committee of the whole on the state of the Union, without a division. This decision is precisely what I wished; though, having moved for a select committee, I did not feel at liberty to assent to it. In committee of the whole on the state of the Union I may leave it to the management of other hands, and may take any part or no part in the debate, as I may think proper. The three members from the city of New York voted to lay the memorial on the table. Cambreleng and White voted against the commitment;

Verplanck for it. I returned to Colonel Richard M. Johnson his note, and told him I had taken a copy of it; which he approved. I thanked him for the part he had taken in this affair, which I believe proceeded on his part from a good intention.

March 11, 1832—I read attentively after church the opinion of the Supreme Court of the United States, delivered by Chief-Justice Marshall, in the case of Worcester, the missionary, against the State of Georgia. It pronounces the law of Georgia under which Mr. [Samuel Austin] Worcester is imprisoned in the penitentiary unconstitutional, null and void. There is no doubt that the execution of this sentence will be resisted and defeated by the Government of Georgia. A case of collision between the judicial authority of the Union and the authority of the State is now brought to an issue. The immediate power is in the hand of the State. The Executive of the Union is leagued with the State authority, and the two Houses of Congress are about as equally as possible divided in the case. It is clear that the Constitution and law of the Union and its judicial authority will be prostrated before the despotic power of the State; and I would it were possible for me to anticipate the course to be taken, and the measure proper to be proposed, when the information shall come back! Convinced that I can effect nothing, my own course will be to withhold myself from all action concerning it.

Adams and his congressional committee worked out a compromise tariff, which passed the House to much acclaim. Yet the president's backtracking on the tariff in his annual message, taken with his stated intention to veto the recharter of the Bank of the United States, seemed of a piece with his support of Georgia. It was not at all clear to the congressman and ex-president that he could do anything that would not backfire politically and personally.

December 4, 1832—In the House of Representatives, the President's message was received and read. It recommends a total change in the policy of the Union with reference to the bank, manufactures, internal improvement, and the public lands. It goes to dissolve the Union into its original elements, and is in substance a complete surrender to the nullifiers of South Carolina.

December 5, 1832—The message of the President gives great dissatisfaction to all those with whom I converse, and will be received with rapture by his partisans. He has cast away all the neutrality which he had heretofore maintained upon the conflicting interests and opinions of the different sections of the country, and surrenders the whole Union to the nullifiers of the South and the land-robbers of the West. I confess this is neither more nor less than I expected, and no more than I predicted nearly two years since, in a letter, I think, to Peter B. Porter. This message already puts my temper and my discretion upon a trial equally severe. Dissimulation I cannot practice. Passion can do nothing but mischief. I walk between burning ploughshares, and have no support upon earth, with a fearful foreboding that every effort I could make for the good of my country would recoil in evil upon myself and my family.

Matters became still more complicated a few days later, when Jackson balanced his reversal on the tariff with a denunciation of South Carolina's nullification of the tariff, and later followed up with a call for federal troops to put down antifederal actions, known as the Force Bill. In a conversation with Congressmen James Findlay and Michael Hoffman, the latter a fellow member of the House Committee on Manufactures, Adams suggested that a larger issue lay behind the conundrums of tariffs and states' rights.

December 24, 1832—Mr. [Michael] Hoffman is a New Yorker, of Dutch descent, a lawyer, of the Democratic Republican party of the Albany Regency, and now a Van Buren man. They are *now* tenacious of State rights, and politically leagued with the anti-tariff policy of the South. But as Jackson men they must be anti-nullifiers; and to these two incoherent elements, subserviency to the slave-holding policy and the personal animosities of President Jackson against Vice-President Calhoun, may be traced the glaring inconsistencies of principle between the message of this year and the proclamation.

I told Hoffman that the real question now convulsing this Union was, whether a population spread over an immense territory, consisting of one great division all freemen, and another of masters and slaves, could exist permanently together as members of one community or not; that, to go a step further back, the question at issue was slavery.

He said he was of that opinion, and that if it should come directly to a point, nine-tenths, if not ninety-nine-hundredths, of his constituents would take side against slavery. He said, too, that if this question with South Carolina should come to a struggle of force, and the nullifiers should be overpowered, the whole population of the State would emigrate to Mexico; but Findlay asked what they would do with their slaves—slavery being abolished in Mexico, and all the South American States, except Brazil.

Adams and others presented petitions against slavery and the slave trade during the nullification crisis, but they were referred to committee, and not considered as important or as dangerous as measures touching on the tariff or states' rights.

January 21, 1833—Attended at the House—Monday; the weekly day for receiving Petitions and Memorials. I presented a Petition from Merchants at Plymouth for an appropriation to build a Custom house and Post Office in that Town. Referred to the Committee on Commerce. Among the petitions presented was one by Coulter of Pennsylvania from inhabitants of the District of Columbia, praying for the gradual abolition of Slavery in the District, and for the prohibition of the Slave-trade in it. Referred to the District Committee. [George] McDuffie presented a resolution of the Legislature of South Carolina, proposing that a Convention of the States be called to consider and determine questions of disputed power, which have arisen between the States and the general government.

In the House on February 4, 1833, Adams replied to an anti-tariff speech by Representative Augustin Smith Clayton of Georgia. Clayton called Southern slaves "our machinery," just as deserving of financial protection as Northern manufacturing's capital investments. "That machinery," Adams retorted, "sometimes exerts a self-moving power." He proceeded to cite the three-fifths clause, the fugitive slave clause, and the federal army that guaranteed protection against "domestic violence," all in accord with the Constitution, as protections for slavery that went far beyond anything Northern industry had. Adams himself wrote to his son a month later that "little did I imagine that my chiffon of a speech upon the Southern Machinery would have been the most popular thing I ever did or said."

He improved on his criticisms of the South and slavery in a minority report on the final tariff compromise, going so far as to portray the Southern landed aristocracy's "holding in oppressive servitude the real cultivators of the soil, and ruling, with a hand of iron, over all the other occupations and professions of men" as "directly leading to the most fatal of catastrophies—the dissolution of the Union by a complicated, civil and servile war." He did not sign this minority report, but its authorship could not have been a secret, given that he was one of two dissenters from the committee majority, and Adams went out of his way to make sure it appeared in newspapers and as a pamphlet.[9]

Although he did not yet reflect in the diary upon the implications, it was becoming increasingly more difficult, or less attractive, for Adams during these years to subordinate his growing sense of slavery's importance to his other agendas. On board a steamboat he found himself arguing with Duff Green, editor of the leading Washington newspaper and a supporter of Calhoun. He continued to keep his distance from both the colonizationists and the abolitionists.

April 12, 1833—I got into a discussion with Duff Green, upon the tariff, domestic manufactures and protection, slave labor, and consolidation, which attracted round us a circle of listeners, to my great annoyance. Another discussion arose between Mr. Messenger and another passenger, upon the project of Earl Grey's Ministry to emancipate the slaves in the British West Indies, from which discussion I with some difficulty kept myself aloof.

April 15, 1833—Mr. N[icholas] Biddle had persuaded Mr. [Abbott?] Lawrence and me to remain at Philadelphia over this day to dine with him. Mr. Thomas Hulme called upon me immediately after breakfast. He is an Englishman, born at Manchester, but has been many years settled here, and has amassed a fortune by manufacturing. He is much devoted to that interest, and he has a project for emancipating the slaves

9. Samuel Flagg Bemis, Adams's foremost biographer, calls Adams's response to Clayton in the House a striking departure: "No longer did the sound of his own voice frustrate him. He suddenly became a compelling speaker." Bemis, *John Quincy Adams and the Union* (New York: Knopf, 1956), 266, 270–72. Bemis calls the minority report, by contrast, "prolix" and "too much of an anticlimax to the nullification controversy," but more recently Fred Kaplan has praised it as "one of Adams' most brilliant achievements as a writer on political and cultural topics." Kaplan, *John Quincy Adams: American Visionary* (New York: Harper, 2014), 462–64.

of our Southern States and making compensation at the public expense to their owners, and for offering to the South an amicable separation of the States as an alternative. This is a subject upon which people here have brought themselves to reason very coolly.

May 24, 1833—My nephew John Quincy was here this Evening and a man brought me a periodical pamphlet called the abolitionist commenced by the Anti-Slavery Society—The first number of a monthly publication to which he solicited my subscription but I declined.

During the early 1830s, the rise of the proslavery argument was as striking an aspect of politics as the rise of abolitionism. The two trends fed each other. One of the most widely read entries in the debate over slavery was the response of Thomas R. Dew, a professor at the College of William and Mary, to the debates over emancipation in the Virginia legislature. Dew opposed all emancipation and colonization plans and relied heavily on both racial and practical arguments against them.[10]

October 13, 1833—. . . and in the evening waded through thirty pages of Professor Dew's review of the debate on the project for slave emancipation. It is a monument of the intellectual perversion produced by the existence of slavery in a free community. To the mind of Mr. Dew, slavery is the source of all virtue in the heart of the master. His argument against the practicability of abolishing slavery by means of colonization appears to me conclusive; nor do I believe that emancipation is the object of the Colonization Society, though it may be the day-dream of some of its members. Mr. Dew's argument, that the danger of insurrection among the slaves is diminished in proportion as their relative numbers increase over those of the white masters, is an ingenious paradox, in which I have no faith.

October 14, 1833—I read further in Professor Dew's review of the slavery debate in the Legislature of Virginia. This pamphlet deserves

10. Thomas Roderick Dew, *A Review of the Debates in the Legislature of 1831 and 1832* (1832); William W. Freehling, *The Road to Disunion: Secessionists at Bay, 1776-1854* (New York: Oxford University Press, 1990), 189–91; Lacy K. Ford, *Deliver Us from Evil: The Slavery Question in the Old South* (New York: Oxford University Press, 2008), 379–81.

grave meditation, and has in it the seeds of much profitable instruction. Slavery is, in all probability, the wedge which will ultimately split up this Union. It is the source of all the disaffection to it in both parts of the country—a disaffection deeply pervading Mr. Dew's pamphlet.

During the winter–spring term of 1833–34, Adams noted a rise in the number of antislavery petitions and the ritualized nature of Congress's dismissals. He wrote to abolitionist Moses Brown that he still would not speak in favor of the abolition of slavery in the District of Columbia: "Bound as I am by the Constitution of the United States, I am not at Liberty to take a part in promoting it. The remedy must arise in the seat of the evil."[11]

January 27, 1834—Mr. W. W. Ellsworth, of Connecticut, presented sundry petitions, without saying from whom, or in what numbers, praying for the abolition of slavery in the District of Columbia. He moved that they should all be referred, without reading, to the committee on the District, but said, and repeated with emphatic gravity, that his own sentiments concurred entirely with those of the petitioners. They were referred "sub silentio."

April 7, 1834—There were also sundry petitions from various parts of the country for the abolition of slavery in the District of Columbia. These are always turned over to the Committee on the District, with a Chairman and a majority of the committee slave-holders, and the House hears no more about them. W. W. Ellsworth, of Connecticut, this day presented one or two of these petitions, and, with much solemnity of manner, said he wished the House to understand that he concurred entirely in the views and sentiments of the petitioners on this subject, and then moved that the petition, without reading, should be referred to the Committee on the District of Columbia.

Political prospects seemed especially bleak to Adams in 1834. While he still did not go out of his way to say that slavery itself lay behind recent developments, he did not always avoid public conversations on these topics—even aboard

11. John Quincy Adams to Moses Brown, December 9, 1833, quoted in Bemis, *John Quincy Adams and the Union*, 331–32.

steamboats, where, on October 20 and 21, he found himself participating in an animated discussion on "the subject of slavery and emancipation and the capacity of the Negro race."

July 30, 1834—Rode over and visited Mr. John Bailey, at Dorchester, and had with him two hours of conversation. There is at present a great calm in the political world, and no prospects upon which I can dwell with satisfaction. The system of administration for the government of the Union is radically and, I believe, irretrievably vitiated— vitiated at the fountain. The succession to the Presidency absorbs all the national interests, and the electioneering contests are becoming merely venal. My hopes of the long continuance of this Union are extinct. The people must go the way of all the world, and split up into an uncertain number of rival communities, enemies in war, in peace friends. Were it otherwise, and were the future destinies of the nation to be as prosperous and as glorious as they have been hitherto, my lease of life is so near its close that I should live to witness little of it. My own system of administration, which was to make the national domain the inexhaustible fund for progressive and unceasing internal improvement, has failed. Systematically renounced and denounced by the present Administration, it has been undisguisedly abandoned by H. Clay, ingloriously deserted by J. C. Calhoun, and silently given up by D. Webster. These are the opposition aspirants to the Presidential succession, not one of them having a system of administration which he would now dare to avow, and at this time scarcely linked together by the brittle chain of common opposition to the unprincipled absurdities of the present incumbent.

August 29, 1834—I went immediately after dinner to my garden, but was called back to two other visitors, from Charleston, South Carolina Mr. [Richard] Yeadon—editor of the Charleston *Courier*, who brought me a letter from Joel R. Poinsett, and Mr. Levy, whom he introduced to me as a citizen of Charleston.[12] Mr. Yeadon spoke with some concern of the political condition of South Carolina, where the Nullification and Union parties are still at issue with each other, and still mutually inveterate.

---

12. Joel Poinsett was a former congressman and diplomat from South Carolina.

I observed that in that controversy the Union party had conceded too much to their adversaries.

Levy said that, if so, Mr. Jefferson's doctrine was the cause of it, and that if the Union party had not held out a strong adhesion to State rights they would have been officers without an army.

Mr. Yeadon said they had much anxiety about the appointment of a Judge of the Supreme Court in the place of Judge Johnson, and hoped it would be Mr. Pettigru—Colonel [William] Drayton having, by his removal to Philadelphia, ceased to be considered a citizen of South Carolina. He said, further, that when President Jackson's first Cabinet was broken up, he offered the office of Secretary of War to Colonel Drayton, by whom it was declined; and that Drayton was the real head and founder of the Union party. He said, too, that at the next session of the Legislature the Nullification party would call a convention of the people, and thereby procure an amendment to the Constitution of the State prescribing the test oath, to establish the State authorities as the only sovereign powers in this Union. And he alluded to the apprehension always prevailing in the South, that the people of the North have a perpetual propensity to promote the abolition of slavery in the South. This ghost, I believe, will haunt them till they bring it up in reality. I said I had no longer the confidence in the long duration of the Union that I once had; but did not say why.

Nullification and tariff controversies had left considerable bitterness in Congress. After observing debates over the boundaries of Maine devolve into defenses of sectional virtue and states' rights, Adams resolved to pick his battles wisely.

December 24, 1834—There is no trial of temper more provoking than that of conflicting with a majority of a deliberative assembly, and none where a manifestation of temper is more useless and unwise. I have fallen into this error more than once, and occasionally made myself exceedingly obnoxious by it. The manifestation of temper must be carefully distinguished from resistance to the will of a majority, which is sometimes a duty of the highest order.

Adams continued to see the presentation of petitions as a duty but did not yet press the issue of how they would be treated by the House.

February 2, 1835—This was the day for receiving memorials and Petitions; but Mr. John Dickson one of the members from the State of New York made a Speech of upwards of an hour in support of a petition signed by 816 ladies of the City of New York for the abolition of Slavery and the Slave-trade in the District of Columbia—of which he moved the reference to a Select Committee and that it should be printed—the chairman of the Committee on the District of Columbia moved to lay the petition and the motion of reference on the table which was carried by yeas and nays 117 to 77.

February 14, 1835—At the House, immediately after the reading of the journal, I obtained leave to present two petitions from citizens of the county of Oneida, in the State of New York, for the abolition of slavery in the District of Columbia. I referred to remarks I had made on presenting similar petitions in December, 1834, said I had not changed my opinions then expressed, and moved the reference of these petitions, without reading, to the Committee on the District of Columbia; which was done. I then asked leave of the House to say a few words by way of explanation; which was granted. It was upon my having said last Saturday that the Senate had dodged the question of the dispute with France, and upon the commercial excitement produced by the stand taken by me on the same occasion. My explanation amused the House.

February 16, 1835—Stephen Phillips, of Massachusetts, presented a memorial from twelve hundred and forty-nine men and three thousand six hundred ladies of his district for the abolition of slavery in the District of Columbia. After a few remarks, he moved that, without reading, it should be laid on the table. Dickson, of New York, then presented a similar memorial from Rochester, in that State, and moved that it should be laid on the table and printed, with the names. [Ratliff] Boon, of Indiana, called for a division of the question. The motion for printing was agreed to, and then a question arose upon the printing of the names, which led to a motion by [Henry] Wise, of Virginia, *who had not voted* on the order for printing being made, for reconsideration of that vote, which gave rise to a snarling debate. The vote for reconsideration was carried, by yeas and nays—one hundred and twenty-five to eighty-one; and, after sundry motions for the previous question and others, a motion to lay the memorial and the motion to print on the table was carried, by yeas and nays—one hundred and thirty-nine to sixty-three. [Harmar] Denny [of Pennsylvania] presented two memorials, one from ladies, for the same abolition of slavery in the District of Columbia. Chinn,[13] from the Committee on the District of Columbia, moved the assignment of next Saturday for the consideration of bills relating to the District; which was refused.

February 23, 1835—A number of petitions for the abolition of Slavery within the District of Columbia with a multitude of signatures were presented by sundry members all without reading laid upon the table.

The upsurge in petitions by abolitionists had a corollary in a striking, and what seemed to white Southerners surprising and outrageous, campaign to use the mail to spread the antislavery word. Partially as a result, 1835 became known as the "riot year," with much of the upsurge credited to anti-abolition mobs and their opponents. Abolitionists had effectively forced the issue to the center of public life and politics in the United States.[14]

August 11, 1835—I received a letter from Mr. Frye, at Washington, about my private business, and in great distress and agony at an attempt of a negro slave of Mrs. Thornton's, at Washington, to murder her and her mother, Mrs. Brodeau. There is a great fermentation upon this subject of slavery at this time in all parts of the Union. The emancipation of the slaves in the British West India Colonies; the Colonization Society here; the current of public opinion running everywhere stronger and stronger into democracy and popular supremacy, contribute all to shake the fetters of servitude. The theory of the rights of man has taken deep root in the soil of civil society. It has allied itself with the feelings of humanity and the precepts of Christian benevolence. It has armed itself with the strength of organized association. It has linked itself with religious doctrines and religious fervor. Anti-slavery associations are formed in this country and in England, and they are already co-operating in concerted agency together. They have raised funds to support and circulate

13. William N. Shinn, representative from New Jersey.
14. David Grimsted, *American Mobbing, 1828-1861: Toward Civil War* (New York: Oxford University Press, 1998); Leonard L. Richards, *Gentlemen of Property and Standing: Anti-Abolition Mobs in Jacksonian America* (New York: Oxford University Press, 1970).

inflammatory newspapers and pamphlets gratuitously, and they send multitudes of them into the Southern country, into the midst of the swarms of slaves. There is an Englishman by the name of Thompson, lately come over from England, who is travelling about the country, holding meetings and making eloquent inflammatory harangues, preaching the immediate abolition of slavery. The general disposition of the people here is averse to these movements, and Thompson has several times been routed by popular tumults. But in some places he meets favorable reception and makes converts. There has been recently an alarm of slave insurrection in the State of Mississippi, and several white persons have been hung by a summary process of what they call Lynch's law; that is, mob-law. Add to all this the approach of the Presidential election, and the question whether the President of the United States shall be a slave-holder or not. They never fail to touch upon this key in the South, and it has never yet failed of success. Rouse in the heart of the slave-holder the terror of his slave, and it will be a motive with him paramount to all others never to vote for any man not a slave-holder like himself. There are now calls in the Atlas, the Webster paper, and the Morning Post, the Jackson and Van Buren paper, at Boston, for a town-meeting to put down the abolitionists; but the disease is deeper than can be healed by town-meeting resolutions.

August 12, 1835—[Isaac P.] Davis had a handbill from the Atlas newspaper office, containing an account of continued riots at Baltimore on Saturday and Sunday last, in which the houses of Reverdy Johnson, John Glenn, and John B. Morris were destroyed by the mobility. In those two days the authorities of the city and of the State appear scarcely to have made an effort to sustain the laws and the rights of property. The riotous spirit manifested itself also last night at Charlestown and Roxbury, by an attempt to celebrate in a tumultuous manner the anniversary of the destruction of the Roman Catholic nunnery at Charlestown. It is said this was suppressed; but Edward Everett says there were riotous assemblages in the streets, very noisy, till late last night. The Baltimore riot was directed against all the persons implicated in the fraudulent failure of the Bank of Maryland, which happened nearly eighteen months ago. Mr. Abbott Lawrence told me that they were going to have a very great meeting at Boston to put down the anti-slavery abolitionists; but, he said, there was no diversity of opinion upon that subject here. That,

I think, will depend upon the measures to be proposed. If the measures are vaporing resolutions, they will pass unanimously, and be inefficient. If the measures are efficient, there will be diversity of opinion.

August 14, 1835—The accounts of the riots in Baltimore continue. In the State of Mississippi mobs are hanging up blacks suspected of insurgency, and whites suspected of abetting them. At Charleston, South Carolina, mobs of slave-holding gentlemen intercept the mails and take out from them all the inflammatory pamphlets circulated by the abolitionists, who, in their turn, are making every possible exertion to kindle the flame of insurrection among the slaves. We are in a state of profound peace and over-pampered with prosperity; yet the elements of exterminating war seem to be in vehement fermentation, and one can scarcely foresee to what it will lead.

As the mail controversy heightened, Boston Brahmins including both his son's father-in-law, Peter Chardon Brooks, and his old sparring partner, Mayor Harrison Gray Otis, sought to appease Southern planters by leading (what they hoped would be nonviolent) public demonstrations against the abolitionists. Adams was dismayed by their hypocrisy. In October, however, he would write to an associate that "with Slave and Abolition whirligig I hope to have no concern."[15]

August 18, 1835—I received from Washington a Richmond Enquirer containing the address of the Baltimore Van Buren Convention to the Democratic Republicans of the United States. There is something extraordinary in the present condition of parties throughout the Union. Slavery and democracy, especially the democracy founded, as ours is, upon the rights of man, would seem to be incompatible with each other. And yet at this time the democracy of the country is supported chiefly, if not entirely, by slavery. There is a small, shallow, and enthusiastic party preaching the abolition of slavery upon the principles of extreme democracy; but the democratic spirit and the popular feeling is everywhere against them. There have been riots at Washington

15. John Quincy Adams to Benjamin Waterhouse, October 15, 1835, in Richards, *Life and Times of Congressman John Quincy Adams*, 110.

not much inferior in atrocity to those at Baltimore. A slave of Mrs. Thornton's made an attempt to murder her and her mother with an axe in the night. He was prevented from accomplishing his purpose by his own mother; and, in revenge for this, mobs of white people at Washington have destroyed sundry negro houses, school-houses, and a church. In the State of Mississippi they have hanged up several persons for circulating abolition pamphlets. In Charleston, South Carolina, the principal men of the State, with the late Governor, Hayne, at their head, seize upon the mails, with the co-operation of the Postmaster himself, and purify it of the abolition pamphlets; and the Postmaster-General, Amos Kendall, neither approves nor disapproves of this proceeding. At Washington, a man named Crandall has been imprisoned for circulating incendiary pamphlets, and in Halifax County, Virginia, a man named David F. Robertson, a Scotch teacher, was in danger of his life, because another man named Robertson was suspected of having dropped in a steamboat the first number of a newspaper printed at New York with the title of Human Rights. In Boston there is a call for a town-meeting, signed by more than five hundred names, with H. G. Otis and P. C. Brooks at their head. This meeting is to be held next Friday, and is to pass resolutions against the abolitionists to soothe and conciliate the temper of the Southern slave-holders. All this is democracy and the rights of man.

August 21, 1835—There was a town-meeting also at Boston this evening to pass resolutions against the proceedings of the abolitionists, as they are called—the preachers of slave emancipation.

August 22, 1835—The Rev. Samuel Nott, Jr., minister of a Congregational Church and Society at Wareham, in the county of Plymouth, paid me a morning visit of kindness and curiosity, and gave me a small volume of sermons published by him, and entitled Sermons from the Fowls of the Air and the Lilies of the Field. He told me that he had been some time a missionary in India, and that he had seen me once in London at a meeting of the British and Foreign School Society, in the year 1816 (13th May). We had some conversation upon the most agitating topic of this time—slavery and its abolition. He thought that the abolition of slavery must come, but that it should be gradual, beginning by attaching the slave to the soil, like the serfs in the north of Europe.

I said Mr. Rufus King had expressed a similar opinion in a speech on the Missouri question in the Senate of the United States; but I believed the slave-holders would never consent to it. My own opinion is, that the planters of the South will separate from the Union, in terror of the emancipation of their slaves, and that then the slaves will emancipate themselves by a servile war. This consummation may be yet remote, and must be preceded by the sacrifice of the public lands to the Western States, effected by the co-operation of the South to purchase that of the West in perpetuating the servitude of their negroes. This coalition accomplished the election of Andrew Jackson as President of the United States, and is now in full vigor to secure the election of his successor. This is the under-current, with the tide of democracy at the surface.

Adams's long-standing tendency to see slavery as a side issue and a dangerous one still kept him aloof from abolition. Yet as antislavery spread in the North, like many others he began to see other issues, such as capital punishment, in light of antislavery reform and the backlash against it, as in this reflection on the movement against capital punishment at the time of the "riot year" controversies.

September 1, 1835—Harvey Field brought me a printed petition to the Legislature of the Commonwealth for the abolition of capital punishment. He asked if I would sign it. I declined, and told him I had not brought my mind to the conclusion that it would be for the good of the community. We have by the laws of the Commonwealth only five crimes punishable with death—treason, murder, burglary, arson, and rape. Now, a law to save the precious lives of men guilty of either of those crimes has, in my judgment, little claim to the merit of humanity. They are a class of people with whom humanity cannot sympathize. A law to prohibit the killing of rattlesnakes would be as rational, and might be urged also upon principles of humanity. There is another point of view in which the abolition of capital punishment at this time is specially objectionable. While such exceeding tenderness is felt for the lives of traitors, murderers, and robbers, here is the sovereign people hanging up, without judge or jury, gamblers, and even the mere circulators of printed papers recommending the abolition of slavery.[16] On one hand we have the most reckless disregard of human life, and the punishment of death summarily inflicted for offences comparatively light, and even for that which is no offence at all; on the other, traitors and murderers are taken into peculiar favor, and their lives must be preserved and guarded as if they were the very jewels of the land. The signs of the times are portentous. All the tendencies of legislation are to the removal of restrictions from the vicious and the guilty, and to the exercise of all the powers of government, legislative, judicial, and executive, by lawless assemblages of individuals. I have, however, no doubt that the punishment of death will be abolished in this Commonwealth, and in all probability throughout this Union.

John Howard Payne was an actor and author who in 1835 traveled to Cherokee territory to collect material on Cherokee traditions. He was the guest of Chief John Ross, leader of the anti-removal part of the Cherokee nation, and was arrested by officials in Georgia on ambiguous charges.

December 13, 1835—I read in the Knoxville Register the long dramatic narrative of John Howard Payne—He has suffered an abominable outrage, but I fear it is we that prospect of a remedy. There is no security for the right Life, of Liberty of property or of reputation, in any of the Slave holding States, with reference to Negroes, or Indians—I can at least give no aid to procure for him a remedy, or satisfaction.

At the outset of the new session of Congress in 1835, it became apparent that the issue of petitions had taken on a more serious cast. Antislavery mail had been suppressed in Charleston and other places with the collusion of Treasury Secretary Amos Kendall. In his annual message, President Jackson had proposed federal action—a law banning "incendiary" publications in the mail. He went so far as to call antislavery activism "unconstitutional and wicked."[17] This statement further emboldened Democrats to make suppression of abolitionists a partisan issue in national politics. Yet the anti-Jacksonian senator

16. In one of the best-known cases of 1835, gamblers in Mississippi were hung by a lynch mob.
17. Freehling, *Road to Disunion*, I, 309.

John C. Calhoun objected to the implications for federal powers, suggesting instead that Kendall had it right the first time: the states could and should protect themselves. In this context, abolitionist publicity and protest of any kind outside the North, including in Washington, DC, took on a different meaning—and so did its suppression. Meanwhile, Adams continued to suggest that antislavery trade petitions be referred to the committee on the federal district, even without a reading.

December 16, 1835—At the House, the day was absorbed in receiving Petitions and memorials from all States and Territories—John Fairfield, a new member from Maine, presented two Petitions for the abolition of Slavery in the District of Columbia. He moved that the first should be referred to the Committee on the District. John Cramer of New York moved that it should be laid on the table—upon which Mason of Virginia called for the yeas and nays—[Horace] Everett of Vermont asked if the motion to lay on the table was made by the member who presented the petition and Fairfield answered yes. The yeas and nays were taken twice, first on laying on the table carried 181 to 36 and to lay on the table the motion to print also carried 168 to 50. I voted on both questions in the negative.

After the suppression of abolitionist propaganda in the South, the movement stepped up its petitions to Congress, particularly on the tricky issue of slavery and the slave trade in the federal district. Some Southern congressmen proceeded to interpret petitions as the equivalent of unsolicited propaganda aimed at slaves and citizens and now demanded their suppression as well.

The first salvo in the petitions controversy came when a freshman congressman, James Henry Hammond of South Carolina, made a motion that a particular petition should not be accepted in any fashion. Adams initially saw this new development as partisan and in part determined by the upcoming presidential election, in which it was expected that New Yorker Martin Van Buren would be the Democrats' successor to Jackson.

December 18, 1835—[Nathaniel B.] Borden [of Massachusetts] presented a petition from Wrentham for the abolition of Slavery in the District of Columbia and moved its reference to a select Committee. Hammond of South Carolina moved that the petition should be rejected—This proposition which was wholly unexpected to Polk the speaker disconcerted him and he blundered in the tangles of the Rules—a debate of four hours arose between the fury of the Southern Slave holders and wiley compliances of the Kinderhook school, in which the rest of the House took no part.[18]—[Francis] Granger of New York came to me and asked me if this was to be tolerated. I told him it would be tolerated—That the Presidential Election was crushing every elementary principle of Freedom, in the free States and that I saw no prospect of useful resistance at this time.

December 19, 1835—Mr. Lawrence[19] and Mr. Granger spoke also of the debate yesterday in the House upon the petition to abolish Slavery in the District of Columbia and both urged me to address the House on the subject. I fear I must.

Beginning on December 21, Representative William Slade of Vermont took the lead in attacking the resolution to not even receive antislavery petitions. Adams suggested that the petitions be referred again to the standing committee, "to sleep the sleep of death."[20]

December 22, 1835—The speaker then said the unfinished business of yesterday was the reconsideration of the reference to the Petition from Cummington for the abolition of slavery in the District of Columbia to the Committee on the District. The debate was then continued by Speeches from [Henry] Wise of Virginia, [George C.] Dromgoole of Virginia, [Francis] Granger, [William] Mason, and [Samuel] Beardsley of New York, and Ingersoll of Pennsylvania. After 3 O'Clock Slade of Virginia moved an adjournment, announcing his intention to speak upon the subject to-morrow. Granger's speech was short but spirited and pungent. Wise and Dromgoole made frequent and direct allusion to what I said yesterday—Wise maintained that Congress had no right to abolish Slavery in the District of Columbia, and quoted the provision

18. The "Kinderhook school" is a reference to New York Democrats under the leadership of Martin Van Buren, known as the red fox of Kinderhook.
19. Abbott Lawrence, a Massachusetts congressman and longtime friend of Adams.
20. Richards, *Life and Times of Congressman John Quincy Adams*, 117.

that private property shall not be taken for public uses without compensation and he complained that runaway Slaves should not be recovered in the north notwithstanding the Constitutional provision that they should be restored—Joseph R. Ingersoll [of Pennsylvania] proposed a Resolution declaring in the broadest terms that the Constitution of the United States recognizes the right of the People of the Southern States to hold slaves. A strange concession for a Pennsylvanian.

In the meantime, petitions continued to arrive in Adams's mailbox, from outside his district.

January 4, 1836—I attended the House with feelings of no small anxiety. After the reading of the journal, the Speaker called the States for petitions, beginning with Maine. When he came to Massachusetts, I presented the memorial of F. C. Gray, and others, praying for an Act similar to that which passed the Senate at the last session of Congress to indemnify them for French spoliations prior to the year 1800. The memorial was, at my motion, without reading, referred to the Committee of Foreign Affairs. I next presented the petition of Albert Pabodie and one hundred and fifty-three inhabitants of Millbury, in the county of Worcester and Commonwealth of Massachusetts, praying for the abolition of slavery and the slave-trade in the District of Columbia. The petition was couched in the same language with that which [George N.] Briggs [of Massachusetts] had presented last week, and which, after it had been referred to the Committee of the District of Columbia, was by a reconsidered vote laid on the table, together with the motion that it should be printed. I therefore now, after stating the contents of the petition from Millbury, said it was my intention to move that, without reading, it should be laid on the table.

I was instantly interrupted by my next neighbor, John M. Patton [of Virginia], who enquired whether the petition had been received; to which the Speaker answered that it had not; whereupon Thomas Glascock, a new member from Georgia, moved that it be not received, and was proceeding to make a speech, when I called him to order; and, appealing to the forty-fifth rule of the House, which prescribes that there shall be no debate upon petitions on the day when they are presented, I demanded that the debate should now be postponed to a day certain; that this day might be free for the receipt of petitions from all the States. The Speaker decided that as the petition had not been received, it was not in possession of the House, and that the fortieth rule of the House, interdicting debate, did not apply. From this decision I appealed, and asked for the yeas and nays; which were ordered, and a debate arose upon the appeal, which consumed the day. I spoke twice, the second time after a clamorous call for the question; but after I had spoken, Vinton, of Ohio, moved an adjournment; which was carried, leaving the question undecided.

By January it was no longer possible to deflect petitions quietly to committees: radical Deep South representatives like Hammond insisted on equating petitions with abolitionist mail. If one type could be suppressed, or had to be, why not the other? On January 6, 1836, Representative Glascock presented a resolution condemning "any attempt to agitate the question of slavery in this House [that] is calculated to disturb the compromises of the Constitution, to endanger the Union, and if persisted in, to destroy, by a servile war, the peace and prosperity of the country." John C. Calhoun presented a similar resolution in the Senate.[21] *But such resolutions raised constitutional issues beyond that of Congress's authority over the District of Columbia, and they did not pass. Democrats tried to tighten the rules on the District of Columbia petitions in particular, with more radical Southerners such as the Virginia Whig Henry Wise trying to strengthen the resolutions into a categorical statement of disapproval that could be extended further at some later date.*

January 6, 1836—[Leonard] Jarvis, of Maine, offered, as he said, at the request of [George W.] Owens, of Georgia, a resolution declaring that the House will not entertain any petitions for the abolition of slavery in the District of Columbia, and he said that it was almost the universal opinion of the North that Congress had no right to interfere with slavery. He read resolutions apparently to that effect adopted at some meeting last summer in the State of Maine.

21. Bemis, *John Quincy Adams and the Union*, 336; Freehling, *Road to Disunion*, 322; William Lee Miller, *Arguing about Slavery* (New York: Knopf, 1996), 115–19.

I asked him to consent that the consideration of his resolution should be postponed, to give an opportunity to other members to offer resolutions; but he declined.

[Adam] Huntsman, of Tennessee, came to my seat and asked me to move to lay the resolution on the table, and said they would support that. I made the motion accordingly, and it was rejected, by yeas and nays—one hundred and twenty-three to sixty-six, Huntsman himself voting with the majority.

Wise then moved two or three resolutions as substitutes for those offered by Jarvis; and they declared that Congress had no power to abolish slavery in the District of Columbia. Owens had said last week that he would move the resolution now offered by Jarvis, and would immediately call for the previous question upon it. Wise now, in offering his substitute, said he should like to see who would move the previous question upon it. Glascock offered a resolution as an amendment to those of Wise, but Wise accepted it as a modification of his resolutions. Cambreleng had been some time calling for the orders of the day; the hour for resolutions having expired, he now succeeded.

Adams remained committed to the petitioning process, and the procedures for receiving and presenting them, as the basis for his activity on the slavery question.

January 12, 1836—At the House, my appeal from the decision of the Speaker, that the forty-fifth rule of the House does not apply to a motion that a petition be not received, was the special order of the day. Before calling the House to order, Mr. Polk came to my seat and spoke somewhat doubtingly whether he should first announce it to be taken up or the unfinished business of yesterday. I said I supposed the special order would come up of course. He did accordingly announce it. [Aaron] Ward, of New York, moved that it should be postponed till next Monday; which gave rise to a short debate. The postponement was a Van Buren or majority measure, upon which the division was not sectional, but political. I opposed the postponement, on the grounds that the question to be decided on the appeal was not confined to petitions upon the subject of slavery, but to all petitions; but that it must be decided before the question could be taken whether the petition presented by me should or should not be received. As the petitioners had thought proper to send their petition to me, I wished to be able to inform them what disposition of it has been made by the House. I objected also to the postponement to next Monday, because, that being the day for receiving petitions, the debate, if renewed, would again interfere with the performance of that duty. The postponement was, however, carried.

January 13, 1836—Jarvis called up his resolution declaring that the subject of abolishing slavery in the District of Columbia ought not to be entertained by Congress, and that all petitions that may be presented demanding it should be laid on the table without printing. This was Jarvis's resolution, but he had borrowed it from Owens, of Georgia, who had given notice that he would move it and then immediately move the previous question. But when Jarvis moved his resolution, Wise immediately moved as an amendment a declaration that Congress have no power to abolish slavery, and said he would see who would move the previous question on that.

Glascock moved as an amendment to Wise's amendment a declaration that any attempt to agitate the question of abolishing slavery in the District of Columbia would lead to the danger of a servile war.

He meant this as a substitute for Wise's amendment; but Wise disconcerted him by accepting the amendment as part of his own.

Chilton Allan [of Kentucky] now moved to lay the whole triad of resolutions upon the table; but this was rejected, by yeas and nays—fifty-eight to one hundred and fifty-five.

For Adams, maintaining decorum and equal treatment of members and constituents was essential. On the next day for presenting petitions, however, it became clear that the status quo of referring petitions had become unworkable. During the coming weeks, more and more petitions were introduced and then "laid on the table," the other traditional way of receiving petitions but not acting on them. Adams continued to discuss procedure with a range of congressmen, from the anti-abolitionist Glascock of Georgia to the freshman Massachusetts representative Caleb Cushing.[22]

22. Diary, January 22, 25, 1836.

January 14, 1836—Mr. Granger, of New York, came to my seat, and said that Mr. [Waddy] Thompson, of South Carolina, was desirous of being introduced to me, but felt some scruple, under an apprehension that I might have taken offence at some remarks made by him in one of his speeches censorial upon me.

I told Granger that I scarcely ever noticed in any manner any personality bearing upon me by any member of the House, and that nothing said by Mr. Thompson had given me the slightest offence.

Granger afterwards brought Thompson to my seat and introduced him. I found him much of a gentleman.

January 18, 1836—Petition day at the House. My appeal from the decision of the Speaker had been postponed to this day, and was now, at the motion of [Albert G.] Hawes [of Kentucky], postponed again till Thursday next. . . . When the turn of Massachusetts came, I presented, first, a petition from sundry persons, sent to me under a blank cover, praying for the construction of a harbor at the mouth of the river St. Joseph, in the Territory of Michigan, which was referred to the Committee of Commerce; then, a petition from three hundred and sixty-six inhabitants of Weymouth, in my own Congressional district, praying for the abolition of slavery and the slave-trade in the District of Columbia.

Hammond, of South Carolina, interrupted me, and moved that the petition be not received. He had no right to interrupt me, and the Speaker said I was entitled to the floor.

[Henry L.] Pinckney, of South Carolina, then entreated me to allow a motion to postpone the question of the receipt of the petition, so that the reception of other petitions might have free course this day; to which I consented, and for which he thanked me. The question of reception was then postponed, and I presented another petition to the same effect, of one hundred and fifty-eight ladies, citizens of the Commonwealth of Massachusetts; for, I said, I had not yet brought myself to doubt whether females were citizens.

The question upon the reception of this petition was also postponed.

A great number of other petitions with the same prayer were presented by many members, and all were postponed, on motions of Hammond that they should not be received, and by a new motion of Gideon Lee, of New York, that the motion not to receive be laid on the table.

The Speaker varied the manner of putting the question—sometimes, that it should not be, and sometimes, whether it should be, received, and finally put it upon the preliminary question, which he has decided is debatable, but that a motion to lay it on the table is in order, and that is not debatable.

[Thomas M. T.] McKennan, of Pennsylvania, on presenting an abolition petition, moved its reference to a select committee, and, upon the motion to lay that motion on the table, called for the yeas and nays. Wise moved a call of the House—which was refused. The yeas and nays for laying on the table were one hundred and seventy-seven to thirty-seven, and I was obliged to vote with the affirmatives, by the consent I had given that the petitions presented by me should be so disposed of.

Henry Laurens Pinckney of South Carolina proposed in early February that a special committee of the House report resolutions on dealing with antislavery petitions. The understanding was that the committee would propose a diluted Gag Rule. According to the new rule, petitions against the slave trade were constitutional, but all petitions in any way related to slavery were to be automatically tabled.[23]

February 9, 1836—[Hopkins] Holsey of Georgia, moved a question, with a view subsequently to move a reconsideration of the Resolution yesterday moved by H. L. Pinckney and carried, but the Speaker declared Holsey's motion not in order. Rice Garland of Louisiana, Glascock of Georgia, and [John] Robertson of Virginia moved a suspension of the Rules, to enable them spread upon the Journal a protest against the vote of the House, to instruct the Committee on the Slavery Memorial to declare that Congress have not the power to interfere with Slavery in the States. The question of suspending the Rules was rejected by yeas and nays.

The Pinckney idea was closer to the administration's line, and Speaker James K. Polk jumped on board enthusiastically—but more ambitiously. The committee

23. Corey M. Brooks, *Liberty Power: Antislavery Third Parties and the Transformation of American Politics* (Chicago: University of Chicago Press, 2016), 19–20.

was to be instructed to fashion its resolutions to make it clear that Congress could not legislate slavery in the states and "ought not" consider it in the District of Columbia. Politicians of various commitments wanted to get the issue off the floor. Southern radicals quickly objected to the implication that Congress could legislate slavery in the federal district. Meanwhile, even after the matter had been sent to the select committee, the issue of petitions recurred every day that was set aside for petitions (usually part of each of the first thirty days of a session and once every two weeks thereafter).

On February 23, for example, Adams noted that a petition from New York "started again the Slavery debate which occupied the remainder of the day." The new expedient of referring the petitions to the select committee itself, which Adams described on February 29 and March 21, did not help much either. In mid-April, a new "snarl" occurred when William Slade presented a petition against the admission of Arkansas to the union with slavery.

Finally, in May, Pinckney's committee returned with a report that included the key word "unconstitutional." Pinckney and his colleagues had chosen to compromise with Henry Wise and the states' rights radicals—to a point. The new gag rule would be ironclad: all slavery-related petitions "relating in any way, or to any extent whatsoever, to the subject of slavery" would be "lain on the table," not referred to a committee. Still, the "unconstitutional" language appeared in the resolution on congressional interference with slavery in the states. The "ought not" remained in the resolution on the District of Columbia—until a resolution was proposed to change it.[24]

May 18, 1836—Immediately after the reading of the journal, H. L. Pinckney presented the report of the select committee to whom all the abolition petitions were referred, and said that the report had the unanimous assent of the committee. He moved that five thousand copies of the report should be printed for the use of the House.

It was immediately attacked with extreme violence, and a fiery debate arose, which continued until one o'clock, and then, by a suspension of the rule, for another half-hour. Motion was made to print ten thousand and twenty thousand copies, and Waddy Thompson said that he would commit it to the flames or to the hangman. Ben Hardin [of Kentucky],

24. Freehling, *Road to Disunion*, 335–36.

who was a member of the committee, declared his dissent to the main sentiment of the report, and protested against it.

May 21, 1836—At the House, the motion of Robertson to recommit H. L. Pinckney's incendiary petition report with instructions to report a Resolution declaring that Congress have not the power to abolish Slavery in the District of Columbia, was first taken up and Robertson made a Speech to the Walls of about three quarters of an hour—and when the time for the order of the day came, [Joseph] White of Florida prevailed upon the House to take up a Bill for paying certain unpaid Volunteers in the Florida Indian War.

On May 25, Adams tried to explain his votes on the different revised Pinckney resolutions; he wanted to be sure he was understood as objecting to the notion that it was unconstitutional for Congress to legislate slavery in the states generally. When he was repeatedly interrupted and not granted a few minutes to speak, he famously turned the silencing of petitions to himself, asking, "Am I gagged or am I not?"

What occurred later in the day, though, had a more immediate impact. Adams seized the opportunity of a bill for relief of refugees in the Second Seminole War to call Speaker Polk and thus the Jackson administration to task—linking the gag rule, the ongoing controversy over the possible annexation of Texas, and the long-standing issue of Indian removal in the South. The only conceivable justification for congressional action lay in the war powers under the Constitution. That power lay with Congress, and it was "tremendous." Congress could not declare that it had no power to interfere with slavery because to do so would disavow its own constitutional responsibilities in time of war. A civil war, indeed, was under way in Mexico and Texas between nationals who had abolished slavery and settlers who wanted to reintroduce it. This was "a war of aggression, of conquest, of slave making."

The new, second Seminole conflict replayed the drama of slave raids that had spurred the first war in Florida eighteen years before. What if Mexico retaliated? "Mr. Chairman, are you ready for all these wars?" he asked, singling out Speaker James K. Polk, on the heels of accusing him as an "Anglo-Saxon, slave-holding, exterminator of Indians," of hating "the Mexican-Spanish-Indian, emancipator of slaves and abolisher of slavery." Drawing an apocalyptic vision of North American conflict and possible European interference, the former president insisted that the present and predictable future wars

would either require the government to protect slave property or, if neces-
sary, sacrifice slave property. "From the instant that your slaveholding states
became the theatre of war, civil, servile or foreign, from that instant the war
powers of Congress extend to interference with the [institution] of slavery in
every way by which it can be interfered with, from the claim of indemnity for
slaves taken or destroyed, to the cession of the State burdened with slavery to
a foreign power. "[25] As late as 1842, Adams proudly noted evidence of slave-
holders' terror at "my exposure of the danger to Southern slavery of eventual
emancipation by martial law. "[26]

May 25, 1836—At the House, the motion of Robertson, to recommit
Pinckney's slavery report, with instructions to report a resolution declaring that Congress has no constitutional authority to abolish slavery in
the District of Columbia, as an amendment to the motion for printing
an extra number of the report, was first considered. Robertson finished
his speech, which was vehement; and he read the letter from Mr. Van
Buren on the subject of the power of Congress to abolish slavery in the
District, and he charged him with evading the question.

I asked that so much of the letter as he had referred to should be
read; and it was. Immediately after the conclusion of Robertson's speech
I addressed the Speaker, but he gave the floor to Owens, of Georgia,
one of the signing members of the committee, who moved the previous question, and refused to withdraw it. It was seconded and carried,
by yeas and nays—one hundred and ten to eighty-nine. I asked what
the main question would be. The Speaker decided that it would be the
adoption of the resolutions of the committee, which have not been in
the slightest degree discussed.

I appealed from the decision, which the House confirmed. The question on the first resolution was taken—one hundred and sixty-eight

25. Adams, *Speech of John Quincy Adams, on the Joint Resolution for Distributing
    Rations to the Distressed Fugitives from Indian Hostilities in the States of Alabama
    and Georgia, Delivered in the House of Representatives, Wednesday May 25, 1836*
    (Washington, DC, 1836), 3–4, 7–8. For the long-term significance of the war pow-
    ers argument, see James Oakes, *Freedom National: The Destruction of Slavery in the
    United States, 1861-1865* (New York: W. W. Norton, 2013), 34–42.
26. Diary, December 23, 1842.

to nine. Glascock asked to be excused from voting. I required that the reasons for excusing him should be entered on the journal. The Speaker was doubtful. The hour of one came, and the order of the day was called—a joint resolution from the Senate, authorizing the President to cause rations to be furnished to suffering fugitives from Indian hostilities in Alabama and Georgia. Committee of the whole on the Union, and a debate of five hours, in which I made a speech of about an hour, wherein I opened the whole subject of the Mexican, Indian, negro, and English war.

Answered by Joab Lawless [of Alabama], [Charles E.] Haynes [of Georgia], Waddy Thompson, and Wise.

The resolution was carried through all its stages and passed, and the House adjourned between seven and eight o'clock, and I came home much exhausted, and soon sought my bed.

The vote on the revised three-part Pinckney gag rule resolutions was held the next day. Adams reinforced the notion of his having been gagged by rising to insist on the unconstitutionality of the first resolution and being shouted down by cries of "Order."[27]

May 26, 1836—At the House, the first subject was the question upon Glascock's assigning the reasons for his asking to be excused from voting on the slavery report resolutions.

The Speaker announced that he had recurred to the only precedent on the journals of the House, which was in my own case, and that the House then determined to proceed in the call of yeas and nays, and announce the decision, without waiting first to decide any question on the refusal of the member to vote; but that such question would remain to be afterwards decided by the House.

I rose, and began to prove that the case was totally different from that of 1832, which could not, therefore, apply as a precedent; but I was called with great vociferation to order, and not permitted to proceed.

The Speaker went on, and announced the result of the vote on the first resolution.

27. Miller, *Arguing about Slavery*, 209–10.

On the call of yeas and nays upon the second resolution, I asked to be excused from voting, and the call was continued, passing me by. Others declined voting, and they were also passed by.

On my name being called on the third resolution, I answered, "I hold the resolution to be a direct violation of the Constitution of the United States, of the rules of this House, and of the rights of my constituents."

They passed on.

Granger asked to be excused from voting on the second resolution, because the resolution is different from that which the committee was instructed to report. He was passed over, and not allowed to offer his reasons.

A scene of great disorder ensued. Glascock claimed the floor to assign his reasons. The Speaker gave him the floor, and then took it away from him by arbitrary, absurd, and in-consistent decisions, all of which were sustained by the House by large majorities by yeas and nays, as were the three resolutions reported by the committee.

Contemporaries recognized immediately the importance of Adams's war powers speech and he quickly published it in the newspapers and in a pamphlet version. In early May, Adams had received draft essays about the proslavery aspects of the Texas Revolution from the abolitionist Benjamin Lundy, who had visited the region himself. On May 27, Lundy wrote to him, "I perceive the ice is broken in the H of R. Perseverance, perseverance, *my friend!"*[28]

The accelerated back and forth between antislavery activists and sympathetic congressmen began to yield a rush of petitions against slavery in the proposed new state of Arkansas—petitions that were now themselves subject to the gag rule. Soon Adams identified himself, for the first time, wholeheartedly with anti–Slave Power politics as a "cause." And in mid-June he ultimately voted against the admission of Arkansas as a slave state.

May 29, 1836—I was occupied all the leisure of the day and evening in writing out for publication my speech made last Wednesday in the House of Representatives—one of the most hazardous that I ever made,

28. Richards, *Life and Times of Congressman John Quincy Adams*, 156–59; Lundy to Adams, May 27, 1836, in Charles Francis Adams Jr., "John Quincy Adams and Martial Law," *Proceedings of the Massachusetts Historical Society*, 2nd Ser. 15 (1901–02), 449.

and the reception of which, even by the people of my own district and State, is altogether uncertain.

June 1, 1836—Mr. Gales sent this morning for the manuscript of my speech last week on the resolution for granting rations to the fugitives from Indian hostilities in Alabama and Georgia, and I sent it to him for publication in the Intelligencer tomorrow, having just then finished writing it out.

June 2, 1836—My speech on the distribution of rations to the fugitives from Indian hostilities in Alabama and Georgia was published in the National Intelligencer of this morning, and a subscription paper was circulated in the House for printing it in a pamphlet, for which Gales told me there were twenty-five hundred copies ordered. Several members of the House of both parties spoke of it to me, some with strong dissent.

After the reading of the Journal several propositions for the receipt of petitions—and several by consent were received G[ideon] Lee of [New York] offered a Resolution to which I objected unless the House would allow me to present twenty Petitions, remonstrances, and memorials against the admission of Arkansas as a Slave State.

June 5, 1836—I made out also a list of memorials and remonstrances against the article concerning Slavery in the Constitution of Arkansas, which I shall attempt to present to-morrow.

June 6, 1836—I presented twenty-two Memorials and Remonstrances against the admission of Arkansas into the Union as a Slave State, and against the Article in the Constitution of that State respecting Slavery. They were all laid on the table, by the Resolution of the 25th of May. I presented also two other Petitions, which were referred one to the Committee on Revolutionary Pensions and the other to the Committee on the Judiciary—There were a multitude of other Petitions, against the Slavery Article in the Constitution of Arkansas—all laid on the table without debate.

June 8, 1836—The next bill in order was the Michigan bill, which Wise agreed to postpone till next Monday, to take up first the Arkansas bill, to make it sure that the slave State shall first come in. Another fiery debate. Wise expressed a fear that a restriction upon slavery would be proposed, and, if adopted by the House, he said he would propose a section to introduce slavery into Michigan. [Joel K.] Mann [of

Pennsylvania] and [Aaron] Vanderpoel [of New York] gave a sort of promise that no proposition concerning slavery should be made in the debate on the Arkansas bill.

I said if no other member would offer such a proposal I would.

A question then arose whether both bills *must* be referred to the committee of the whole or not, as indirectly making a charge upon the people. The Speaker, after much hesitation, decided, upon a precedent of 1832, that they *must* be referred to the committee of the whole. The House immediately went into committee on the Michigan bill.

June 10, 1836—I then, at five in the morning, offered my amendment to the third section of the bill for the admission of Arkansas. It was very short, and I said very little in presenting it, but it kindled a fiery debate of three hours, in which Wise, Cushing, Briggs, [Samuel] Hoar, [Gideon] Hard, of New York, took a part, and Dromgoole, drunk with whiskey, and [Jesse] Bynum [of North Carolina], drunk with slavery, used insulting language, which I demanded should be taken down by the Clerk, but which Speight, the Chairman, would not notice.

My amendment was rejected by tellers—thirty-two to ninety.

About eight o'clock Slade came in, and offered a much stronger amendment, which was rejected. [Joseph] Underwood offered an amendment to the Michigan bill, which was rejected. Wise spoke till ten o'clock, when Chambers, of Kentucky, made a point of order, whether the Speaker was not bound to take the chair for this day. He would not. Wise spoke another hour.

Then the committee rose and reported the two bills, and the House adjourned at eleven o'clock.

June 13, 1836—Then followed the bill for the admission of Arkansas— upon which I offered the amendment I had proposed in committee of the whole. It was read, and I remained on my feet to address the House in support of it. [Sherrod] Williams, of Kentucky, started up, and moved the previous question. I claimed the floor, and the Speaker gave it to me. Williams insisted on his right to it, and the Speaker gave it to him. I appealed from the decision, and the House sustained the Speaker, by a vote of ninety-seven to eighty-seven. The previous question was carried. The bill passed to a third reading by one hundred and forty-seven to fifty-two. Both bills were passed without amendment, by the previous question. Adjourned about six.

June 19, 1836—I have been some days occupied in preparing my Report of the proceeding in Committee of the whole, and in the House upon my proposed amendment to the Bill for admitting the State of Arkansas into the Union—My correspondence consequently falls into arrears again. My speech on the rations comes back with echoes of thundering vituperation from the South and West, and with one universal shout of applause from the North and East. This is a cause upon which I am entering at the last stage of life, and with the certainty that I cannot advance in it far; my career must close, leaving the cause at the threshold. To open the way for others is all that I can do. The cause is good and great.

In the wake of this speech, Adams began to receive more correspondence and visits from Lundy and other abolitionists. He began to formulate his role as a fellow traveler with a distinct role to play as a congressman. He would break bread, trade texts, and strategize with abolitionists, but would not join them formally.

July 8, 1836—After breakfast I had visits from Benjamin Lundy and Lewis C. Gunns, Editor of the Times and Independent Press—They wished me to address the Anti-Slavery Societies which I declined.

July 9, 1836—Philadelphia, 9th.—Atlee, Edwin B.; Barton, Isaac; Semple, Matthew; Buffum, Arnold. The four persons named came this morning as committees—1. Of the Pennsylvania Society for Promoting the Abolition of Slavery; 2. Of the Philadelphia Anti-Slavery Society, with votes of thanks to me and to the other members of Congress who, at the late session of Congress, opposed the influence of the slavery predominant party in that body.

I desired them to return my thanks to the respective societies for the honor they had done me by these resolutions, and to assure them of the grateful sentiments with which I received them. One of the resolutions contained also an invitation of attendance at a public meeting—which I declined; and I gave them a full and candid exposition of my own principles and views with regard to the institution of domestic slavery, differing from theirs under a sense of the compact and compromise in the Constitution of the United States. I declined attendance at any public meeting of the societies, and said I believed the cause itself would be more benefited by such service as I could render to it in the discharge of my duty in Congress than by giving notoriety to any action on my part in support of the societies or in connection with them. They acquiesced in these determinations, and declared themselves well satisfied with the result of this interview.

July 11, 1836—With praise and prayer to God, and a solemn sense of my earthly condition, and hopes of a better world, I enter upon the seventieth year of my pilgrimage. Benjamin Lundy came this morning, and, in a conversation of about two hours, made me acquainted with his principles, prospects, and purposes relating to slavery. He was heretofore the editor of the Genius of Universal Emancipation, and has now the intention of commencing the publication of a newspaper devoted, like that, to the extinguishment of slavery—a cause which, within the last two or three years, has fallen into great discouragement. He solicited assistance from me for the matter of his proposed publication, but I thought best not to give him any expectation of it.

After dinner, Mr. William B. Reed came in, but I had no time to converse with him. Benjamin Lundy came at six, and I walked with him to the house of his friend James Mott, No. 136 North Ninth Street, where there was a large tea and evening party of men and women—all of the Society of Friends. I had free conversation with them till between ten and eleven o'clock, upon slavery, the abolition of slavery, and other topics; of all which the only exceptionable part was the undue proportion of talking assumed by me, and the indiscretion and vanity in which I indulged myself. Lucretia Mott, the mistress of the house, wife of James Mott, is a native of the island of Nantucket, and had heard of my visit there last September. She is sensible and lively, and an abolitionist of the most intrepid school. Benjamin Lundy and another friend came home with me to Mr. Riddle's, and Lundy came in, and conversed with me nearly another hour.

James Madison, whom Adams always spoke of with respect and admiration, died on June 28, 1836. Invited to give a eulogy by the city of Boston, Adams worried that this performance, too, could not avoid the politics of slavery. Ultimately he decided that the question of Madison's views on nullification,

*which he might seem to have supported with the Virginia Resolutions of 1798
but had publicly opposed during the early 1830s, could not be avoided.*[29]

August 31, 1836—The preparation for the Eulogy of Mr. Madison occu-
pies my time with much reading and my progress in writing upon it
is slow and very irksome—There are circumstances in the Life of Mr.
Madison, of which I cannot speak with praise, and of which I would
therefore gladly not speak at all. But I cannot pass them over in silence—
Nor will it be possible for me to treat them without giving offence to a
large portion of the People of this Union—Should I suppress the truth?

September 28, 1836—I read the article from the North American
Review upon nullification, sent to me by Mr. Edward Everett, and
written by him in 1830.[30] I read also the letters from Mr. Madison to
him upon the subject, of the same date. I have undertaken to mark, in
very explicit terms, the difference between the opinions, the purposes,
and the conduct of Mr. Madison and Mr. Jefferson with reference to
the Alien and the Sedition Acts. They were very remarkably different.
I foresee that this may engage me in a controversy with the Jeffersonian
school of the South, and that it will be specially unpalatable in Virginia.
There are many considerations which make this exceedingly hazardous at my time of life, but after long deliberation I have concluded
that there is a duty for me to perform—a duty to the memory of my
father; a duty to the character of the people of New England; a duty to
truth and justice. If controversy is made, I shall have an arduous and
probably a very unthankful task to perform, and may sink under it;
but I will defend my father's fame. I will vindicate the New England
character, and I will expose some of the fraudulent pretences of slave-
holding democracy. I pray for temper, moderation, firmness, and self-
control; and, above all, for a pure and honest purpose; and, if it so
please Heaven, for success.

November 25, 1836—I wrote a few lines to Governor Edward Everett,
and to John H. Eastburn, of whom I have asked another hundred

29. John Quincy Adams, *An Eulogy on the Life and Character of James Madison* (Boston:
J. H. Eastburn, 1836), 53–58.
30. For Everett's role, see Matthew Mason, *Apostle of Union: A Political Biography of
Edward Everett* (Chapel Hill: University of North Carolina Press, 2016), ch. 3.

copies of the eulogy on James Madison. This is occasioned by a number of applications which I have received from various persons, strangers to me, and who have just curiosity enough to see the work, without being at the cost of a quarter of a dollar to pay for it. There are in the eastern, central, and western parts of the country multitudes of collectors of pamphlets of this description, who bedaub me with flattery for gratuitous copies of my speeches and orations, while others do them about equal honor by malicious and caustic reviews. There is in the Boston Courier, which Gales this day sent me, such a review of the eulogy on Madison, by a blue-light federalist of the Hartford Convention school, while in the Telegraph newspaper of this day there is a deadly onset upon me from the clanking chains of a Southern slave-holder for my speech upon the Texan imposture last June.

6

Antislavery Whig Congressman (1836–46)

By 1836, John Quincy Adams had become a full-fledged and open opponent of slavery and slaveholders in American politics, but by no means did that make slavery a straightforward political proposition for him. For he had done nothing so simple as move on to easily labeled "antislavery" ground. Few if any Americans held such idealized positions. Instead, they inhabited very specific positions in specific contexts along a finely graded spectrum of opinion and action on slavery. Furthermore, while his fight against the gag rule associated him with that issue in minds then and since, in this as in previous eras of his career slavery entered American politics and his consciousness in such a variety of ways that it could never be considered a simple issue. Only on the surface, then, is it surprising that Adams could write in 1843, as if it had been 1820, that his "ideas" on slavery "are yet crude, indigested, and confused."[1]

So while in the last decade-plus of his life Adams worked alongside abolitionists and Liberty Party activists such as Joshua Leavitt, he found himself in continued tension with other abolitionists. In part that was because their method of angrily agitating the issue struck Adams as out of step with his own very Whiggish vision that the abolition of slavery, war, and other major

---

1. Diary, June 26, 1843.

ANTISLAVERY WHIG CONGRESSMAN   199

ills in human society would come only on Providence's timetable. For all his tensions with the Whig Party proper in the 1840s, his very Whig faith in the ethic of Improvement was part of what distinguished him from less patient abolitionists.

Nevertheless, Adams's thoughts and public expressions had traveled a great distance in the antislavery direction by this phase of his career, and they proved highly influential, and helpful, to antislavery activists during and after his lifetime. His continued complaints that he was a voice in the wilderness were more in keeping with the lone-wolf self-image that he had cherished for more than four decades than with the reality of the small but growing band of antislavery politicians who cohered around him during this phase of his career.

Adams remained torn both personally and politically about how to approach this vortex of slavery-related questions, and nowhere is that confusion clearer than in the contradictory and sometimes tortured entries in his diary. In some of them he confessed the enormous pride—sometimes verging well past the brink of self-aggrandizement—he took in leading the small but growing antislavery phalanx in Congress, and talked candidly about his relish for the strife with slaveholders and their allies. In other accounts of these battles he chided himself for unstatesmanlike imprudence and prayed for protection from his own vaunting ambition. In yet others he vacillated in the same entry between whether his cause demanded prudence or heat. It had become unequivocally Adams's cause, but that in no meaningful way simplified his life or his politics. He had plenty of work and experienced boosts of energy and inspiration that surprised even him, as he noted his advancing age. On the other hand, the very necessity of such a politics seemed to reflect the failure of the Democratic-Republican and Whig versions of nationalism.

Over time, the push to annex the republic of Texas as one or more slave states, led by Southern Democrats, assumed growing importance in Adams's mind. His commentary on a conversation with conservative Massachusetts Whig Caleb Cushing in the following diary entry made it plain that concerns about parliamentary process being violated, in addition to other concerns, helped attract his attention to the Texas affair.[2]

2. See also Diary, September 18, 1837.

December 24, 1836—I asked Cushing if there would be a report from the [House] Committee of Foreign Affairs on the President's message concerning Texas. He had some doubts.

Cushing, as a member of that committee, concurred in their excellent senseless report of the 4th of July last, on Texas, screwed through the House by the previous question, without allowing one word of discussion.[3] The tone is now totally changed. ... [A South Carolina legislature's report] represents the Texans as a people struggling for their liberty, and therefore entitled to our sympathy. The fact is directly the reverse—they are fighting for the establishment and perpetuation of slavery, and that is the cause of the South Carolinian sympathy with them. Can this fact be demonstrated to the understanding, and duly exhibited to the sentiment, of my countrymen? with candor, with calmness, with moderation, and with a pencil of phosphoric light? Alas! no!

As the Second Session of the Twenty-Fourth Congress convened in December 1836, its members reinstated the ultimate abuse of parliamentary procedure in Adams's mind, the gag rule. Multiple diary entries from early 1837 make it clear that Adams's desk had become the central clearinghouse for a flood of abolition petitions, and he fought to present them in spite of the gag. The inconsistency with which Speaker James K. Polk (a Tennessee Democrat) applied the rule—for instance, in silencing abolition petitions but not those for aid to the ACS or even a mocking one from Virginians "praying Congress to furnish husbands at public expense to all female petitioners upon subjects relating to slavery"—grated on Adams. Inconsistency would become the least of Adams's worries by February 1837, as attempts by his House colleagues to censure him for his course—he referred to them as "Resolutions against me"—proliferated. All this combined to make slavery an all-engrossing topic in Adams's mind. Accordingly, he read and pondered deeply on slavery in a broad Atlantic context that now included Great Britain's prominent experiment in gradual emancipation in the West Indies. But he would not profess himself either ready or eager for this fight.[4]

---

3. The resolution was that the US government recognize Texan independence. For these maneuvers and Adams's objections, see *Congressional Globe*, 24th Congress, 1st Session, 611, 615–16; Diary, July 4, 1836.

4. Diary, January 30, October 6, February 7, April 1, 8, 1837.

ANTISLAVERY WHIG CONGRESSMAN   201

April 2, 1837—I . . . read the printed letter of Gerrit Smith to the Rev. James Smylie, late Stated Clerk of the Presbytery of Mississippi, author of a book in defence of slavery, to which this letter is an answer.[5] I have read scarcely anything upon this controversy, and am quite incompetent to discuss it myself. I come to the conclusion without examining the premises. I have an abhorrence of slavery, but how bad it is no one can imagine without understanding the details. Smylie defends slavery as an institution sanctioned by the Scriptures. But the extermination of the Canaanitish nations was also sanctioned by the Scriptures. The punishment of death was prescribed for a multitude of what we should consider very trivial offences. The theory of the rights of man was then utterly unknown; and Mr. G. Smith shows that the servitude of that time was a milder condition than the slavery of the present age and of this country. This subject of slavery, to my great sorrow and mortification, is absorbing all my faculties.

April 19, 1837—I answered a letter from John G. Whittier,[6] inviting me, on the part of the Managers of the Massachusetts Anti-Slavery Society, to attend the meeting of the New England Anti-Slavery Convention at Boston, to be held on the last Tuesday of May.[7] I have not absolutely declined to attend, but have assigned reasons for not attending which will probably be decisive to my own mind. Upon this subject of anti-slavery my principles and my position make it necessary for me to be more circumspect in my conduct than belongs to my nature. I have, therefore, already committed indiscretions, of which all the political parties avail themselves to proscribe me in the public

5. Gerrit Smith, *Letter of Gerrit Smith to Rev. James Smylie: of the State of Mississippi* (New York: R. G. Williams, 1837).
6. John Greenleaf Whittier was a Quaker poet and one of the leading lights of New England abolitionism.
7. In this letter Adams asked Whittier and other abolitionists to respect the sincerity of his difference of opinion with them on abolition in general and in the district, and assuring them that if he did not accept their invitation it would be due to no disrespect of them on his part. He also asked Whittier to consider that while he had only advocated the right of petition rather than calling for abolition, that had "brought down upon myself the bitterest animosities of the South, and of the whole slave representation in the House, without being sustained by one single member upon the floor." He seemed to be suggesting that if this limited stance proved hopeless, anything smacking more truly of abolitionism would be only more so. See John Quincy Adams to Whittier, April 19, 1837, Adams Family Papers, Microfilm Edition, MHS.

opinion. The most insignificant error of conduct in me at this time would be my irredeemable ruin in this world, and both the ruling political parties are watching with intense anxiety for some overt act by me to set the whole pack of their hireling presses upon me.

It is also to be considered that at this time the most dangerous of all the subjects for public contention is the slavery question. In the South, it is a perpetual agony of conscious guilt and terror attempting to disguise itself under sophistical argumentation and braggart menaces. In the North, the people favor the whites and fear the blacks of the South. The politicians court the South because they want their votes. The abolitionists are gathering themselves into societies, increasing their numbers, and in zeal they kindle the opposition against themselves into a flame; and the passions of the populace are all engaged against them. The exposure through which I passed at the late session of Congress was greater than I could have imagined possible; and, having escaped from that fiery furnace, it behooves me well to consider my ways before I put myself in the way of being cast into it again.

On the other hand, may God preserve me from the craven spirit of shrinking from danger in the discharge of my duty! Between these two errors let me pursue the path of rectitude unmoved, and put my trust in God.

Although Adams was approaching the age of seventy, he proved himself a dedicated worker in gathering and presenting abolitionist petitions.[8] Far from shirking this onerous work, as the congressional session wound down he sought ways to become more efficient in the future.

April 28, 1837—The abolition Petitions which I received in the course of the Session, nearly 300 in number; a large portion of them accompanied with Letters and the . . . persecution which they excited against me so entirely absorbed my faculties, that they disconcerted all my system of orderly method, and warned me that if please God to spare me for attendance at the 25th Congress I must adopt an improved method at least for assistance to my failing Memory.

8. See, for example, Diary, January 31, April 24, September 15, 1837; January 29, February 4, 8, March 4, September 7, 8, 10, 17, 18, October 19, 1838.

Adams's return to Massachusetts between congressional sessions brought him into more regular contact with that state's radical abolitionists. These encounters were apt to feature "argumentative conversation." When the town leaders of Newburyport, Massachusetts, invited Adams to address their July 4 fete that summer, he used the occasion to articulate a strongly Whig-flavored antislavery position. At this celebration of the Declaration of Independence, he urged that it was for the current generation to uphold that document's spirit of national unity and popular rights against threats including Southern nullifiers' extreme doctrine of state sovereignty. Supporters of the Declaration must uphold its ideal of "Union as one People,—*Union* so as to be divided by no act whatever.*" It was no surprise, he offered, that apostasy from the Declaration was centered "in that portion of the Union, the civil institutions of which are most infected with the gangrene of slavery," which was itself a great contradiction of the founding document's ideals. It was also no wonder that the slaveholding authors of the gag rule "shrink from the light of free discussion," but Northerners must resist slavery's attempted "conquest over the domain of freedom." Emancipation, he added, would be a blessed part of the overall improvement of man, and no true believer in Christianity would hear "of impossibilities, when human improvement is the theme."[9] Though he ended with this apparently gratuitous passage yearning for the abolition of slavery, this speech—with its emphasis on Union and the ideal of Improvement—was in all other respects eminently Whiggish rather than abolitionist. And in his diary, he revealed personal and political reasons for the distance between himself and abolitionists.*

September 1, 1837—I then went to the Anti-Slavery office, 223 Arch Street; thence to Samuel Webb's house, and afterwards to Benjamin Lundy's office. I saw and had long conversations with them both, and with two or three others whom I found with them. . . . Lundy returned with me to my lodgings. He and the abolitionists generally are constantly urging me to indiscreet movements, which would ruin me and weaken and not strengthen their cause. My own family, on the other

9. Diary, June 6, 14, August 1, 1837; John Quincy Adams, *An Oration Delivered before the Inhabitants of the Town of Newburyport, at Their Request, on the Sixty-First Anniversary of the Declaration of Independence, July 4th, 1837* (Newburyport, MA: Morss and Brewster, 1837), quotations on 48, 50, 52, 53, 55.

hand—that is, my wife and son and Mary—exercise all the influence they possess to restrain and divert me from all connection with the abolitionists and with their cause.[10] Between these adverse impulses my mind is agitated almost to distraction. The public mind in my own district and State is convulsed between the slavery and abolition questions, and I walk on the edge of a precipice in every step that I take.

As Adams found himself marginalized in the House as an antislavery Whig, the twin foes of slavery and the Democratic Party merged ever closer in his mind.[11] The occasion of the second entry here was a debate over a Democratic banking measure.

September 11, 1837—The standing committees were announced ... [the chairs of the leading ones being] all rank Van Burenites. I am still Chairman of the Committee of Manufactures, which has this session nothing to do. [James] Buchanan, of Pennsylvania, a new member, is Chairman of the Committee of Elections; three others of the members are new; a majority slave-holders, and a majority, though not the same persons, Administration men. ... There are six slave-holders upon the Committee upon the District of Columbia, with [James] Bouldin, of Virginia, at their head. The party drill on both points, of slavery and Administration, is complete.

October 10, 1837—The Divorce or Sub-Treasury bill from the Senate was called up—not by [Churchill C.] Cambreleng [of New York], but by [Francis W.] Pickens, of South Carolina, who ... is a fixture to the house of Calhoun, and Van Buren bought him with Calhoun. ... Pickens is a coarse sample of the South Carolina school of orator statesmen—pompous, flashy, and shallow. [Hugh] Legaré [of South

10. For some useful speculation on these family members' reasons for an anti-abolitionist position, see Alison T. Mann, "Slavery Exacts an Impossible Price: John Quincy Adams and the Dorcas Allen Case, Washington, D.C." (PhD diss., University of New Hampshire, 2010), ch. 3. That family connection to slavery that Mann demonstrates, including at times a slave working in Adams's own household, may well explain his feeling of helplessness in the face of this stubborn, deeply entrenched institution. For a brief diary glimpse of how African American labor affected Adams's household and working life in Washington, see Diary, December 26, 1838.
11. See also Diary, September 28, 1837.

Carolina] is another, much more polished, better educated, and better disciplined; a fine speaker, a brilliant scholar, but yet a shallow bottom. He opposed the taking up of this bill; but it was carried against him. Pickens's speech was a jumble of indigested political economy, of abuse upon Jackson for his war against the bank, of abuse, repeated from Calhoun, upon banks, banking, and the bank, of South Carolina nullification, of slave-driving autocracy, and of ranting radicalism. He said, if the abolitionists of the North would preach insurrection to the Southern slaves, he would retort upon them by preaching insurrection to the laborers against the capitalists of the North. He said he supposed he should pass for a Loco-foco;[12] but he had recently heard it said that John Milton[13] was a Loco-foco. Then he passed a panegyric upon John Milton as the intrepid supporter of the *rights of man*, and concluded that if John Milton was a Loco-foco he was content to be called so too. All this was delivered with an air of authority and a tone of dogmatism as if he was speaking to his slaves.

The following entry signals Adams's first awareness of a case that would take up much of his attention, the tragic case of a re-enslaved woman, Dorcas Allen, who had killed two of her children after they had been sold to a slave trader. After careful inquiry, Adams would end up intervening by donating fifty dollars to help liberate Allen. Although he saw the case itself as a clear-cut one of both "illegality" and "iniquity" by slave drivers, he would never be sure that he had "not imprudently engaged myself in this matter."[14] In this diary entry Adams captured the complexity and the pathos of the incident, and reflected directly on what a tightrope slavery was for him at this point in his career. It is also curious that he ended his written contemplations in despondency over the political prospects of antislavery, given that in recent sessions of Congress he clearly was far from alone in fighting the gag rule. Several other Northern congressmen boldly presented petitions in challenge to that rule and Adams held strategy meetings with them, so that a more optimistic

12. A newly minted slang term, used derisively by Whigs, for radical Democrats, usually those centered in New York who emphasized working men's rights.
13. Presumably this is the revered seventeenth-century English poet.
14. See Diary, October 28, 30, November 1, 2, 9, 13, 1837. For an extended study of this case that gives full attention to Adams's part, see Mann, "Slavery Exacts an Impossible Price."

(and perhaps a less self-important) man might have felt himself at the head of a slowly growing movement.[15]

October 23, 1837—There was in the National Intelligencer this morning an advertisement signed James H. Birch, and Edward Dyer, auctioneer, headed "Sale of Slaves"—a sale at public auction, at four o'clock this afternoon, of Dorcas Allen and her two surviving children, aged about seven and nine years (the other two having been killed by said Dorcas in a fit of insanity, as found by the jury who lately acquitted her). The advertisement further says that the said slaves were purchased by Birch, on the 22d of August last, of Rezin Orme, warranted sound in body and in mind; that the terms of sale will be cash, as said slaves will be sold on account of said Rezin Orme, who refuses to retake the same and repay the purchase-money, and who is notified to attend said sale and, if he thinks proper, to bid for them, or retake them, as he prefers, upon refunding the money paid and all expenses incurred under the warranty given by him.

I asked Mr. Frye[16] what this advertisement meant. He seemed not to like to speak of it, but said the woman had been sold with her children, to be sent to the South and separated from her husband; that she had killed two of her children, by cutting their throats, and cut her own to kill herself, but in that had failed; that she had been tried at Alexandria for the murder of her children, and acquitted on the ground of insanity; and that this sale now was by the purchaser at the expense of the seller, upon the warranty that she was sound in body and mind.

I called at the office of the National Intelligencer, and saw Mr. Seaton;[17] enquired of him concerning the advertisement of the sale of slaves in the paper of this morning. He answered with reluctance, and told me the same story that I had heard from Mr. Frye, adding that there was something very bad about it, but without telling me what it was. It is a case of conscience with me whether my duty requires or forbids me to pursue the enquiry in this case—to ascertain all the facts and expose

---

15. See Diary, September 26, October 2, December 7, 1837; January 5, 15, 1838.
16. Adams's brother-in-law and longtime DC resident Nathaniel Frye.
17. William W. Seaton, long-standing publisher of this influential paper.

them in all their turpitude to the world. The prohibition of the internal slave-trade is within the constitutional power of Congress, and, in my opinion, is among their incumbent duties. I have gone as far upon this article, the abolition of slavery, as the public opinion of the free portion of the Union will bear, and so far that scarcely a slave-holding member of the House dares to vote with me upon any question. I have as yet been thoroughly sustained in my own State; but one step further and I hazard my own standing and influence there, my own final overthrow, and the cause of liberty itself for indefinite time, certainly for more than my remnant of life. Were there in the House one member capable of taking the lead in this cause of universal emancipation, which is moving onward in the world and in this country, I would withdraw from the contest, which will rage with increasing fury as it draws to its crisis, but for the management of which my age, infirmities, and approaching end totally disqualify me. There is no such man in the House.

Adams's record of a conversation with a leader of the ACS gave him the opportunity to identify where he stood on the antislavery spectrum. By the late 1830s, the Northern supporters of the ACS had become well known for a conservative brand of antislavery sentiment that both alarmed many slaveholders and disappointed many radical abolitionists.

October 31, 1837—Mr. R. R. Gurley, a Secretary of the Colonization Society, . . . called upon me. He mentioned that he had it in contemplation to set up here a periodical journal partly religious and partly political, but chiefly to promote the objects and views of the Colonization Society. He proposed at the same time an unqualified approbation of my course in Congress upon the subject of Texas and of the right of petition—I told him that I was much gratified at having the assurance of his approbation upon my conduct on trying questions—That my own views, with regard to the abolition of slavery throughout the United States, concurred more with those which I understood to be avowed by the leading members of the Colonization Society than with those of the Abolition and Anti-Slavery Societies in general. But that to be frank and candid with him, I did not think it possible that a paper to be conducted on the principles which he had exposed could be sustained in this place. It would be as the Colonization Society itself is obnoxious to both the opposite parties—to the abolitionists and to the Slave-holders. I believed there would henceforth be no middle term between them. After a long conversation with him, which more fully confirmed me in those opinions, he left me, apparently not convinced by my remarks, but admitting that he had little to say in reply to them—.

Adams likewise diagnosed a polarizing political climate over slavery in his perspicacious analysis of the politics of slavery in Massachusetts and how that would end up resonating nationally. He was proved correct in every one of his predictions of the short- and long-term political consequences for Edward Everett in his public answers to these election-year abolitionist queries.[18]

November 7, 1837—I found at the office a Boston daily advertiser, containing Letters from a Mr. Atwill[19] and from William Jackson to Governor Edward Everett, about his opinions concerning the abolition of Slavery in the District of Columbia, and the annexation of Texas to this Union, with his answers—He is somewhat embarrassed, with his opinions heretofore expressed upon Slavery; but he is explicit enough now, and will lose very few if any votes this year for his anti-abolitionism—It will give him trouble hereafter—

Although he was not possessed of a political tin ear, Congressman Adams was no more a man of the people in the Jacksonian sense than President Adams had been. Jacksonian democracy run wild was the sort of mobocracy that threatened "the cause of human freedom" as he now understood it. This was part of why he read slavery and freedom into President Van Buren's first annual message to Congress, despite admitting that "in the message there was not a word about" slavery.[20]

18. See Matthew Mason, *Apostle of Union: A Political Biography of Edward Everett* (Chapel Hill: University of North Carolina Press, 2016), ch. 4–5. The "trouble hereafter" was when Southern senators attempted to block his confirmation as US minister to Britain in 1841, citing his election-year letters to abolitionists.
19. Winthrop Atwill, Whig-leaning editor of the *Northampton Courier,* who had written to Everett inviting him to defend himself against abolitionist attacks.
20. Diary, December 5, 1837.

November 22, 1837—There was a riotous assemblage of people, perhaps three hundred in number, with a cannon, who went round last
night to the President's house and the houses of some of the heads of
Departments, discharged their cannon, and made much disturbance,
in celebration of the Whig victories in the late elections, especially in
the State of New York. I heard little of it myself, though it once awoke
me out of sleep, and I knew not what it was. This effervescence of
popular feeling is too common and too little discountenanced by any of
the predominant parties; both of them use the populace to glorify their
triumphs and to depress their enemies, and both of them suffer for it
in turn. The most atrocious case of rioting which ever disgraced this
country happened on the night of the 7th of this month at Alton, in the
State of Illinois, where a man by the name of [Elijah P.] Lovejoy, one
of the leading abolitionists of the time, has been striving to establish a
newspaper. . . . [The mob] shot Lovejoy dead. . . .

This Lovejoy wrote me a letter last January, which I answered in
April.[21] He was a man of strong religious, conscientious feeling, deeply
indignant at what he deemed the vices and crimes of the age. Such men
are often fated to be martyrs; and he has fallen a martyr to the cause of
human freedom.

December 5, 1837—The message gave me a fit of melancholy for
the future fortunes of the country. Cunning and duplicity pervade
every line of it. The sacrifice of the rights of Northern freedom to
slavery and the South, and the purchase of the West by the plunder of
the public lands, is the combined system which it discloses. It is the
system of Jackson's message of December, 1832, covered with a new
coat of varnish. Jackson was dashing and daring; this man is insinuat-
ing and plausible.

*Adams found it increasingly curious that the agitation of the petitions issue by
Adams and his allies provoked hysterics in slaveholding congressmen, despite
the fact that the latter controlled the levers of power and habitually used
them to defend slavery. In the following entries it becomes clear that Southern*

---

21. In this letter Adams agreed with Lovejoy's dire estimate of the low levels of public
  morality prevalent among the leaders of the United States of both parties. See John
  Quincy Adams to Lovejoy, April 15, 1837, Adams Family Papers, MHS.

histrionics and abuse of power combined to sustain his efforts and encourage him to come out openly on the relevant issues.

December 20, 1837—Slade's[22] motion of Monday, to refer a petition for the abolition of slavery and the slave-trade in the District of Columbia to a select committee, came up.

Polk, the Speaker, by some blunder, had allowed Slade's motion for leave to address the House in support of the petition without putting the question of laying on the table. So Slade to-day got the floor, and, in a speech of two hours on slavery, shook the very hall into convulsions. Wise, Legaré, Rhett, Dawson, Robertson,[23] and the whole herd were in combustion. Polk stopped him half a dozen times, and was forced to let him go on. The slavers were at their wits' end. At last one of them *objected* to his proceeding, on the pretence that he was discussing slavery in Virginia, and on this pretence, which was not true, Polk ordered him to take his seat. A motion to adjourn, made half a dozen times before out of order, was now started, and carried by yeas and nays.

Formal notice was immediately given by a member of a meeting of all the slave-holding members in the chamber of the Committee on the District of Columbia. Most, if not all, of the South Carolina members had left the hall.

December 21, 1837—H.R.U.S. The journal had disfigured and falsified the transactions [of the day previous]. Slade moved to amend the journal so as to state the facts correctly; but his motion was rejected. Patton[24] had a resolution ready drawn, agreed upon at the slavery meeting of yesterday—a resolution ... that no petitions relating to slavery or the trade in slaves in any State, district, or Territory of the United States shall be read, printed, committed, or in any manner acted upon by the House.

I objected to the reception of the resolution, and Patton moved to suspend the rules; which was carried—one hundred and thirty-six to

22. William Slade, a Vermont Whig who had become a key Adams ally.
23. Henry A. Wise (Whig, Virginia), Hugh Legaré (Democrat, South Carolina), Robert Barnwell Rhett (Democrat, South Carolina), William C. Dawson (Whig, Georgia), John Robertson (Whig, Virginia).
24. John M. Patton (Democrat, Virginia).

sixty-five; and, after a speech, he moved the previous question; which was carried, as was the resolution.

When my name was called, I answered, "I hold the resolution to be a violation of the Constitution, of the right of petition of my constituents, and of the people of the United States, and of my right to freedom of speech as a member of this House."

I said this amidst a perfect war-whoop of order. In reading over the names of the members, the Clerk omitted mine. I then mentioned it, and the Speaker ordered the Clerk to call my name again. I did not answer, but moved that my answer when first called should be entered on the journal. The Speaker said the motion was not in order; that the only answer that could be given was aye or no. I moved that my motion might be entered on the journal, with the decision of the Speaker that it was not in order; to which he made no answer.

December 22, 1837—H.R.U.S. On the reading of the journal, I found my motion, yesterday made, to insert on the journal my answer to the gag resolution. I moved to amend the journal, by inserting that when my name was called, I rose, and said, "I hold the resolution to be a violation of the Constitution of the United States, of the right of petition of my constituents, and of the people of the United States, and of my right to freedom of speech as a member of this House."

Boon[25] asked if my motion was debatable. I said I hoped it was, and that the House would allow me to debate it. Boon moved to lay my motion on the table. I asked for the yeas and nays, but they were refused, and the motion was laid on the table; but my answer was entered on the journal.

Patton had come charged with a speech to prevent the entry upon the journal. Boon's motion to lay mine on the table balked him, and I bantered him upon his resolution, till he said that if the question ever came to the issue of war, the Southern people would march into New England and conquer it.

I said I had no doubt they would if they could, and that it was what they were now struggling for with all their might. I told him that I entered my resolution on the journal because I meant his name should go down to posterity damned to ever-lasting fame.

25. Ratliff Boon (Democrat, Indiana).

He forced a smile, and said we should then go down together. I replied, precisely; side by side; that was what I intended. So conscious was he of the odious character of his resolution that he dared not resent these remarks, but he dared not object to Boon's motion to lay mine on the table; which precisely answered my purpose, of having my answer entered upon the journal. He soon after rose from his seat and left the House.

These provocations by slaveholders failed to push Adams into the abolitionist camp. Instead, he remained the go-to man for Northern Whigs who wanted help negotiating their partisan and antislavery loyalties.[26] *He had a Christmas gift for those who wished to stake out non-abolitionist ground from which to assault the gag rule.*

December 25, 1837—H.R.U.S. Four members from New York— Fillmore, Marvin, Mitchell, and Peck[27]—came and requested me to draw up a paper to address to their constituents, assigning their reasons for voting against the resolution for laying all abolition petitions on the table. They said they wished to guard against the imputation of favoring abolitionism, but to adhere inflexibly to the right of petition. I drew up, accordingly, a sketch of an address to the people of the State of New York according to their ideas.

December 26, 1837—H.R.U.S. I gave to Mr. Fillmore the paper that I had, at the request of him and his three colleagues, drawn up, and told him it was entirely at their disposal, to use in whole or in part, or to alter or reject, as they might please. He said it was rumored to be the intention of the members from New York who voted for the speech-smothering resolution to address the people on their side.

26. See also Diary, January 5, 1838.
27. Millard Fillmore, Richard P. Marvin, Charles F. Mitchell, and Luther C. Peck, all Whigs. A search of the *Daily Commercial Advertiser* (Buffalo) and of Gale's Nineteenth Century U.S. Newspapers database for late December and early January finds no such address, nor does it appear to have been printed in pamphlet form. These congressmen may have decided that it would be drowned out in much of New York by the explosive news of conflict along the state's border with Canada, which dominated newspapers' columns in these weeks.

Even as Adams served as a lightning rod for the gag and Texas controversies, he recoiled when he thought he saw needless sectional strife in this era of escalating conflict.[28] *Such was his reaction to a Washington Presbyterian minister's sermon, and may explain his declining of an invitation from Pennsylvania abolitionists a few days later.*[29] *It certainly helps account for his nuanced position on abolition in the District of Columbia, and for his sense that he was walking a treacherous (if rewarding) path with his gag rule fight.*

January 7, 1838—It was a review of the transactions of the past year occasional for the first Sunday of the present. There were allusions to the suppression of the Freedom of Speech and of the Press, which I thought bolder than most of his auditory would relish; for in this community there is now no freedom even of thought upon of any topic tainted with Slavery. . . . [Thus, this minister's engagement of the issue of] freedom of speech, though very guarded [was] not suited to his own success in this meridian—I thought his Sermon this day imprudent, for alluding at all to the rights of human Nature—He bewailed in pathetic terms the deep dissensions of the Presbyterian Church, which flow from the same cause, Slavery, though he did not mention it, and which in the course of the last year has terminated in a schism—But in other respects, he affirmed that the cause of religion and morality had made cheering progress in the course of the year—

January 20, 1838—I answered a letter from Samuel Webb and William H. Scott, of Philadelphia, inviting me to deliver an address to the Pennsylvania Hall Association upon the opening of the hall which they are erecting in that city for free discussion; to be opened about the first week in May.[30] I declined.[31]

28. See also Diary, January 24, February 14, 1838.
29. For other examples of Adams refusing abolitionist speaking invitations, see Diary, July 24, 28, 1838.
30. For the turbulent, brief history of this hall, see Beverly C. Tomek, *Pennsylvania Hall: A "Legal Lynching" in the Shadow of the Liberty Bell* (New York: Oxford University Press, 2013).
31. In this intriguing letter, Adams anticipated that if he were to speak at this event, the anti-abolitionists of Philadelphia would attack him not only as an incendiary but also as an outsider who had no business lecturing Philadelphians on the first principles of the American Republic. "I should have no answer," he admitted,

January 23, 1838—T. T. Whittlesey, one of the members from Connecticut who voted against the resolution of 21st December,[32] sought a conversation with me upon the subject, and asked my opinion of the abolition of slavery in the District of Columbia. I told him I had always been against it, and that I thought the South had been ill advised in putting the issue upon the right of petition. I said I should move to rescind that resolution. He said he must adhere to the vote he had given for this session, because it would otherwise appear as if he had yielded to a threat, but at the next session he would vote for referring the petitions.

January 28, 1838—I received this day thirty-one petitions, and consumed the whole evening in assorting, filing, endorsing, and entering them on my list, without completing the work. With these petitions I receive many letters, which I have not time to answer. Most of them are so flattering, and expressed in terms of such deep sensibility, that I am in imminent danger of being led by them into presumption and puffed up with vanity. The abolition newspapers—the Liberator, Emancipator, Philanthropist, National Enquirer, and New York Evangelist, all of which are regularly sent to me—contribute to generate and nourish this delusion, which the treacherous, furious, filthy, and threatening letters from the South on the same subject cannot sufficiently counteract. My duty to defend the free principles and institutions is clear; but the measures by which they are to be defended are involved in thick darkness. The path of right is narrow, and I have need of a perpetual control over passion.

For all the nuance of his own position, Adams was losing patience with Northern congressmen who hesitated to join his crusade. Disheartened to find Massachusetts Whig members particularly divided about how to respond to the gag rule and related issues, he questioned his longtime allegiance to the Whig Party. His disgust with the famous millennialist preacher Harriet Livermore, when taken with his response to the sermon of January 7, makes one wonder how ministers could win with him.

"satisfactory to myself to give to such enquiries." So while he strongly encouraged free discussion of slavery in Philadelphia, he believed "that voice must come from among themselves." See John Quincy Adams to Webb and Scott, January 19, 1838, Adams Family Papers, MHS.

32. See entry for December 21, 1837.

March 7, 1838—It is evident that they are all averse to any action which may countenance the anti-slavery excitement at home. Their wish is as much as possible to suppress it. Their policy is dalliance with the South; and they care no more for the right of petition than is absolutely necessary to satisfy the feeling of their constituents. They are jealous of Cushing, who, they think, is playing a double game. They are envious of my position as the supporter of the right of petition; and they truckle to the South, to court their favor for Webster.[33] He is now himself tampering with the South on the slavery and the Texas questions. [Stephen C.] Phillips differs from the rest in opinion, but does not venture to part from them in policy. [Richard] Fletcher ... is a cipher, and will drop from his seat or decline a re-election. I will keep with them as long as I possibly can, but may be forced to separate from them, even before the close of the present session of Congress.

June 3, 1838—I took Mary and her daughter Fanny with me this morning to the Capitol, where, in the Representative Hall, Harriet Livermore preached from Luke xxiii. 34: "Then said Jesus, Father, forgive them; for they know not what they do"—a discourse, on the absolute and unqualified forgiveness of injuries. Indirectly only against duelling; not even indirectly against slavery.

As Adams continued to find ways to challenge the gag rule, he received anti-slavery resolutions from his state's legislature. His attempt to introduce these resolutions, and Southerners' attempts to gag them, raised the issue of whether the personal abuse they had directed to him would be carried over to a sovereign state's legislature. The mingling of the gag issue with that of Texas only ratcheted up the tensions that led to such hostile treatment of states and their representatives.[34]

June 4, 1838—The presentation of petitions took not more than two hours. . . . I stated that I had received certain resolutions of the Legislature of Massachusetts, adopted at their recent session, relating to slavery

33. A reference to Daniel Webster's perpetual presidential ambition in this era, which almost all Massachusetts Whigs supported.
34. For more of Adams's reactions to perceived mistreatment in the House, see Diary, June 23, 1838.

and the slave-trade in the District of Columbia and in the Territories, which, under ordinary circumstances, I should deem it my duty now to present. But it would be recollected by the House that last week one of my colleagues, W. B. Calhoun,[35] had presented to the House certain resolutions of the same Legislature of a kindred character, though not the same. They related to the admission into the Union of any new State with a Constitution tolerating the existence of slavery within its borders; that the Speaker of the House, by a construction, which I deemed erroneous, of the resolution of the 21st of December last, had decided that those resolutions presented by my colleague should be laid on the table without being read, printed, referred, or considered; that my colleague, on a subsequent day, had applied to the House for leave to withdraw those resolutions, with the avowed purpose of making known to his constituents and mine the manner in which they had been treated by the House; that this leave had been granted, and that, afterwards, my colleague had offered a resolution, now pending, for the future consideration of the House, declaring that the order of the 21st of December, 1837, shall not be construed to include the resolutions of any State Legislature; that I should not now present the resolutions of the Legislature of Massachusetts, with which I was charged, but should reserve them until, by the action of the House upon the resolution offered by my colleague, it should be ascertained whether the resolutions of the Legislature of my native Commonwealth would be treated by this House with the respect to which they are entitled, or with contempt.

While I was making this statement, [John] Campbell, of South Carolina, first rose and made a question of order.

The Speaker said that if I had resolutions of the Legislature of Massachusetts to present....[36] I said I was stating to the House the reasons why I should not present them, and must, therefore, necessarily refer to the proceedings of the last week and the resolution offered by my colleague. There were two or three other faint calls to order before I finished, and the Speaker was apparently much inclined to arrest me, but did not venture to do so. I went through.

35. William B. Calhoun, a Massachusetts Whig.
36. These ellipses are Adams's.

June 5, 1838—Waddy Thompson [of South Carolina], with more candid disclosure of real purpose, opposed the bill [surveying boundaries between Wisconsin and neighboring states and territories] on the avowed ground of maintaining the balance of power between the slave-holding and non-slave-holding States. He said he would never consent, and hoped no Southern man would ever vote for making new Territories or admitting new States from the Northwest into the Union, so long as the Northern fanatics were pouring in floods of petitions against the admission of that great and glorious people of Texas which had applied for admission into our Union, as was desired most earnestly by a large portion of our own country, and for which proposals in this House had been made, but not considered.

June 6, 1838—I took the occasion, while up, of answering Waddy Thompson's declaration that he would vote for no new Northern Territory while Northern fanatics were pouring in petitions against the annexation to this Union of the great and glorious republic of Texas. I objected to the peculiar glory of Texas, which consisted of having made of a land of freemen a land of slaves. I said we had too much of that sort of glory already, and was proceeding to illustrate by the achievements of the late Philadelphia mobs,[37] when the stunning cries of "Order!" emboldened the Speaker to order me to take my seat.

Thompson entreated that I might be allowed to proceed, insisting that I was strictly in order. But I had said as much as I wished to say then, and I did not appeal from the Speaker's decision.

Abolitionists with a political bent never stopped seeking to more fully enlist Adams. The message of political abolitionist Alanson St. Clair was consistent with other evidence that antislavery was becoming a force to be reckoned with in Northern politics.

July 27, 1838—A Mr. St. Clair was here the whole afternoon; an agent of the State Anti-Slavery Society—Long and various conversation with him—He spoke of a public enquiry of my Sentiments as to the expediency of immediate abolition of slavery in the District of Columbia.

37. Who burned Pennsylvania Hall just weeks previous; see Tomek, *Pennsylvania Hall.*

Enquired what would be the prospect of preventing the admission of a Slave State in Florida. Exceedingly sanguine as to the growth and spread of abolitionism. Thinks the abolitionists hold the balance of power now in all the free states; and that in six years they will have strength enough to abolish slavery in the District—He said Isaac Knapp[38] wished to give an order for 1000 copies of my pamphlet speech, and I gave him the names of Gales and Seaton to whom he might apply for them—[39]

One of the latest tactics of the gag rule's proponents was to argue that women had no business petitioning Congress, because many of the abolitionist petitions had come from women. To prepare a response, Adams researched past examples of women's public engagement that most American men had deemed acceptable.[40] Thus armed, he told a gathering of ladies in Quincy, Massachusetts, that their antislavery petitioning constituted lofty patriotism, not sordid politics. Such a conception of this controversy surely also sustained Adams's own efforts.

September 4, 1838—I then addressed the ladies for about five minutes, thanking them for their kindness, and alluding to the testimonials of approbation and confidence which I had received last summer from the men of this Congressional district after the fiery trial of the preceding winter. I said that this had made a deep and abiding impression upon my heart, but that at the two sessions of the present Congress new trials, of a different character, had come, in which the rights and the reputation of the women of my country, and particularly of the district, were involved. I stated the number of petitions which I had received from the several towns in the district from women; the violent outrage by the Chairman of the Committee of Foreign Affairs, Howard,[41]

---

38. Abolitionist publisher, cofounder with William Lloyd Garrison of *The Liberator* and of the New England Anti-Slavery Society.
39. John Quincy Adams, *Speech of John Quincy Adams of Massachusetts, upon the Right of the People, Men and Women, to Petition* . . . (Washington, DC: Gales and Seaton, 1838). Joseph Gales and William W. Seaton were the publishers of the highly influential Washington newspaper the *National Intelligencer*. Knapp was not the only abolitionist who successfully asked Adams if he could copy and distribute this speech; see Diary, August 31, September 4, 1838.
40. See Diary, July 30, 1838.
41. Benjamin Chew Howard (Democrat, Maryland).

upon the petitioners, and the insult upon the sex, which I had felt myself called upon to repel, and the defence of the rights and fair fame of women which ensued. It was to this, I presumed, that I was indebted for the present kind notice of approbation from the ladies of Quincy, and to another of a similar nature in another town of the district. I then made some re-marks on the right of women to petition, and on the propriety of their taking a part in public affairs. This was a point to be left to their own discretion, and there was not the least danger of their obtruding their wishes upon any of the ordinary subjects of legislation—banks, currency, exchange, Sub-Treasuries, internal improvement, tariffs, manufactures, public lands, revenues and expenditures, all which so profoundly agitate the men of the country; the women, so far from intermeddling with them, could scarcely be prevailed upon to bestow a thought upon them; and, knowing that, it was scarcely consistent with civility so much as to name them in their presence. I now alluded to them only to discard them. But, for objects of kindness, of benevolence, of compassion, women, so far from being debarred by any rule of delicacy from exercising the right of petition or remonstrance, are, by the law of their nature, fitted above all others for that exercise. I said I hoped their right would never again be questioned. I was sure if the gentleman who, I believed, in an unguarded and inconsiderate moment had indulged himself by casting the reflection which I so earnestly reprobated could be present to witness the scene now before me, he would never again be tempted to express so ungentle a sentiment. I hoped no member of the House of Representatives of the United States would ever again be found to treat with disrespect the sex of his mother, but would feel for every woman the sentiment which I would now tender in thanks to every female present, whether mother, daughter, wife, or sister, as expressed in the beautiful lines of an English orator and poet—

Had I a heart for falsehood framed, I ne'er could injure you,
For, though your tongue no promise claimed, your charms would
    keep me true.
To *you* no soul can bear deceit, no stranger offer wrong,
But friends in all the aged you'll meet, and lovers in the young.[42]

42. Lines from "Had I a Heart for Falsehood Framed" by Richard Sheridan (1751–1816).

Thus I closed, and then the collation followed.

As the vote on Adams's re-election to the House neared in 1838, the election-eering tactics of both Democrats and abolitionists only increased his distaste for both groups. The latter group again included the public written inter-rogation of candidates regarding their positions on key antislavery issues. In William Ellery Channing, Adams found someone who had a similarly ambiguous relationship with both mainstream Whigs and abolitionists. Adams would go on to win his re-election, but not by the hoped-for comfort-able margin.[43]

November 8, 1838—John A. Green . . . told me that the Administration democrats of this District were to vote for William Morton Jackson of Plymouth, a warm abolitionist against me. They had made no nom-ination but would act in secret concert together. Their choice of an abolitionist to support the Van Buren Administration is a specimen of electioneering honesty.

November 10, 1838—I had a morning visit from Dr. Channing,[44] Dr. Tuckerman, Mr. Phillips, son of the late Lieutenant-Governor Phillips, and Dr. Channing's son. They were here nearly two hours, and I had a long conversation with them upon slavery and anti-slavery, abolition societies, and slave-holding policy.

Dr. Channing asked my opinions upon two points: one, the present test question of the abolitionists—the immediate abolition of slavery in the District of Columbia and the Territory of Florida; and the other, whether, in the event of the adoption of those measures, the Southern States would secede from the Union.

43. See Diary, November 13, 15, 1838.
44. The influential Boston preacher and moral reformer William Ellery Channing. Adams thought that Channing's 1836 pamphlet on slavery, which caused an enormous stir in Boston and beyond, was "an inflammatory, if not an incen-diary, publication," for all its surface smoothness (Diary, January 8, 1836). The others mentioned here include Joseph Tuckerman, Channing's close friend and fellow Unitarian preacher and social reformer. By Phillips he probably referred to Jonathan Phillips, another Boston reformer who was a close friend of Channing; and "the late Lieutenant-General" was probably William Phillips Jr., who served in that capacity from 1812 to 1823 and died in 1827.

I said, first, that to make a test question upon the *immediate* abolition was absurd, and had something captious in it, because it was notoriously impracticable. There is in the present House of Representatives (a majority) of nearly two to one opposed to the consideration or discussion of the subject; and if the proposition should be made, they would refuse to consider it.

Mr. Phillips said he wished I would take some method of publishing this opinion.

I told him of the letter I wrote to Mr. C. P. Kirkland,[45] and said I should probably take some occasion to express similar opinions at the approaching session of Congress; but that my opinions will have no influence upon the abolitionists, who have already given me repeated warnings that they will desert and oppose me if I do not come over to *them* in the creed of *immediate* abolition. I said it was necessary to consider the spirit of abolitionism as a fact as well as a theory—as a phenomenon to be studied, and over which no individual can have much control. As to the second question, I did not believe that the South would dissolve the Union if slavery should be abolished in the District of Columbia and in Florida. South Carolina might perhaps secede, but she could not carry the South with her.

Dr. Channing appeared to entertain great apprehensions for the Union, and deep concern at the violence of the abolition spirit.

---

45. In his response to the queries of this upstate New York abolitionist, Adams declared forthrightly that "I am not for the *immediate* abolition of slavery in the District of Columbia or the Territory of Florida; but I am for the abolition of slavery in both; and throughout the United States, and throughout the Globe; with all practicable diligence and speed." Part of what made both impracticable was that there would be no effective support for either in Congress. But even in principle he would only support abolition in either place if it could "be accomplished without injustice to the white inhabitants . . . and without violation of the Faith pledged in the Constitution of the United States" to slaveholders' and others' property rights. Rather than wishing the Constitution had been otherwise, "I must take it and the Treaties concluded under it as they are; and wait for the appointed time, advancing it [emancipation] by all lawful means in my power when the wrongs of one portion of mankind may be redressed without inflicting wrongs not less deplorable upon the other." See John Quincy Adams to Kirkland, October 15, 1838, Adams Family Papers, MHS.

November 12, 1838—Between breakfast and dinner I visited Dr. Channing. I had a conversation again of two hours or more with him upon the subject of the abolition of slavery. The Doctor was heretofore an idol of the party now calling themselves Whigs, but has become very obnoxious to them. They had almost worshipped him as a saint; they now call him a Jacobin. He is deeply sensitive to this change in his worldly fame, and exceedingly fearful that the abolition cause will go to ruin, or that the abolitionists will stir up an insurrection of slaves and lead to a dissolution of the Union. In his youth he resided some time in Virginia, and is well acquainted with the character of the planters in that State, which, he thinks, has undergone a great and remarkable change since he lived there; that is, within the last forty years. He was then struck with the great and unbounded security in which they lived in the midst of their slaves, and surrounded by them, and nightly at their mercy for their lives. They were also then a people careless of property, improvident, and thriftless, and generally wasting their estates in expenses beyond their means. He thought them now at least as economical, thrifty, and parsimonious as the people of the North. ... The Doctor said there were now at the South many women inclined to favor the abolition of slavery; that in the course of the last summer he had travelled in company with a lady of Baltimore, who told him that she was herself an abolitionist, and that multitudes of Southern women were so at their hearts. But he recurred continually to the fact that the Southern slave-holders would dissolve the Union; said he had heard it had been remarked by Mr. Cushing that there was a growing coldness on the part of the Southern members towards those of the North; and asked me how the Southern members treated me.

I said they all treated me as gentlemen, and most of them with kindness and courtesy; that Mr. Cushing had been desirous of a very intimate personal intercourse with the Southern members, and perhaps had seen some change in their deportment towards him. I had thought it apparent that they generally held in contempt the Northern members who truckled to them, such as John Randolph had nicknamed "dough-faces."[46] But there was so marked a difference between the

---

46. Randolph had originated this derisive term during the Missouri controversy. Adams
    seems to have offered this account of his personal relations with southern members

manners of the South and of the North that their members could never be very intimate personally together. The Doctor appeared to entertain a great distrust of the political action of the abolitionists, and feared they would ruin their own cause and its friends. He asked me to write to him; which I promised to do.

November 24, 1838—I had met Edmund Quincy[47] in the street, and he had promised to come and have some conversation with me this evening. He came, and I conversed with him freely on the political movements of the anti-slavery and abolitionist party. They interrogate all the candidates for the General and State Legislatures what their opinions are upon sundry questions relating to the abolition of slavery; and if the answers are not exactly conformable to their opinions, they vote against the candidate, or scatter their votes to defeat his election. Very few of the candidates answer the questions to their satisfaction, and they show their power by marring the elections. The result of their interposition has been hitherto mischievous, and, I believe, injurious to their own cause. I urged this as strongly as I was able, but apparently without making any impression upon his mind. The moral principle of their interference to defeat elections when they cannot carry them appears to me to be vicious; and I think the first result of their movements will be to bring the two parties together against them. As yet, their political action has only tended to break down the barriers between the parties, the natural consequence of which is to strengthen the Administration which they abhor.[48]

An interaction with an African American charlatan did nothing to improve Adams's view of abolitionists.

of Congress in part to dismiss the effectiveness of the "doughfaces'" strategy of conciliating the South. Given Channing's concerns for the Union, Adams seems to have been trying to assure him—and possibly himself—that his own course of fighting the gag and Texas annexation was not eminently calculated to destroy the Union.

47. A leading Boston political abolitionist.
48. By the end of the 1830s, most political abolitionists came to see the validity of Adams's dim view of the effectiveness of this strategy, pursuing alternatives such as third-party action; see Corey Brooks, "Building an Antislavery House: Political Abolitionists and the U.S. Congress" (PhD diss., University of California—Berkeley, 2010), 22–23, 28–35.

December 10, 1838—A black man came this morning to my house and
sent in a note signed William Lodge asking money for rent; and with
the note, a Bible—I told my waiting man, Moses Smallwood that it
must be a mistake and that the man must be enquiring for some other
person. He then sent in word that he wanted to see me. He came in,
and said that he had got a white man named Reynolds to write the note
for him, but that it was only to get the means of seeing me—That he
had a message to me from the Lord, who had appeared to him, and
commanded him to say to me that the Negroes must be made free.
I enquired of him his name. He said the name given him by his Parents
was that subscribed to the note, William Lodge. But the Lord had given
him the name of John—I asked him of his occupation, and he said
that until last Thursday he had been working with a shoemaker in the
Pennsylvania Avenue, but he had then left him and was now without
work. On further enquiry I found that he had formerly lived with me,
and in the summer of 1830 went with the family to Quincy. He was
then not more than eighteen or nineteen years old, and I was obliged
to turn him off for gross misconduct in the house—The summer afterwards while my son John was living with his family in the House on
the President's Square, in this City, the House was broken open in the
Night and robbed by a gang of which this Messenger from the Lord
was the pilot and perpetrator. He was taken up, and lodged sometime
in jail; but was finally released for want of positive proof to convict
him—I had not heard of him since, and did not recognize him now,
till upon pressing enquiries he acknowledged that he had lived with me
and he said that the Lord had told him that after my father's death his
Estate at Quincy belonged to him—I told him to go away, and to deliver
no more such messages from the Lord to any one for so sure as he did,
he would be taken up, and committed to jail, and sold—That I would
not complain of him to the police, but others would if he should make
any more revelations from the Lord.

*The advent of the Third Session of the Twenty-Fifth Congress saw a renewed
fight over the gag rule. In his effort to amass enough votes to strike it down,
Adams re-emphasized the revered Constitution. Although this session saw
halting progress toward even-handed procedural treatment of the North and*

South, he was not encouraged by the overall result, at least in the short term.[49]
*Neither was he prepared to accept as a merely granted privilege—as opposed
to an absolute right and duty—his ability to speak on the floor of the House.*

December 13, 1838—I . . . offered [my motion]:

> Resolved, that the powers of Congress being conferred by the
> Constitution of the United States, no resolution of this House can
> add to or deduct from them.

Objection was made to its introduction. I moved a suspension of the
rules to introduce it; which was refused, by yeas and nays—seventy-five
to one hundred and twenty-four.

Wise then offered a string of what he called Southern resolutions,
ultra servile; but the suspension of the rules was again refused.

Slade offered a resolution declaring the infamous nature of the
slave-trade as carried on in the District of Columbia, and concluding that therefore so much of [the gag rule] as related to that subject
be rescinded. Suspension of the rules refused—yeas fifty-five, nays one
hundred and fifty-seven.

John Calhoun, of Kentucky, offered a resolution instructing the
Committee on the Judiciary to report bills for enforcing in the non-
slave-holding States the restitution of fugitive slaves. Suspension again
refused. The comparison of the yeas and nays upon these different questions might perhaps lead to some useful conclusions. They indicate the
rallying of the whole South to the Van Buren standard, the close adhesion to it of the Northern and Western serviles, and the total want of
settled principle in the Northern and Western opposition Whigs.

I doubt if there are five members in the House who would vote
for a bill to abolish slavery in the District of Columbia at this time.
The conflict between the principle of liberty and the fact of slavery
is coming gradually to an issue. Slavery has now the power, and falls
into convulsions at the approach of freedom. That the fall of slavery is

49. See also Diary, December 12, 14, 15, 17, 1838; January 7, 1839.

predetermined in the counsels of Omnipotence I cannot doubt; it is a part of the great moral improvement in the condition of man, attested by all the records of history. But the conflict will be terrible, and the progress of improvement perhaps retrograde before its final progress to consummation.

December 22, 1838—I then took up and refuted Legaré's argument [in favor of the gag], but was soon called to order by the Speaker, and by sundry Southern members. I was perfectly in order, and therefore persevered till Bynum objected to my being permitted to proceed. Upon which Briggs[50] moved that I might proceed *in order*. The question was taken by yeas and nays, and the vote was one hundred and fourteen to forty-seven that I might proceed.

The Speaker said, "The leave to proceed is granted;" to which I replied, "Mr. Speaker, I have not asked leave to proceed." But I did proceed.

Adams continued to try to influence the Whig Party without fully identifying himself with the party.

December 25, 1838—Morning visits from my colleagues. Reed, Hastings,[51] and Briggs. There has been a proposal from the Kentucky delegation in the House to ours for a conference on the subject of the next Presidential election; and Cushing asked me one day last week if I would attend such a conference.

I said, no; that, from the peculiar position in which I stood, I had since 1829 taken no part in the Presidential elections, and should take none for the remnant of my life, unless called to vote as a member of the House, in which case I should vote for the candidate favored by the majority of my constituents. I had afterwards some conversation with Mr. Reed, and advised him to suggest caution to the members of our delegation against committing themselves at all to the Kentuckians upon the subject of the Presidency. Reed, whom I met yesterday in the street, said that they had postponed for a week the conference with the

50. Jesse A. Bynum (Democrat, North Carolina) and George N. Briggs (Whig, Massachusetts).
51. John Reed and William S. Hastings, like Briggs, both Massachusetts Whigs.

Kentucky delegation. The Governor of Kentucky and the members of the delegation from that State in the House are now so deeply committed upon all the slavery questions that it is impossible to get the vote of Massachusetts for Mr. Clay; and his only chance of election is by the Southern and slave-holding interest.

The degree to which Adams had changed his political style was revealed in a conversation in which publisher William Seaton sounded very much like the Adams of the 1810s and 1820s. The new Adams was so deeply engaged intellectually with questions surrounding slavery and abolition in America and beyond that he sometimes got carried away. But he never carried himself onto truly abolitionist ground, as the abolitionists themselves were all too willing to remind him. But that went both ways; Adams meant by his two open letters to abolitionist petitioners to put "dampers" on both "their senseless and overbearing clamour" for abolition in the District of Columbia and a growing tendency by antislavery Americans to think him more favorable to their cause than he was.[52]

April 16, 1839—I . . . called at the office of the National Intelligencer and told Mr. Seaton I should to-morrow or the next day bring him a letter to the petitioners who entrusted me with their petitions to be presented to H. R. U. S., to be published with the closing list, and which would cover from four to five columns of the paper.

He appeared to be somewhat shy, and regretting that this subject was to be again agitated. I expected as much, and said if, after reading my manuscript, he should decline to publish it, I would simply notify the petitioners of the fact, and publish the letter in another newspaper; and if so, I should use it as an illustration of the suppression of the freedom of the press, necessarily consequent of the suppression of the right of petition and freedom of speech in the House.

He thought there was another view of the freedom of the press, which consisted of editorial independence in refusing to publish what ought not to be published.

52. See Diary, January 27, March 11, 19, 22, April 6, July 3, 9, 15, 23, August 5, September 28, 1839.

I thought there might be editorial independence in this, but not much freedom of the press.[53]

April 23, 1839—I wrote a Letter to Samuel Webb of Philadelphia; to return as he requested a Letter from him containing his plan for the emancipation of all the Slaves in this Union. Webb proposed to me to bring forward his plan or to return his Letter, which I now do. I intended to write him a Letter of four lines, and wrote four pages, which consumed the morning.[54]

May 21, 1839—I finished my second letter to the Petitioners[55] which I intended to make very powerful but upon reading it over I find so

53. Adams succeeded in getting this paper to print his letter, which was then reprinted and discussed in many other newspapers. He dedicated the bulk of the letter to vindicating the petition as a natural and constitutional right. Only in the last two paragraphs did he reiterate that he did not favor the immediate abolition of slavery either in the District or in Florida, adding that he needed to balance the wishes of these abolitionist petitioners with the dictates of "justice, the Constitution, and prudence." He ended with an emphatic statement that he neither identified himself as an abolitionist nor harbored a wish to lead that movement. *National Intelligencer*, April 23, 1839.

54. Adams told this Philadelphia abolitionist that his "most anxious efforts have been, and still are directed to preserve the free institutions of my native Commonwealth ... from the encroachments and the infection of Slavery." But that was as far as he could go. "To the compromises of the Constitution I must submit," in large part because he had "many times sworn to support the Constitution of the United States." Moreover, he did not believe abolition—which "I would gladly promote"—would be "effected by an arm of flesh, and certainly not by the coercion of Law, against the People." He rather boldly affirmed that while he shared with Christ and his ancient disciples a dedication to "the cause of human freedom," he had learned from their example not to meddle unduly with established governments in pursuit of that cause. In sum, slavery could only be abolished peacefully and constitutionally with consent of the Southern states, and therefore that was the only mode that he could support. See John Quincy Adams to Webb, April 23, 1839, Adams Family Papers, MHS. Adams had taken his time in answering Webb's letter, as Webb had sent him his detailed, seven-page letter prefacing this subject almost two months previous; Webb to Adams, February 28, 1839, Adams Family Papers, MHS. Webb's follow-up letter, detailing his emancipation scheme, does not appear in the relevant "Letters Received" reels of the microfilm edition of the Adams Family Papers.

55. This letter, also widely republished, lamented that so many Americans had retrogressed from the antislavery principles of their Revolution, and assured readers that "I adhere to the ethics of the Revolution." But the immediate abolition of slavery in the District would be "utterly impracticable" given that state of opinion nationwide. He also opposed that measure because it would be forced on the residents of the District without their consent, which would be "contrary to the first principles of our institutions." Indeed, given the core American principle of the

feeble, and at the same time so unsparing that I hesitate whether to send it—I have promised however and cannot consistently withhold my reasons for being opposed to the immediate abolition of Slavery in the District of Columbia, and in the Territory of Florida. There is a great want of method in the composition of this paper, which will not give satisfaction to any party—and there is in it perhaps too little respect for persons—The obligation of meeting adversaries face to face, and the admonitions of Prudence are greatly at variance with each other. This letter weighs much upon my spirits—but it must go.

June 27, 1839—I answered the letter from Henry Williams[56] asking for publication [of] my opinion upon the constitutionality and expediency of the fifteen-gallon license law,[57] and I received a letter from Joshua Leavitt and Henry B. Stanton[58] for the committee of arrangements of the American Anti-Slavery Society, earnestly inviting my attendance at a National Anti-Slavery Convention, to be held at Albany on the 31st of July next. These appeals to me for my opinions upon subjects convulsing the public mind, with the conflict of interest and passions, are at once flattering and perplexing—so flattering that they have an evident tendency to engender self-conceit and a fatuitous over-estimate of my own importance. I ought to know, and never for a moment forget, that my opinion is not of the weight of a straw to influence that of the public upon any great question of politics or of morals.

consent of the governed, it was not for some Americans to impose their beliefs on others. So a massive change of opinion would be required to legitimately abolish slavery anywhere in the South, and unfortunately the abolitionists were impatient, meddling dreamers if they thought this would be accomplished anytime soon. In short, "I adhere faithfully to the stipulations of the Constitution of the United States, which I have pledged my faith before God to support; and I can lend my hand to no project for the abolition of slavery in these United States without the consent of their masters." *National Intelligencer*, May 28, 1839.

56. Williams suggested to Adams that "your written opinion on the subject" would weigh heavily in this controversy. Henry Williams to Adams, June 22, 1839, Adams Family Papers, MHS.

57. A Whig measure banning the sale of alcohol in quantities less than fifteen gallons, which had just passed the Massachusetts legislature. Adams was correct in his prediction that it would redound to the benefit of the Democrats in Massachusetts, including by ousting Governor Everett in the fall 1839 election.

58. Stanton and his wife, Elizabeth Cady Stanton, were among the most prominent of American abolitionists and social reformers.

Common prudence should warn me not to mingle unnecessarily with controversies without a distinct and unequivocal call of duty. And this is the more incumbent upon me because my opinions, without being useful to others, draw down a load of obloquy upon myself, and even upon my family. Yet when my opinions are formally asked, common civility requires an answer; the refusal to give an opinion would manifest either churlishness or a selfish timidity affecting discretion. This license law is an ill-advised measure, intended to promote the virtue of temperance, but infringing the personal freedom and habits of the people. A profligate use of the passions of the people is made to overthrow the present State Administration and turn it to the benefit of Van Buren. And it is among the strange anomalies of party management that the political agency of the anti-slavery party produces the same effect. This National Anti-Slavery Convention will be followed by the same result. My answer to Mr. Williams will not satisfy him, nor anyone else. And while the abolition champions are importuning me to attend their Convention, all their newspapers with one voice have opened in a grand chorus against my letters to the petitioners.

July 14, 1839—I have answered a very earnest invitation of Joshua Leavitt and H. B. Stanton to attend a grand National Anti-Slavery Convention to be held at Albany on the 31st of this month.[59] I have declined attending, on the express ground of my dissent from the declaration of sentiment of the American Anti-Slavery Society of 1835, and especially to the belief and affirmation "That every American citizen who retains a human being in involuntary bondage as his property is (according to Scripture, Exodus xxi. 16) a MAN-STEALER." I have taken a direct issue upon that affirmation with the American Anti-Slavery Society and all its affiliated associations. The conflict is fearful; but, certain as I am that this declaration is neither true nor just, I have no doubt of ultimate success in the encounter.

---

59. This was, like other letters to abolitionists, a respectful but vigorous and in-depth expression of disagreement with the means by which they pursued abolition. In this case he engaged their biblical argument as well, stating flatly that "slaveholding is not man Stealing," and concluding that like other abolitionist extremism, this charge was ultimately counterproductive to their cause. See John Quincy Adams to the Rev. Joshua Leavitt and H. B. Stanton, July 11, 1839, Adams Family Papers, MHS.

Adams remained skeptical enough of both abolitionists and Britons that he investigated but ultimately resisted their claims that emancipation was proving a complete success in the West Indies. This visit was very much of a piece with these political abolitionists' attempts to get American opinion leaders to sign off on this interpretation of the British experiment. In this reaction Adams differed from normally conservative associates such as Edward Everett, but accorded with the majority of Americans.[60]

August 19, 1839—Mr. Francis Jackson and Mr. Edmund Quincy visited me, with Mr. John Scoble, an English abolitionist, who has been travelling in the West Indies, and has been about a month in this country, lecturing upon abolition. . . . Mr. Quincy said they had induced Mr. Scoble to come out to give me any information that I might desire concerning the condition of the English islands where slavery has been abolished. I had much conversation with him. His reports upon the condition of the islands are all rose-colored as to the results of emancipation; but he is evidently a prejudiced and interested witness. As to the ultimate issue, he admitted that the islands must finally pass into the exclusive possession of a mongrel half-breed of African and European blood, from which the white race will gradually retire, but will not be expelled; and that, as a further necessary consequence, the colonial supremacy of England over them will cease.

I spoke of the despotic measures of the English Ministry, suppressing the Legislature of the island of Jamaica to carry through the emancipation laws, and of the convulsions in the English Government itself occasioned thereby. He said that it was all occasioned by the intractable obstinacy of the Legislative Assembly of Jamaica in resisting an Act of Parliament for the reform of the prison. The proposal had only been to suspend the Legislative Assembly of Jamaica for two years and a half, to which it had been reduced from five years. The bill had finally passed in the House of Commons by a majority of ten, but had been thrown out, with the exception of a single section, by the

60. Diary, July 16, 1839, May 1, July 22, 1840; Mason, *Apostle of Union*, ch. 4; Edward Bartlett Rugemer, *The Problem of Emancipation: The Caribbean Roots of the American Civil War* (Baton Rouge: Louisiana State University Press, 2008), 145–290.

House of Peers. Mr. Scoble was much dissatisfied with the compensation granted by the British Parliament to the emancipated slaves'
masters, which, he said, was carried entirely by intrigue, against the
will of the abolitionists. The conversation was animated, but good-
humored, and we parted with all the forms of politeness and civility.

September 22, 1839—[In] the Queen Victoria's speech at the close
of the Session of Parliament . . . the queen declares . . . her determination to persevere in her efforts to persuade all the Christian powers
to abolish the Slave-trade. It is hardly conceivable that if the British
Government were sincere in their zeal for the abolition of the Slave
trade, they should after so many years of negotiation have accomplished
nothing but Treaties. The British Nation drive their Government along
in this Career; but the Government never have been and never will be
hearty in the cause—

*The cautious Adams usually did not provide material aid to enslaved African
Americans who approached him. He completely discounted biblical theories
of the racial inferiority of Africans and lamented his countrymen's treatment
of Native Americans, but those statements hardly ever translated into action
on behalf of supplicants from these groups.*[61] *But as with the Dorcas Allen
incident, the case of the Spanish slaving vessel* Amistad *pulled him in when
a leading Boston abolitionist called his attention to it. The human cargo of
that ship rose in successful rebellion on the high seas, and by surviving the
white crewmen's trickery were able to land in the United States rather than
on the African coast. How to treat these rebels became a hot American and
international political and legal issue. Almost immediately upon hearing of
the case, Adams wrote that it "now absorbs [a] great part of my time and all
my good feelings," as he searched to "make up opinions for which I am willing
to be responsible."*[62]

September 26, 1839—I called . . . at Mr. Ellis Gray Loring's Office and
had some conversation with him concerning his Letter to me on the
case of the Amistad and her cargo of Africans. . . . Mr. Loring was

61. Diary, July 8, December 30, 1838; August 3, 1839; June 30, 1841.
62. Diary, October 1, 2, 7, 1839; January 19, 1840.

extremely anxious to obtain my opinion as to the right of the President to deliver up the negroes, upon the demand of the Spanish Minister yet the time has not yet come when it would be proper for me to give an opinion for publication—Prudence would forbid my giving an opinion upon it at any time; and if I ever do, it must be with great consideration and self-control.

As earthly wrongs including war and slavery in its multiple guises continued to haunt Adams's waking thoughts, he came to the very New England Whig conclusion that abolition could only follow God's unknowable plan. What that meant for his own course on slavery remained at least partially obscure. He tried to work this out in diary entries ranging from poetry to a curious history of the presidency of the United States, written as if he had never been either a candidate or president.

October 19, 1839—On the morning upon which I received John G. Whittier's Letter,[63] I saw Venus, just risen dazzling bright as morning Star. The thought occurred to me of taxing her for some lines for the Philadelphia female Anti-Slavery Society and I have elaborated them thus.

To the Morning Star-Seen Rising 5 A.M. 16 October 1839,

> Bright Star of Morning! Welcome to mine eyes!
>   More lovely, than at even-tide's decay.
>   For now thou comest with the dawning ray;
> And soon the glorious lord of light shall rise
> Anon his splendor shall emblaze the skies;
>   And thy own flame in his shall melt away
>   But mingled with his radiance, thine shall play,
> With lustre, though unseen, that never dies.
> Oh! Morning Star of Man's immortal soul!

63. Whittier wrote on behalf of the Female Anti-Slavery Society of Philadelphia, which was assembling "a small volume of poetry" to sell as a fundraiser. They were soliciting writings from "such of our American Poets as are willing to contribute toward the collection," and Whittier wrote to Adams as a likely contributor. John G. Whittier to Adams, October 11, 1839, Adams Family Papers, MHS.

> When shall thy beams irradiate the pole,
>   Redeeming Earth from Midnight's Ebon Sway?
> Dispel the gloom of Slavery's deadly shade –
> Turn to the plough share Wars ensanguin'd blades;
>   And glow with promise of unclouded day?

December 22, 1839—There was no afternoon church-bell, and I had a day of bodily repose. Of mental repose I can enjoy none while witnessing the wrong that I cannot prevent, and suffering at once from the injustice of man and the chastising hand of Heaven—disease, bereavement, afflictions not to be named, and the temptations of the adversary to conclude, with Brutus, that virtue is but a name. Yet there is in Providence a "vis medicatrix"—a healing, repairing, redeeming hand. Let me never despair of its power, never be weary of well-doing. Perhaps the severest trial of righteousness is the patient fortitude which endures, without yielding to, the perverseness of mankind. In adversity, consider. I employed part of this day in preparing for the presentation of petitions and in assorting papers. Upon that most vexatious and portentous subject of slavery and the slave-trade, I am yet to fix upon the course it will be my duty to pursue. I see clearly that it is not for me to volunteer in bringing it forward, and as clearly that it will be impossible for me to steer clear of it altogether; it will be forced upon me. It will not be for me in walking to direct my steps; may they be directed from above!

January 1, 1840—A very curious philosophical history of parties might be made by giving a catalogue raisonné[64] of the candidates for the Presidency voted for in the Electoral Colleges since the establishment of the Constitution of the United States. It would contain a history of the influence of the Presidential office upon the Government of the United States, and the reaction of the Government upon the President's office. Would not the retrospect furnish as practical principles in the operation of the Constitution—1, that the direct and infallible path to the Presidency is military service coupled with demagogue policy; 2, that, in the absence of military service, demagogue policy is the first and

64. A comprehensive, annotated listing.

most indispensable element of success, and the art of party drilling is the second; 3, that the drill consists in combining the Southern interest in domestic slavery with the Northern riotous Democracy; 4, that this policy and drill first organized by Thomas Jefferson first accomplished his election, and established the Virginia dynasty of twenty-four years, a perpetual practical contradiction of its own principles; 5, that the same policy and drill, invigorated by success and fortified by experience, has now placed Martin Van Buren in the Presidential chair, and disclosed to the unprincipled ambition of the North the art of rising upon the principles of the South; and 6, that it has exposed in broad day the overruling influence of the institution of domestic slavery upon the history and policy of this Union? How this power may be counteracted is no deep mystery; but I have not time to set the machine in motion, and shall say nothing about it, but leave it to posterity to wait the good time of the Lord.

As the crucial presidential election year of 1840 dawned, Adams continued to pose, even in his diary, as the outsider bemused by the sometimes contradictory ways in which partisans both North and South deployed slavery against each other.[65] But his reaction was not so detached when he saw congressmen coming more unequivocally forward to champion his cause. Indeed, he thought that the time might be right to "propose a plan of co-operation" for this growing anti-gag rule group, and he was willing to proceed with caution lest he fracture that nascent coalition.[66] And he was never so indifferent to politics that he would allow that cause to be conflated with that of the abolitionists.

January 20, 1840—On entering the House, I found Mr. Slade on the floor upon Waddy Thompson's resolution for a rule to exclude abolition petitions; into the vortex of which he had drawn the whole subject of slavery, slave-trade, and abolition. He took nearly three hours to conclude the speech that he had commenced on Saturday, and delivered himself of the burden that has been four years swelling in his bosom.

65. See Diary, January 16, 25, April 13, 1840.
66. Diary, February 3, 1840.

January 24, 1840—Bynum spoke nearly four hours, with all his characteristic venom and vehemence and his usual disregard of truth. At an early part of his speech he alluded repeatedly to me, and said I had contended that the people of the South ought to be influenced by the abolition doctrines of foreign English periodical journals and reviews.

I rose, and said, "Mr. Speaker, the gentleman refers to me what I never said."

He persevered, and said, "Well, sir, the gentleman's speech will be published; and, unless he suppresses what he said, it will then appear."

I said, "Mr. Speaker, I never said one word of what the member has imputed to me, nor anything like it; and now he may proceed and impute to me what he pleases."

January 29, 1840—Morning visits from John G. Whittier, Isaac Winslow, and Samuel Mifflin, all of the Society of Friends, and all abolitionists. Whittier is now the editor of the Pennsylvania Freeman newspaper, published weekly at Philadelphia. Whittier said he thought this last outrage upon the right of petition, the establishment of a rule refusing to receive or entertain any abolition petition,[67] might perhaps be the best thing that could have been done to promote the cause of abolition. It was, at least, casting off all disguise.

I said it would depend upon the impression which it would make on the people; and I had little expectation from that. They had been familiarized to the privation of the right, and could not be roused to take an interest in it. The difference between the resolution of the four preceding sessions of Congress and the new rule of the House is the difference between petty larceny and highway-robbery. I had much conversation with these men upon the dissensions among the anti-slavery men and abolitionists, and concerning the late Benjamin Lundy.

February 5, 1840—Meeting of the Massachusetts delegation in the House. . . . It was my wish to present the abolition petitions committed to my charge together with the rest. But the unanimous opinion of all the other members present was, not to offer this day any that they called abolition petitions—that is to say, that touched at all upon slavery—but only business petitions. It was said that by avoiding the obstruction

---

67. A refinement of the gag rule passed the previous day; see Diary, January 28, 1840.

to the presentation of other petitions we should not excite resentment, and that, as the daily receipt of petitions is continued until the 15th of this month, we shall have ample time and occasion to present the anti-slavery petitions between this time. I gave it as my opinion that if we once let slip the opportunity of presenting the anti-slavery petitions, they would never allow us another. I said that I had attended the meeting intending to propose measures of increasing concert and energy to recover the prostrate right of petition; and I mentioned those that I minuted in this diary of the day before yesterday; but, I said, I would not set my face against the whole delegation, and would, accordingly, abstain from presenting any anti-slavery resolutions this day—not even either of the two sets of resolutions of the Legislature of Massachusetts bearing upon slavery.

By 1840, Adams's priorities had so reversed since he had been secretary of state that he joined other antislavery congressmen in pressing the government to investigate every instance of "the abuse of the flag of the United States" in the illicit Atlantic slave trade.[68] What he learned in this process helped convince him that many American slaveholders would stop at nothing to pursue their interests.[69] He needed little convincing in light of continued procedural favoritism toward the South in the House by the new Speaker of the House, Robert M. T. Hunter, and after another interaction with one of slavery's victims.[70]

April 6, 1840—The morning was devoted principally to the perusal of the dispatches from N. P. Trist,[71] Consul of the United States at the Havanna, concerning the fraudulent use of the flag of the United States for carrying on the African slave-trade. They are voluminous, and manifest either the vilest treachery or the most culpable indifference to his duties. For the last three years it is apparent that there has been the most shameful prostitution of the American flag to carry on that traffic; that it has been openly notoriously practised before his face; that as Consul

---

68. Diary, April 2, 1840.
69. See also Diary, May 8, 1840; February 1, March 5–6, 1841.
70. See Diary, February 11, March 9, 1840.
71. Nicholas Trist, a Jackson appointee to Havana, was born in Virginia in 1800 and was deeply connected to the Madisons and other leading Virginia families.

of the United States, and at the same time Acting Consul for Portugal, he has actively lent his aid to it, and, when detected in malpractices by the members of the British and Spanish mixed commission, held a most grossly insulting and insolent correspondence with them, and then, in a long series of letters to the Secretary of State, charges all this unlawful and unhallowed trade to defects in the laws.

There is a very long letter from Mr. Fox[72] to the Secretary of State, denouncing both the abuse of the flag and the conduct of Trist; and Forsyth's[73] answer is as if one of the gang of pirates were appealed to pass sentence upon the rest—an accomplice judge. . . .

I offered [a resolution] to discharge the committee of the whole on the state of the Union from the consideration of so much of the message as relates to this fraudulent use of our flag, and to refer it to the Committee of Commerce, with instructions to investigate the subject and to report a bill to suppress the frauds. Turney[74] objected, and the slavers were all agog.

April 17, 1840—A dark-colored mulatto man, named Joseph Cartwright, a preacher of a colored Methodist church, came this morning with a subscription-book to raise four hundred and fifty dollars to purchase the freedom of his three grandchildren—two girls and one boy, all under three or four years of age. He told me that he had been upwards of twenty years in purchasing his own freedom and that of his three sons; that after this, Henry Johnson, late a member of the House of Representatives from Louisiana, had bought his son's wife and her three children, with many other slaves, to carry them away to Louisiana; that after the purchase he had been prevailed upon to consent to leave them here for a short time in the charge of a man to whom he had ostensibly sold them, but with the consent that this Joseph Cartwright should purchase them for one thousand and twenty-five dollars. He had actually purchased and paid for the mother, and was now endeavoring to raise four hundred and fifty dollars for the three children. There were in the subscription-book certificates of two white Methodist ministers,

72. Henry Stephen Fox, Britain's minister to the United States.
73. Secretary of State John Forsyth of Georgia.
74. Hopkins L. Turney (Democrat, Tennessee).

Hamilton and Cookman, to the respectability of this man—a preacher of the gospel! What a horrible exemplification of slavery!

In his diary reaction to Methodist minister and Senate chaplain George G. Cookman's commentary on Psalm 72:16–20, Adams revealed some ambivalence about whether beneficial changes in mankind's lot were best achieved by patiently awaiting Providence or by human pursuit of improvement.

April 26, 1840—He analyzed and commented with great ingenuity and fervor upon every part of this text, as prophetic of the Messiah's kingdom—of that blessed time when war shall be banished from the earth. The theme is to me delightful. These promises of the Scriptures, these transcendently sublime prophecies of the old covenant, and these practicable means and irresistible tendencies to their fulfilment in the new, are the most precious pledges of my faith. If I did not believe them I should be compelled to reject the whole book. I do most faithfully believe them. Peace—perpetual peace! What an inexpressible blessing to the race of man! Not that I deem it necessary to believe that the nature of carnivorous beasts shall be changed—these I suppose to be figures of speech; but that the murderous and treacherous passions in the heart of man shall be so far eradicated or restrained that there shall be no more public or private war. With the practice of war slavery must of course be extinguished. Mr. Cookman was sufficiently enthusiastic in this belief to gratify me and my faith and hope in the future advent of the kingdom of the Messiah, [and] to pass among my friends for insane. That Christianity has already made immense progress in checking and controlling the anti-social passions of man is undeniable. A religious principle that man has no right to take the life of man will soon accomplish the abolition of all capital punishments, and the principles of liberty are daily rendering the life of man more and more precious.

As his conflict with Southerners and Democrats wore on, Adams's epithets for these enemies multiplied. He branded "the reasonings of the mock democracy" as "venomous sophistical and disingenuous." The "slavers" numbered all too many "party slaves" in their "servile phalanx." One Northern Democrat, he sighed, "would be an honest man if he could." But he was allied with

Southerners who were incapable of "fair dealing," "a compound of wild democracy and iron-bound slavery combined with the feudal cramp of State sovereignty—the mongrel brood of doctrinal nullification."[75] As personal as this rhetoric was, it bespoke his strong conviction that business as usual in Washington threatened the future of his beloved country.

July 25, 1840—The late session of Congress has been painful to me beyond all former experience, by the demonstration which it has given of degenerating institutions. Parties are falling into profligate factions. I have seen this before; but the worst symptom now is the change in the manners of the people. The continuance of the present Administration will, if accomplished, open wide all the flood-gates of corruption. Will a change produce reform? Pause and ponder! Slavery, the Indians, the public lands, the collection and disbursement of public moneys, the tariff, and foreign affairs: what is to become of them?

For all his posturing that he was outside the political mainstream, as voting on his own re-election neared Adams thought political abolitionists no better than party hacks. Although he could easily dismiss as lunacy William Lloyd Garrison's increasingly radical embrace of women's rights and rejection of American government and politics, he found more threatening the work of political abolitionists who for the 1840 election had organized a third party, the Liberty Party.

October 13, 1840—Mr. [Ellis Gray] Loring . . . told me that the administration party of the 12th congressional District had held their meeting yesterday, and had nominated Morton Jackson as their Candidate for the next Congress, and he seemed apprehensive that the abolitionists of the District would also vote for him, and he was evidently more uneasy for the result than he was willing to acknowledge—The aggregate vote of the 24 towns in the District, last year was a majority for Governor Morton,[76] although the abolitionists voted for Mr. Everett. The abolitionists, this

---

75. Diary, June 8, 12, 19, 20, 27, 1840.
76. Marcus Morton, the Democrat who after several tries had succeeded in unseating Everett.

year have nominated Seth Sprague junior but he is absent in Europe, and Loring thinks they will vote for Jackson, a fiery abolitionist. He said that Mr. May[77] of Scituate was friendly to me and wished to see and converse with me, upon the subject—That he had been sore upon my declaration against the immediate abolition of slavery in the District of Columbia, but that he was disposed [to] overlook that on a pledge from me in favour of a prohibition of the slave trade in the District—I told him I should be glad to see and converse with Mr. May; but I gave no encouragement to the idea of calling upon me for a pledge. The whigs of the District are to hold their Convention at Plympton to-morrow. It is probable, but not certain that they will nominate me. If they do, and the abolitionists vote for Jackson, he will carry the election against me. If they vote for Sprague[78] there will be no choice. There is not in the United States a District in which the issue is more uncertain, and my mind must be made up to bear the last stroke of dismission from the public service, by the total abandonment of the people—

October 24, 1840—Mr. Wright[79] came and . . . [w]e conversed much upon abolition and anti-slavery Societies, about which, and their dissensions I gave him very freely my opinions—I told him that many of them acted like Bedlamites than reasonable men, and instanced the ferocious attacks of Garrison upon him, and his crack brained woman, no government and non-resistance balderdash—He gave me a Massachusetts abolitionist extra of which he said he had several with him, but of which he is no longer the Editor. He charged Garrison with having wronged him in publishing a private and confidential Letter which he Wright had written but spoke of him with much reserve, and said the cause of abolition would prosper and triumph, in spite of all these snarlings among its advocates– He adhered tenaciously to the third party nominations and was sure that however feeble they may now be, they would ultimately triumph—

The political demise of a leading Virginia Whig convinced Adams further that slavery's influence on American politics was killing all that was good.

77. Samuel May, one of the leading practitioners of the election-year interrogation of candidates.
78. Boston lawyer and Whig politician Peleg Sprague.
79. Leading abolitionist Elizur Wright.

November 22, 1840—Met at the breakfast-table Mr. Charles Fenton Mercer, who, after twenty-two years of service in the House of Representatives of the United States, last winter, in a fit of despair, accepted an office as cashier of a bank at Tallahassee, in Florida, and is now going to England—I suppose to raise the wind for that institution. Mercer is one of the most respectable natives of Virginia, and has devoted his life to the internal improvement of the country and to the gradual extinction of slavery in the State. In both of these benevolent and exalted purposes his exertions have been abortive. The savage and barbarous genius of slavery has not only baffled them all, but has kindled a flame of popular odium against him, from which he has shrunk into the cashier of a bank at Tallahassee. A noble spirit doomed to drudge in the mines.

After securing re-election once again, Adams proceeded to Washington. At New Haven, Connecticut, he met with Roger Sherman Baldwin, a lawyer working on the Amistad *case. They conversed for two hours about the case, which had been heard by the district and circuit courts and was now headed for the US Supreme Court. Baldwin and Adams then went to visit the Africans in the New Haven jail, and Adams thought their two leaders had "very remarkable countenances." Once in Washington Adams consulted with relevant officials about the case, which he had agreed to help argue before the Supreme Court.[80] He felt so keenly about pursuing justice for the* Amistad *rebels that he was able to overcome his prejudice against political abolitionists and consult one of their publications.*

December 12, 1840—I thought it necessary to look into the case of the Amistad captives, to prepare for the argument before the Supreme Court in January—of which I dare scarcely to think. I read, especially, the article in the American and Foreign Anti-Slavery Reporter of 1st October, 1840, entitled "The Amistad Case," p. 48–51, with deep anguish of heart, and a painful search of means to defeat and expose the abominable

80. Diary, November 17, December 11, 1840. For other entries detailing his work and worry on this case, see Diary, December 27, 1840; January 1, 3, 8, 10–13, 15, 17, 19–20, 1841.

conspiracy, Executive and Judicial, of this Government, against the lives of those wretched men. How shall the facts be brought out? How shall it be possible to comment upon them with becoming temper—with calmness, with moderation, with firmness, with address, to avoid being silenced, and to escape the imminent danger of giving the adversary the advantage in the argument by overheated zeal? Of all the dangers before me, that of losing my self-possession is the most formidable. I am yet unable to prepare the outline of the argument, which I must be ready to offer the second week in January. Let me not forget my duty.

January 14, 1841—To the Capitol, where I went into the Supreme Court room just before the Judges came and opened the Court. F. Key,[81] the District Attorney, came to me and enquired when the case of the blacks was to come on. I said we had filed a motion to the Court to dismiss the case, which, I understood, was to come up for argument on Saturday. He said he was afraid there was not any chance for the poor creatures; that the case of the Antelope was precisely in point against them.[82] He had argued that case for the freedom of the negroes, but it had been overruled. Yet it would never do to send them back to Cuba. The best thing that could be done was to make up a purse and pay for them and then send them back to Africa.

I said we hoped to prove that the case of the Antelope would not be conclusive in its bearing upon our clients; but he continued very positive in the impression that it would. I went, therefore, into the Supreme Court library-room, and took out the volume of Wheaton's Reports[83] containing the case of the Antelope. I read as much of it as I could, and longed to comment upon it as I could; but I have neither time nor head for it—nothing but the heart. . . .

81. Francis Scott Key, a Jackson appointee as US attorney for the District of Columbia in 1833. In addition to composing the national anthem, this DC-area slaveholder was a staunch opponent of abolitionism.
82. In 1820, American authorities seized a Spanish slaver (which had previously been seized by Latin American privateers) off the coast of Florida on suspicion that its crew meant to illegally sell the 281 Africans on board into slavery. This complex case that involved questions such as whether the United States could prosecute the slave trade as piracy reached the US Supreme Court in 1825. Chief Justice Marshall led a divided court in ruling that the US seizure of this vessel had been illegal.
83. Henry Wheaton, *Reports of Cases Argued and Adjudged in the Supreme Court of the United States* (Philadelphia: Mathew Carey, 1816–27).

I pursued this evening my examination of the documents in the case of the Amistad captives, but am yet utterly unprepared for the argument.

January 16, 1841—This day the motion, signed by Mr. Baldwin and myself, and filed by him in the Supreme Court, to dismiss the appeal by the United States from the decree of the District and Circuit Courts in the case of the Amistad captives, was to have been argued, Saturday being, by the rules of the Court, the weekly day for the argument of motions. I was not half prepared, and went to the Court with a heavy heart, full of undigested thought, sure of the justice of my cause, and deeply desponding of my ability to sustain it

When the Court was opened, the Chief Justice, Roger B. Taney, said that the Court had thought it best to postpone the Amistad case to await the arrival of Judge Story,[84] who was expected to be here on Monday or Tuesday. It was desirable that there should be a full Court for the hearing of the case, and the Court would take it up on any day of the week immediately after his arrival.

Mr. Baldwin stated that he was under the necessity of leaving this city next Saturday, to attend a Court in Connecticut. The postponement of the case afforded me a momentary relief, but left a state of suspense scarcely less distressing than the agony of the ordeal itself.

In this interval in the Amistad *case, Adams entered some intriguing thoughts in his diary about the escalating clash between North and South. In these entries it appears that he thought the conflict itself less disturbing than the idea of the North losing the battle over the future of slavery and the nation because of lack of spirit, and that he fully retained his sense that he stood bravely alone in goading and bearing the fury of the hysterical South. Nothing but that heroic self-image could have suggested that he was alone, for he had powerful and similarly provocative allies, notably Joshua Giddings of Ohio.[85] Yet it was never more than a part of him that relished this combat.*

January 20, 1841—The correspondence between the Governors of New York and Virginia has absorbed two of my evenings, and is of

84. Massachusetts' Joseph Story, who served on the court from 1811 to 1845.
85. See Diary, February 8–9, 1841.

awful import. Its most alarming feature is the tameness of tone on the part of W. H. Seward, the Governor of New York, and the insolence of Hopkins, the Lieutenant-Governor, and of Gilmer, the Governor of Virginia, throughout the whole correspondence.[86]

January 21, 1841—At the House, ... about a dozen petitions were presented before it came to my turn. I had upwards of thirty to present. I presented only five, three of which were referred to appropriate committees. The other two contained each three several prayers: 1, the abolition of slavery and the slave-trade in the District of Columbia; 2, the prohibition of the slave-trade between the States; 3, to refuse the admission of any new State whose Constitution tolerates slavery. I moved the reference of each of them to the Committee on the Territories.

The Speaker said that only the prayer of a refusal to admit new slave States could be received—whereupon Connor,[87] of North Carolina, moved that this part of each of the petitions should be laid on the table; which was done. But, upon my remarking that the petitions must be cut in two, Black, of Georgia,[88] and Wise, of Virginia, took fire, and blazed into a conflagration with me, with each other, and with the Speaker. The votes of laying on the table the receivable parts of the petitions were reconsidered by yeas and nays—one hundred and four to fifty. Black appealed from the Speaker's decision. Wise insisted that the petitions had not been received. I braved them both. The House got into a snarl. The Speaker knew not what to do. The morning hour expired, and Lewis Williams[89] called the orders of the day. Black fumed and raved, and moved to suspend the rules to take the question on his appeal; but they would not give him the yeas and nays, and refused to suspend the rules.

86. This controversy hinged on Governor Seward's refusal to extradite citizens accused by Virginia authorities of "slave-stealing." It came at a time when Georgia and Maine had a similar squabble, and both took place very much in public with other states weighing in. See Herman V. Ames, ed., *State Documents on Federal Relations: The States and the United States* (1911. Repr. New York: Da Capo Press, 1970), 40–45. Governor Thomas W. Gilmer's belligerent stance likely alarmed Adams all the more because he was a Southern Whig, and that branch of the party had a largely deserved reputation for sectional moderation.

87. Henry W. Connor, a Democrat.

88. Edward J. Black, newly converted from the Whigs to the Democrats.

89. A Whig from North Carolina.

February 4, 1841—On my return to the House, I found Charles Shepard on the floor, discussing the topics of the Treasury Note bill, as a Southern planter, for an hour; followed by James Garland, of the same interest.[90] I then took my turn for an hour, and arraigned before the committee, the nation, and the world, the principles avowed by Henry A. Wise, and his three-colored standard, of overseer, black, duelling, blood-red, and dirty, cadaverous, nullification, white. Of its effect I will not now speak. I have discharged what I believe to be a solemn and sacred duty. At the close of his reply, his gang of duellists clapped their hands, and the gallery hissed. William Cost Johnson[91] began his usual rhodomontade,[92] but the whole committee was in fermentation; they rose, and the House adjourned at half-past four.

February 5, 1841—Sleepless night. The step that I have taken yesterday absorbs all the faculties of my soul. Deliberately taken, to have any useful effect it must be calmly, firmly, judiciously, perseveringly, alas! skilfully pursued. I fear I have estimated too highly its importance. I fear my own incompetency to sustain it effectively and successfully. I know not what support I shall receive in or out of the House; I stand alone in this undertaking. Few, if any, of my colleagues appear to understand my purpose, and, from their deportment yesterday, I should conclude they thought it one of my eccentric, wild, extravagant freaks of passion.

Trumbull, of Connecticut,[93] alone, came to me after it was over, took me by the hand, and thanked me. Mr. Barnard[94] thought I ought to have dwelt more emphatically upon the disclaimer of all motives personally offensive to Wise; though he admitted I had disclaimed them. Brockway[95] this day asked if my speech would be printed. . . .

Mr. Merrick, Senator from Maryland,[96] and David Hoffman, of Baltimore, visited here this day, and told my wife that Mr. Webster[97] had been highly delighted at hearing of my speech; but all around me

90. Shepard was a North Carolina Democrat, Garland a Virginia Democrat.
91. A Whig from Maryland.
92. Bragging, blustering speech.
93. A Whig.
94. Daniel D. Barnard (Whig, New York).
95. John H. Brockway (Whig, Connecticut).
96. William D. Merrick, a Whig.
97. Daniel Webster, soon to join the William Henry Harrison administration as secretary of state.

is cold and discouraging, and my own feelings are wound up to a pitch that my reason can scarcely endure. I trust in God to control me.

While waiting to argue the Amistad *case, Adams continued diligent research, especially on a prior slave-ship revolt case (the* Antelope*), and avoided another slavery-related trial—surely in part to keep his focus on this one.*[98] *Beyond the merits and stakes intrinsic to the* Amistad *controversy and trial, Adams clearly also found it a practical, direct way of acting against slavery. Although his advocacy of the* Amistad *rebels won him the admiration of leading abolitionists, he and Baldwin knew better than to base their argument before the Southern-friendly court of Chief Justice Roger Taney on provocative abolitionist sentiment.*

February 21, 1841—Meditative devotion, as it kindles, is apt to mislead the judgment; but my impending duties brought me again down to the earth. At the last hour, I was yet to prepare a frame for my argument on the case of the Amistad captives. I must accommodate my plan of extemporaneous discourse to that of the Attorney-General, scarcely yet unfolded, and much also to my colleague's argument, which is yet to come. I began this evening an index to the documents that I am to review, that I may follow some order in extemporizing upon them. Of all that I have written, nine-tenths are waste paper.

February 22, 1841—I walked to the Capitol with a thoroughly bewildered mind—so bewildered as to leave me nothing but fervent prayer that presence of mind may not utterly fail me at the trial I am about to go through. . . .

The Attorney-General, Henry D. Gilpin,[99] then delivered his argument in the case of the Amistad captives. It occupied two hours, and, after a summary statement of the facts as developed in the documents from which he had copiously read on Saturday, he contended that the Amistad was a regularly documented Spanish schooner, employed in

98. See Diary, January 26–28, February 6, 10–11, 15, 17, 1841. On the *Antelope* case, see Jonathan Bryant, *Dark Places of the Earth: The Voyage of the Slave Ship* Antelope (New York: Liveright, 2015).

99. Van Buren had appointed this resident of Pennsylvania and Delaware as attorney general in 1840. His time in this position would end just weeks later.

the coasting trade between the different ports of the island of Cuba; that the passports of the passengers were regularly signed by the Governor-General of Cuba, and proved beyond all controversy that the blacks were the property of Ruiz and Montez;[100] that the Court, by the comity of nations, could not go behind or enquire into the validity of these documents, for which he cited many authorities in the law-books. He attempted no argument to show that the right of property remained unimpaired by the insurrection, and insisted that all the negroes ought to be restored to their owners, and that the Circuit Court erred in pronouncing the negroes free.

Mr. Baldwin followed, in a sound and eloquent but exceedingly mild and moderate argument in behalf of the captives, till half-past three, when the Court adjourned.

February 23, 1841—With increasing agitation of mind, now little short of agony, I rode in a hack to the Capitol, taking with me, in confused order, a number of books which I may have occasion to use. The very skeleton of my argument is not yet put together. . . . Mr. Baldwin occupied . . . four hours, in closing his argument in behalf of the Amistad captives and in the support of the decision of the District and Circuit Courts. The point upon which he dwelt with most emphatic earnestness was the motion to dismiss the appeal of the United States on the contest of their right to appear as parties in the cause, they having no interest therein. His reasoning therein was powerful and perhaps conclusive. But I am apprehensive there are precedents and an Executive influence operating upon the Court which will turn the balance against us on that point. In commenting upon the insurrection of the blacks, Mr. Baldwin firmly maintained their right of self-emancipation, but spoke in cautious terms, to avoid exciting Southern passions and prejudices, which it is our policy as much as possible to assuage and pacify. When he came to the point of questioning the validity of the Governor-General's ladino passports, he left a good deal still to be said. He closed at half-past three, and left the day open for me to-morrow. I went into the Congress library, and took out for use the thirty-seventh volume of Niles's Register, containing the speech of

---

100. Jose Ruiz and Pedro Montez, among the masters of the ship.

James Madison in the Virginia Convention on the double condition of slaves in that State, as persons and as property.

February 24, 1841—I was busied in preparation in the Clerk of the Supreme Court's room nearly an hour—to the moment of the meeting of the Court. ... Chief-Justice Taney announced to me that the Court were ready to hear me. The Judges present were Taney, Story, Thompson, McLean, Baldwin, Wayne, Barbour, and Catron. Judge McKinley[101] has [not] been present during any part of this trial. The Court-room was full, but not crowded, and there were not many ladies. I had been deeply distressed and agitated till the moment when I rose; and then my spirit did not sink within me. With grateful heart for aid from above, though in humiliation for the weakness incident to the limits of my powers, I spoke four hours and a half, with sufficient method and order to witness little flagging of attention by the Judges or the auditory—till half-past three o'clock, when the Chief Justice said the Court would hear me further to-morrow. Mr. Baldwin mentioned that he would stay and hear me to-morrow, but that he should be obliged to leave the city on Friday, to return home. The structure of my argument, so far as I have yet proceeded, is perfectly simple and comprehensive, needing no artificial division into distinct points, but admitting the steady and undeviating pursuit of one fundamental principle, the ministration of *justice*. I then assigned my reason for inviting *justice* specially, aware that this was *always* the duty of the Court, but because an immense array of power—the Executive Administration, instigated by the Minister of a foreign nation—has been brought to bear, in this case, on the side of *injustice*. I then commenced a review of the correspondence between the Secretary of State and the Spanish Ministers Calderon and Argaiz,[102] which I analyzed with critical research as far as I was able, but with not half the acuteness, nor with a tenth part of the vigor, which I would have applied had they been at my command. I did

101. Roger Taney of Maryland (chief justice from 1836 to 1864), Smith Thompson of New York (associate justice from 1823 to 1843), John McLean of Ohio (1829–61), Henry Baldwin of Pennsylvania (1830–44), James M. Wayne of Georgia (1835–67), Philip P. Barbour of Virginia (1836–41), John Catron of Tennessee (1837–65), John McKinley of Alabama (1838–52).
102. Spanish ministers to the United States Angel Calderon de la Barca and Chevalier de Argaiz.

not, I could not, answer public expectation; but I have not yet utterly failed. God speed me to the end!

March 1, 1841—I went to the Supreme Court, and concluded my argument in the case of the Amistad captives. I spoke about four hours, and then closed somewhat abruptly, leaving almost entirely untouched the review of the case of the Antelope, which I had intended, and for which I was prepared. It would have required at least an hour, and I had barely reached it when the usual time of the Court's adjournment came. I was unwilling to encroach upon the time of the Court for half of a third day, so that I cramped into a very brief summary what I had to say upon that case, and finished with a very short personal address to the Court.

March 6, 1841—In the Supreme Court . . . Walker, of Mississippi,[103] came to me and said he wondered how any one could ever have thought that the case of the Amistad had any thing to do with abolition. Peters[104] is too confident of a decision of the Court in our favor. My anxiety for it is intense, and deeply distrustful. . . .

When I came home I found at my house a black man, named John Francis Cook, who left a Letter handsomely written by himself, with an engraved Portrait of Cinque,[105] sent me as a present by Mr. Robert Purvis of Philadelphia. I had received a copy of the same portrait from Mr. Lewis Tappan and another from I know not whom—This Evening I was visited by Mr. Isaiah Thomas and Mr. Jacob M. Howard of Detroit, Michigan. Mr. Thomas is a Grandson of Isaiah Thomas of Worcester; the patriarch of the printing press in New England, and founder of the American Antiquarian Society. Mr. Howard is the member-elect of the House of Representatives from Michigan—They had heard my second day's argument in the case of the Amistad captives, and spoke much of it. . . . [A]lthough I fell immeasurably short of my wishes in that case, I did not utterly disappoint the public expectation.

March 9, 1841—Judge Story delivered the opinion and decree of the Court in the case of the United States appellants *vs.* the Schooner Amistad. It affirms the decision of the District and Circuit

103. Senator Robert J. Walker (Democrat, Mississippi).
104. Richard Peters Jr., the Supreme Court's reporter of decisions.
105. The best-known leader of the *Amistad* rebellion.

Courts, excepting with regard to the negroes. It reverses the decision below, placing them at the disposal of the President of the United States, to be sent to Africa; declares them to be free, and directs the Circuit Court to order them to be discharged from the custody of the Marshal.

Judge Baldwin expressed some dissent from the opinion, which I did not hear, nor did I learn what it was. I went to the chamber of the Committee of Manufactures, and wrote to Mr. Roger S. Baldwin, at New Haven, and to Mr. Lewis Tappan, of New York, to inform them of the decision of the Court, and gave the letters to Mr. [William J.] McCormick, the Postmaster of the House.

The court's decision left the Amistad's *Africans in a sort of limbo at the mercy of unfriendly American presidents and thus ensured that this case was not done for Adams or the other principals. At one point he even ventured to a "startled" Secretary of State Webster that the American courts ought to hand over the* Amistad *to the African rebels as their property.*[106] *Still, he found himself searching for another practical outlet for his growing antislavery energy and ambition (an ambition that he quite naturally perceived in others more readily than in himself).*

March 21, 1841—In the afternoon, at St. John's Church, I heard Mr. Hawley[107] read the service for the fourth Sunday in Lent, and preach from Revelation xxii. 12: "And, behold, I come quickly; and my reward is with me, to give every man according as his work shall be." The preacher remarked how universally all men worked for reward—which he illustrated by sundry specifications, but never bethought himself of the slave. If he had thought of it, he would not have ventured to take the verse for a text. The courtly preacher never mentions hell to ears polite. Massillon[108] sometimes preached to the conscience of Louis the Fourteenth; but no minister of the word of God, south of Mason and

106. See Diary, March 10, 18, 22, May 4, 12, September 22, 1841.
107. William Dickinson Hawley, the same influential Washington clergyman encountered in chapter 3.
108. Jean-Baptiste Massillon, Catholic bishop who preached at Versailles. This was an apt choice of analogy for Adams given Louis XIV's association with absolute power.

Dixon's line, ventures to preach one word against slavery. Not a few preach slavery itself. . . .

I this day took up and made a minute of eight folio pamphlet documents, containing about thirteen hundred pages of papers communicated to the British Parliament in 1839, and forty relating to the slave-trade, divided into classes, A, B, C, D, two sets of each. What can I do with them? It is impossible to separate the discussion upon the African slave-trade from the moral and political aspects of slavery; and that is with us a forbidden topic. I apprehend this is the rock upon which the Harrison Administration will drift and go to pieces, as it is the quicksand upon which that of Van Buren was stranded. The tariff and the bank are but suckers from the root.

March 27, 1841—I . . . waded along nearly through N. P. Trist's dissertation philippic addressed to the British Commissioners at the Havanna in the form of a letter dated 2d July—29th August 1839—an elaborate, insolent, crafty, hypocritical treatise to sustain and justify the African slave-trade and negro slavery, under hollow professions of deep detestation of them both. This paper, and the whole of Trist's correspondence, and his conduct as United States Consul at Havanna, are among the most remarkable phenomena of the death-struggle now in continual operation between the spirit of liberty and the spirit of bondage on this continent of North America. Trist has the ambition to act a prime part in this great convulsion.

March 29, 1841—I completed the assortment and filing of my letters received since the beginning of this year; and find myself with a task before me perfectly appalling. I am yet to revise for publication my argument in the case of the Amistad Africans; and, in merely glancing over the slave-trade papers lent me by Mr. Fox, I find impulses of duty upon my own conscience which I cannot resist, while on the other hand are the magnitude, the danger, the insurmountable burden of labor to be encountered in the undertaking to touch upon the slave-trade. No one else will undertake it; no one but a spirit unconquerable by man, woman, or fiend can undertake it but with the heart of martyrdom. The world, the flesh, and all the devils in hell are arrayed against any man who now in this North American Union shall dare to join the standard of Almighty God to put down the African slave-trade; and what can I, upon the verge of my seventy-fourth birthday, with a

shaking hand, a darkening eye, a drowsy brain, and with all my faculties dropping from me one by one, as the teeth are dropping from my
head—what can I do for the cause of God and man, for the progress
of human emancipation, for the suppression of the African slave-trade?
Yet my conscience presses me on; let me but die upon the breach.

April 2, 1841—My time slips away from under me week after week,
while I am doing nothing. I was all this day absorbed in struggling
to answer a letter from Messrs. Jocelyn, Leavitt, and Lewis Tappan,
about the Amistad Africans, whose case involves deeply perplexing
questions yet to be discussed and adjusted. And I had this day a letter from Mr. Leavitt mentioning that the printer was calling for my
revised argument before the Supreme Court, upon which I have not yet
commenced. Upwards of two hours of my time was consumed in reading documents in the Parliamentary papers relating to the slave-trade,
accumulating proofs of the duplicity of Spain and Portugal in their
treaties with Great Britain and in their edicts against the slave-trade.
With that same duplicity the Government of the United States stand
heavily charged; and with such defences as Forsyth's dispatches and
Trist's dissertations, compared with the last paragraph of Van Buren's
last annual message to Congress, an American must hide his head for
shame. The Consummation of the whole system of policy is disclosed
in N. P. Trist's letter to the British Commissioners of 2d July and 29th
August, 1839.

April 3, 1841—I finished my letter to Simeon S. Jocelyn, Joshua
Leavitt, and Lewis Tappan, declining a proposal made to me by them
to commence a correspondence with Lord Palmerston respecting the
case of the Amistad Africans. On full deliberation, I concluded that it
would be improper, and perhaps an infraction of the Act of Congress
of 30th January, 1799.[109] This subject of slavery is yet festering; and this
morning's National Intelligencer contains the letter of John M. Patton,
acting Governor of Virginia, to William H. Seward, Governor of the

---

109. The burden of Adams's response was that their proposed course would be nothing but "labour lost," but he did cheer on their efforts to secure in some effectual
way justice for the Amistad Africans. See John Quincy Adams to Simeon Jocelyn,
Joshua Leavitt and Lewis Tappan, April 3, 1841. The Logan Act, which Congress
passed in 1799, forbade American citizens to enter unauthorized negotiations
with foreign governments that had a dispute with the US government.

State of New York, announcing his readiness to deliver up a man charged with forgery in New York, arrested in Virginia, and whom the late Governor, Gilmer, had refused to deliver up at the requisition of Governor Seward; also the message from Governor Seward to the Legislature of New York of 26th March last, which is firm, spirited, and well-tempered. Hitherto, the controversy has been much more ably managed by Seward than by the Virginians; but there have been symptoms of the basest defection to the cause of freedom among the New York Whigs, and a disposition to sacrifice Seward to the South, which will excite fearful misgivings of the result.

Sectional conflict combined with partisanship greeted the new William Henry Harrison administration from the very beginning. Southern Democrats in the Senate scrutinized many of Harrison's Northern appointees, from Webster down to Indian agents, for signs of abolitionist sympathies before they would confirm them. As Adams put it, "slavery is already hurling thunderbolts at the President-elect and the Northern portion of his" supporters.[110] *When Harrison died in office and was replaced by nominal Whig John Tyler, Adams understood that this unexpected blow to the Whig Party would hardly calm either the sectional or the partisan waters.*

April 4, 1841—At thirty minutes past midnight, this morning of Palm Sunday, the 4th of April, 1841, died William Henry Harrison, precisely one calendar month President of the United States after his inauguration. The first impression of this event here where it occurred is of the frailty of all human enjoyments and the awful vicissitudes woven into the lot of mortal man. He had reached, but one short month since, the pinnacle of honor and power in his own country. He lies a lifeless corpse in the palace provided by his country for his abode. . . .

The influence of this event upon the condition and history of the country can scarcely be foreseen. It makes the Vice-President of the United States, John Tyler, of Virginia, Acting President of the Union

110. Diary, February 27, September 6, 1841. See also Matthew Mason, "The Local, National, and International Politics of Slavery: Edward Everett's Nomination as U.S. Minister to Great Britain, "*Journal of the Civil War Era* 6 (March 2016): 3–29.

for four years less one month. Tyler is a political sectarian, of the slave-driving, Virginian, Jeffersonian school, principled against all improvement, with all the interests and passions and vices of slavery rooted in his moral and political constitution—with talents not above mediocrity, and a spirit incapable of expansion to the dimensions of the station upon which he has been cast by the hand of Providence, unseen through the apparent agency of chance. To that benign and healing hand of Providence I trust, in humble hope of the good which it always brings forth out of evil.

April 6, 1841—And may the blessing of Heaven upon this nation attend and follow this providential revolution in its Government! For the present, it is not joyous, but grievous. The moral condition of this country is degenerating, and especially that part of its institutions which is organized by the process of unceasing elections. The spirit of the age and country is to accumulate power in the hands of the multitude, to shorten terms of service in high public office, to multiply elections and diminish Executive power, to weaken all agencies protective of property or repressive of crime, to abolish capital punishment, imprisonment for debt, and even the lien upon property of contracts. Slavery, temperance, land-jobbing, bankruptcy, and sundry controversies with Great Britain constitute the materials for the history of John Tyler's Administration. But the improvement of the condition of man will form no part of his policy, and the improvement of his country will be an object of his most inveterate and inflexible opposition. May the omnipotence of God overrule the depravity of man! Of human purpose or human energy I despair.

A conversation with John D. Dickinson, a New York politician in Washington on a mission for Governor William H. Seward, convinced Adams that perhaps the long-simmering controversy between that state and Virginia needed his intervention—interestingly, because of his expertise in international affairs.

April 13, 1841—Mr. Dickinson ... manifested great anxiety to know what were the intentions and the expectations of the Administration with regard to a national bank, a tariff, and the distribution among the States of the proceeds of the public lands.

I told him I knew nothing more upon these subjects than was to be gathered from the newspapers, and advised him to see the President and the Secretaries. I said there was another subject which I deemed of more vital importance to the Union than the bank, the tariff, the currency, or the land and State debts questions, or than all of them together; and that was the controversy between the States of New York and Virginia, and the slavery question generally, about which not one word was said by Mr. Tyler in his address to the people of the United States, intended for an inaugural exposition of his principles of administration.

He said he thought as I did with regard to the importance of the question between New York and Virginia. I enquired if the people of New York would sustain Governor Seward in the stand he had taken. He said, certainly; and that there was but one weighty member of the Senate opposed to it or doubtful of it—Gulian C. Verplanck.[111] I suppose Verplanck to be the ablest man in that Senate; but the nerve is not in him. He is of the class of men whose last resort always is to compromise with principle.

April 15, 1841—I finished my letter to the Governor of New York, which I marked private, but wrote with a constant anticipation that it may be published very soon, and in all probability will be, sooner or later.[112] I have laid down the principle of international law upon which I concur with him in his controversy with the Executive authorities of Virginia. I take what I believe to be the impregnable position, the right of each sovereign party to a contract to construe its provisions for itself, but not to impose its construction upon the other. I have not touched upon the policy or impolicy of delivering up fugitives from justice, nor upon the usages among civilized nations, nor upon the degree of transgression embraced in the definition of the word crime. Upon all these points there is much debatable ground; but the independent right of construction on both sides, the necessity that both parties should understand the words constituting obligation in a compact in the same sense, and the basement story of the controversy—the conflict between freedom and slavery—are parts or auxiliaries of Seward's

111. A Democrat who had represented New York in the US House of Representatives from 1825 to 1833.
112. John Quincy Adams to William H. Seward, April 16, 1841, Adams Family Papers, MHS.

argument which cannot be shaken. Prudence has warned me to stand aloof from this contest; but I cannot. The leading men of the North are all truckling to Southern slavery. They are all ready to desert Seward in the stand that he has taken. I see what it will cost me to stand by him; but I have so little political capital left that the remnant is not worth saving, especially at the cost of base desertion from the cause.

Cases in the Supreme Court and between states came and went, but the constant theme was the battle with slaveholders and their allies in Congress. Adams's entries about these debates continued to record in some detail his personal persecution at the hands of Speaker and members alike.[113] *It was always more political than personal, and as the special First Session of the Twenty-Seventh Congress neared its end, Adams found that the gag rule was as strong as ever.*

June 14, 1841—At the House, immediately after the reading of the journal, Mr. Wise . . . spoke for upwards of six hours, a continual invective upon me. . . . [B]eginning every successive sentence with a loud and vehement clatter, he immediately bowed down over his desk till his head and chest became horizontal, his mouth pouring out all the time his words in a whisper. Abolition, abolition, abolition, was the unvarying cry; and he represented me as a fiend, the inspirer and leader of all abolition. . . .

Several motions were then made, with great confusion and disorder, till a motion was made to adjourn, and carried, by yeas and nays. I came home about eight o'clock, in great tribulation, and perplexed in the dilemma between firm perseverance, intemperate retaliation, and tame submission. What I most need, and fervently pray for, is control over my own temper.

August 9, 1841—The committees were called for reports; and then resolutions were promiscuously offered. I presented one requiring of the Clerk to prepare, and report to the House at the commencement of the next session, a list of the petitions the reception of which has been suspended during the present session. After a long struggle to dodge this resolution,

113. See also Diary, June 7, 9, 15, July 27, November 6, 1841.

from all parts of the House, Gilmer,[114] of Virginia, moved to lay it on the table. I called for the yeas and nays, and, with the utmost difficulty, obtained them. They were one hundred and twenty-four to sixty-two—so utterly prostrate is the right of petition in the House, and so ashamed are they who submitted to the expedient of excluding *all* petitions to keep out the abolitionists, that any record of their prostitution should remain.

As searing as all this congressional abuse was for Adams, and as hostile as he felt toward the Democrats and Tyler supporters, he was not yet ready to write off every Southerner. So while he was sure that slavery was "the root of all evil" at least in American politics, he was not ready to see everything in starkly sectional terms.[115]

September 3, 1841—Colonel Hayne, of South Carolina,[116] came to my seat to request a conversation with me at some convenient time about a plan which he has formed for settling by a compromise the great slavery question, and which he wishes me to undertake. His views are pure and benevolent. I promised cheerfully to see and hear him on the subject, without fixing the time.

September 16, 1841—Edward Stanly, a member of the House from North Carolina,[117] called to take leave. He has excellent principles, and a lofty spirit, with a quick perception, an irritable temper, and a sarcastic turn of mind, sparing neither friend nor foe. He is the terror of the Lucifer party, and Wise made that desperate attempt last week to scale him on the floor, by which he only succeeded in flooring himself. Stanly's spirit is not to be subdued; but the thunderbolt of heaven has fallen upon the Whigs, and he, with all the honest men of the party, is disheartened and perplexed. We have no hope but in the redeeming power of heaven to overrule for good the seemingly most calamitous events.

114. Whig Thomas W. Gilmer, who had just completed his service as governor of Virginia.
115. Diary, October 12, 1841.
116. It is unclear who this was. It could not have been Robert Y. Hayne, the South Carolina senator and governor, for he had died in 1839. There was a Charles E. Haynes who left Congress just days before, but he represented Georgia.
117. Unsurprisingly, Stanly was a Whig.

Adams continued to have major differences with the abolitionists, including two young zealots whom he tried to dissuade from suicide missions preaching antislavery in Southern climes.[118] *As gratifying as his participation in the* Amistad *case was, he received plans to thank him at a special event as typical abolitionist exhibitionism.*

November 19, 1841—I received last week a splendidly bound quarto Bible, presented to me, with an address in manuscript fronting the title-page, signed by Cinque, Kinna, and Kale, for the thirty-five Mendian Africans of the Amistad. Mr. Lewis Tappan has been extremely desirous of having this done by a public exhibition and ceremony, which I have repeatedly and inflexibly declined, from a clear conviction of its impropriety, and invincible repugnance to exhibiting myself as a public raree-show;[119] but, as in common civility an answer was due to the present and the address, I wrote one this day to the address, and one, enclosing it, to Mr. Tappan.[120]

Adams's sense of humor was never his strong suit. It abandoned him entirely as he contemplated the coming session of Congress, with Tyler pushing for Texas annexation and the gag rule renewed by motion of William Cost Johnson.[121]

December 7, 1841—Johnson came to my seat to introduce some friend, and joked about his victory for three or four days. But it is for the Congress; and bitterly does it try my temper. Winthrop and Saltonstall[122]

---

118. Diary, July 24, 1841; February 14, 1842. For more on his ongoing suspicion of "fanatics" of all kinds, see January 21, April 3, 1844.
119. A spectacle.
120. Adams frankly rested his reluctance to accede to this ceremony to his unwillingness to create "the appearance on my part of an ostentatious display of the service which it had been my good fortune to tender" the plaintiffs. He was not ready "to seek for the praise or to hazard the censure of public assemblies" relative to this case. But his gratitude to them for sending the Bible was effusive. See John Quincy Adams to Lewis Tappan, November 19, 1841; and Adams to the Mendian Africans, November 19, 1841, Adams Family Papers, MHS.
121. See also Diary, November 20, 1841.
122. Robert C. Winthrop and Leverett Saltonstall, both Massachusetts Whigs.

have both applied to me and strenuously urged my consent to act again as Chairman of the Committee of Manufactures, to witness the prostration of the whole manufacturing interest by the faction combined of Southern slave-breeders and the Northern Democracy. I despair—at least for my own time. The day of redemption will come, but it is not destined for me.

December 8, 1841—Stanly ... came to my seat to enquire of my motive for voting against his resolution. He thought I felt sore upon the vote adopting the gag-rule excluding petitions. And I do. But the mortification that I feel is not that of mere defeat: it is the disgrace and degradation of my country, trampling in the dust the first principles of human liberty. This is the iron that enters into my soul.

December 18, 1841—This afternoon, Mr. Leavitt called on me, with Mr. Gates,[123] member of the House from the State of New York. They are alarmed at numerous indications of a design to revive the project of annexing Texas to the United States ...; and they asked if anything could now be done to counteract this movement. I know of nothing but to make it as soon and as extensively known as possible. There is apparently in this movement a concert of long standing between Andrew Jackson, Samuel Houston, recently elected for the second time President of Texas, and Santa Anna, now reinstated as President of the Mexican Confederation; and that the project is to be consummated by a cession of Texas from the Mexican to the North American Confederacy. The developments of this project are not yet sufficiently clear and explicit to know how to meet and counteract it.

In early 1842, Adams presented two petitions that were designed to provoke motions of censure against him, which would make it impossible for the gag's proponents to deny him the floor of the House to defend himself. One was a purported petition from a group of Georgians praying that Adams be removed as chairman of the Committee on Foreign Affairs; the second was from the citizens of Haverhill, Massachusetts, asking Congress to investigate mechanisms to break up the Union. He got his wish, gaining an opening to speak while his opponents lacked the votes to censure him. Despite the brilliance of his parliamentary legerdemain, Adams was never above entering detailed and bitter reflections on his enemies and their "conspiracy against me" in his

123. Seth M. Gates, a Whig who later went on to be a leader in the Free Soil Party.

diary. He captured his nervousness, his bitterness, and his feeling of triumph in the following entries.[124]

February 5, 1842—[While I was speaking in the House,] Romulus M. Saunders[125] started up on a point of order on the old pretence—that I had no right to discuss the subject of slavery. The Speaker[126] ruled the point against him. He appealed, and demanded the yeas and nays, which were refused, and the decision of the Speaker sustained—ninety-seven to twenty-five. I saw my cause was gained. ... I came home scarcely able to crawl up to my chamber, but with the sound of "Io triumphe" ringing in my ear.

February 6, 1842—My attention, morning and afternoon, involuntarily wandered from the preachers and their discourses to the critical nature of my own position; confident of my deliverance from this particular assault upon me, so senseless that its malignity merges, by its stupidity, not into innocence, but into harmlessness, but always distrustful of my own control over my own spirit. One hundred members of the House represent slaves; four-fifths of whom would crucify me if their votes could erect the cross; forty members, representatives of the free, in the league of slavery and mock Democracy, would break me on the wheel, if their votes or wishes could turn it round; and four-fifths of the other hundred and twenty are either so cold or so lukewarm that they are ready to desert me at the very first scintillation of indiscretion on my part. The only formidable danger with which I am beset is that of my own temper.

Mr. Barnard came with a manuscript report, by the reporters of the National Intelligencer, of my speech of yesterday, for my revisal. They sent it to Mr. Barnard, supposing that, after their sally against me, I might possibly not incline to receive it directly from themselves. Mr. Barnard told me that intimations had been very distinctly given to Gales and Seaton that their treatment of me could not be tolerated at the North, and that this was the occasion of their sending their

124. Diary, February 3–4, 1842. For a good, brief account of these events, see Leonard L. Richards, *The Life and Times of Congressman John Quincy Adams* (New York: Oxford University Press, 1986), 139–45.
125. A Democrat from North Carolina.
126. The Speaker of the House for this session was John White (Whig, Kentucky).

reporters' notes to me through him. I was up till past midnight, revising the notes of the Friday's debate.

February 7, 1842—Mr. Weld[127] was here this morning, with a cheering report of the impression of my defence of Thursday, Friday, and Saturday, upon the current of popular opinion out of the House. A Mr. Dorsey, a stranger, brought me a document which he supposed might be useful to me in my defence. . . .

I prepared a minute of the outlines of the continuance and conclusion of my defence, which would have occupied at least a week. But I saw on Saturday that the House was tired of the whole subject, and that to close it now would afford relief to all parties. I went to the House, therefore, prepared to proceed, but willing to stop short and dismiss the subject from the consideration of the House forever. I was belated, and the House had been about ten minutes in session when I entered and took my seat. Other business was under consideration, but the question of privilege, or my trial, was soon called up. I then observed that, having perceived on Saturday some impatience on the part of the House to get rid of this subject, and persevering in the determination not to be responsible for one hour of time unnecessarily consumed on this subject, if the House was ready to lay it on the table forever, I would acquiesce in that decision without requiring further time for my defence; of which I should need much if required to proceed.

Botts[128] then moved to lay the whole subject on the table forever; carried, by yeas and nays—one hundred and six to ninety-three. Meriwether, of Georgia,[129] asked to be excused from voting, because he hotly lusted for a vote of the severest censure upon me, but despaired of obtaining it. The House refused to excuse him, and he voted to lay on the table the whole subject. They then took in hand the Haverhill petition, and refused to receive it—one hundred and sixty-six to forty, Briggs, Baker, Cushing, and Hudson voting with the majority.[130]

127. Theodore Dwight Weld, a leading American abolitionist.
128. John Minor Botts (Whig, Virginia).
129. James A. Meriwether, a Whig.
130. George N. Briggs, Osmyn Baker, Caleb Cushing, and Charles Hudson, all noted by Adams because they were Massachusetts Whigs.

I then proceeded with my budget [of petitions], of which I presented nearly two hundred, till the House adjourned. Most of them were excluded by the rule, or laid on the table by objections to their reception. And thus ended the second prosecution of me by the despotic process of contempt.

Though "conspiracy" was a typically strong term, Adams did not have a persecution complex; he did have many inveterate and vocal enemies in the House. This became even clearer after the end of this censure trial, when the Speaker accommodated a wave of Southerners and other anti-Adams men who wished to noisily resign from the committee he chaired.[131] This movement was of a piece with Southern senators' earlier push to deny Northern men confirmation to certain posts, and seemed to many—especially to Southern Whigs—a harbinger of Southern Democrats' dangerous drive toward sectional purity tests.

February 9, 1842—In the House, immediately after the reading of the journal, Gilmer sent to the Speaker two papers; one signed by himself, R. M. T. Hunter, R. Barnwell Rhett, and George H. Proffit,[132] asking to be excused from further service on the Committee of Foreign Affairs, because from recent occurrences it was doubtful whether the House would remove the Chairman, and they were unwilling to serve with one in whom they had no confidence. The other paper was a letter from W. Cost Johnson to Gilmer, apologizing for not attending the meeting of the committee yesterday, but assuring him that if he had attended he would have voted for another Chairman. These papers were received without objection. The four fugitive members were excused from further service by a shout of acclamation. Cost Johnson then asked to be excused, and was excused in like manner.

February 15, 1842—In the National Intelligencer of this morning I found the letters from Mark A. Cooper, Isaac E. Holmes, and Reuben Chapman,[133] asking to be excused from serving on the Committee of

131. See also Diary, February 10, 14, 18, 1842.
132. A Whig from Indiana.
133. These were all Democrats, Cooper from Georgia, Holmes from South Carolina, and Chapman from Alabama.

Foreign Affairs; and the two former were so insulting personally to me that they are unquestionably breaches of privilege, and I confidently believe that the Speaker would have refused to receive or present them had they referred to any other man in the House; certainly not without giving notice to the inculpated member, and to the House, of the accusatory character of the letters. I was very strongly inclined to make it a point of privilege in the House to vindicate my own character. I had given notice to Holmes and Chapman on Saturday of the meeting of the committee this morning: neither of them had hinted his intention to ask to be excused.

At the meeting this morning, the six members in function were all present; but, as there were three vacancies, it was agreed to postpone till the next meeting the regular business of the committee. I read the letters of Mark A. Cooper and Holmes, and said I considered them gross breaches of privilege and had serious thoughts of denouncing them to the House. But Everett and Granger[134] said it would be giving them an importance which the writers earnestly desired; while without such notice they would be, as they were, universally despised. Shepperd and Edward T. White[135] thought the letters insidiously aimed more against them than against me, by the principle assumed that *no* Southern man could in honor consent to serve with me. I determined, therefore, to sacrifice again my personal feelings for the sake of peace, and to take no notice of the letters.

In this poisonous atmosphere, Adams surrendered enough of his lone-wolf self-image to welcome and encourage allies in his fights.[136] Joshua Giddings remained one of the more important of these comrades. In these weeks he had responded forcefully to the Tyler administration's stance on the rebellious slaves of the slaving ship Creole, *who had risen against their captors and gained freedom in the British West Indies. The administration argued that by virtue of international comity the British government should have respected the U.S. Constitution, which rendered these slaves property. Framed in this way, the* Creole *case raised far-reaching questions for people like Giddings and Adams,*

---

134. Horace Everett (Whig, Vermont) and Francis Granger (Whig, New York).
135. Augustine H. Shepperd (Whig, North Carolina) and Edward Douglass White (Whig, Louisiana).
136. See Diary, December 26, 28, 1842.

such as whether the administration would render slavery national rather than
only sectional in its reach and legitimacy. Giddings's belligerent resolutions in
the House against the administration's position led to something all too famil-
iar for Adams: a movement to censure him.

March 3, 1842—Mr. Giddings came to enquire the precise extent to
which I hold the subject of slavery in the States subject to the jurisdiction of the National Government; and I explained it to him. In the case
of a servile war, involving the free States of the Union, the question
of emancipation would necessarily be the issue of the conflict. All war
must end in peace, and peace must be concluded by treaty. Of such a
treaty, partial or universal emancipation would probably form an essential, and the power of the President and Senate of the United States over
it would be coextensive with the war.

March 21, 1842—Giddings, of Ohio, offered a series of resolutions
relating to slavery and the Creole case. . . . After much turbulence and
confusion, Giddings withdrew the resolutions.

Botts then moved a suspension of the rules to offer a preamble and
resolution of censure upon Giddings; yeas, one hundred and twenty-
eight; nays, sixty-eight; not two-thirds. Weller, of Ohio,[137] then offered
the same resolution, it being still the turn of the States, and he moved
the previous question. The question whether Giddings should be heard
in his defence was unsettled at the adjournment.

March 22, 1842—In the House, the resolution of censure upon
Giddings, with a preamble first moved yesterday by Botts, then moved
by Weller, moving at the same time the previous question, was taken
up, and, after two full hours of twistings, decisions by the Speaker
reversed by the House, motions that he should have permission to be
heard in his defence, by reconsideration, by suspension of the rules, by
general consent, the resolution of censure was actually passed, by yeas
and nays—one hundred and twenty-five to sixty-nine; and then the
preamble was adopted—one hundred and nineteen to sixty-six.

I can find no language to express my feelings at the consummation
of this act. Immediately after the second vote, Giddings rose from his

---

137. John B. Weller, a Democrat clearly seeing a chance to take local partisan advan-
    tage of Giddings's vulnerability.

seat, came over to mine, shook cordially my hand, and took leave. I had a voice only to say, "I hope we shall soon have you back again." He made no reply, but passed to the seats of other members, his friends, and took leave of them as he had done of me. I saw him shake hands with Arnold,[138] who voted against him. He then left the House, and this evening the city.

The Giddings debacle, together with abundant other contemporaneous evidence that slavery was infecting both Washington politics and the general political climate of America, made Adams contemplate afresh the relationship between slavery and partisanship, and his relationship to both.[139]

March 25, 1842—Mr. [Horace] Everett presented to me yesterday a paper signed by several members, requesting a meeting of the Whig members from the non-slave-holding States at ten this morning, in the chamber of the Committee of Foreign Affairs. I declined signing the call, acknowledging no party communion with the Whigs of the slave representation; but I said I would attend the meeting.

March 26, 1842—Mr. Sprague and Mr. Robbins[140] called on me this morning, and said they were desirous of having some conversation concerning the duties on cordage to be fixed on the revisal of the tariff. But the conversation immediately became general concerning the present aspect of affairs in Congress and in the country, which is deplorable. I told them that slavery, the support, the perpetuation, and the propagation of slavery, was at the root of the whole system of policy of the present Administration; that an essential part of this system was hostility to the manufactures and to the free labor of the North; that this spirit, in alliance with the mock Democracy of the free States, exercises now absolute control over the majority of both Houses of Congress, and, if unable to carry all its purposes into execution now, will at least defeat every measure which could contribute to promote the manufacturing interest or the domestic industry of free labor.

138. Thomas D. Arnold (Whig, Tennessee).
139. See, for example, Diary, March 18–19, 24, April 26–28, 30, May 2–3, June 24, 1842.
140. Seth Sprague Jr. and Edward H. Robbins, New Englanders in Washington to lobby for the manufacturing interest.

Adams's bone-deep distrust of the Tyler administration led him to positions
that were the complete opposite of those he had once held. For instance, the
president and the secretary of the navy, proslavery Virginian Abel Upshur,
pushed for a much stronger navy. Rather than welcome this suggestion, as the
nationalist Adams would previously have done, he groused that "this sudden
Virginian overflow of zeal for the patronage of the navy comes reeking hot
from the furnace of slavery."[141] *But nothing showed his about-face quite like*
his reaction to an American naval officer's advocacy of the Tyler administra-
tion's desire to limit the breadth of the mutual right of search for slave trade
abolition granted in the 1842 Webster-Ashburton Treaty. He even ascribed to
American officials a philosophy ("do no right and take no wrong") that he
had once used to describe the British navy.[142] *He continued his role as self-*
appointed watchdog of American complicity in the illicit African slave trade
into the next administration.[143]

April 26, 1842—Mr. [Thomas W.] White, editor of the Southern
Literary Messenger, called on me this morning, and took the article
of Lieutenant [Matthew Fontaine] Maury upon the right of search,
which he had lent me last Saturday and requested me to read and give
my opinion of it. He now asked my opinion, and I told him I disagreed with it altogether; that Lieutenant Maury's law was quarter-deck
law—do no right and take no wrong; that he assumed erroneous law,
and principles utterly untenable, and, above all, that the temper of his
article was rancorous and vituperative—a fault of all the diplomatic
papers and dissertations on our side in this recent controversy.[144]

141. Diary, April 24, 1842; see also February 9, 1844. An article by Matthew J. Karp
    illuminates the strength of Adams's analysis here: "Slavery and American Sea
    Power: The Navalist Impulse in the Antebellum South," *Journal of Southern
    History* 77 (May 2011), 283–324.
142. For more on his opposition to the administration on this point, see Diary, June
    13, 1842; March 15, 21, 25, 1843.
143. See Diary, April 15–17, May 10, 1845.
144. White ran this article anyway. It was a vigorous warning of the dangers to
    American sovereignty posed by "British pretensions" and a protestation that the
    United States was doing all it could to effect the abolition of the slave trade—
    much like Adams may have written earlier in his career. See "The Right of
    Search," *Southern Literary Messenger* 8 (April 1842), 289–301.

Adams had become so sectionalist that he saw slavery where others likely did not and talked of "the free and servile sections of this Union" rather than using more generic or neutral terms such as "sectionalism." But he still sought to counsel prudence among his growing band of antislavery Whigs. His own ambivalence continued between his repeated self-exhortations to control his temper and his unstatesmanlike glee in provoking it in the slaveholders. He also seems to have determined to agitate issues only when he thought he stood a reasonable chance of prevailing. But that did not lessen his impatience with those who declined to engage with slavery at all.

May 11, 1842—Mr. Giddings had yesterday requested an interview with me at my house this morning; to which I had agreed, and he came.[145] He said that the Army Appropriation bill would shortly come up for the consideration of the House. There was an item of appropriation in it of one hundred thousand dollars for the prosecution of the war in Florida, which he thought should be struck out. Mr. Slade, with whom he had conversed upon the subject, was of the same opinion, and they had thought it best to consult with me concerning the expediency of making the motion. I said I concurred entirely in the opinion that the item ought to be struck out, but I was not sure that it would be advisable at the present time to make the motion. It would undoubtedly breed a tempest. The whole system of policy of the country, foreign and domestic, war and peace, slavery and the slave-trade, would be opened for debate on this motion, and the public feeling on this topic was so lukewarm and so perverted, even in the free States, that I could not ward off the doubt of the expediency of agitating it at all, by starting the game ourselves.

May 21, 1842—Not a day passes but I receive letters from the North, and sometimes the West, asking for an autograph and a scrap of poetry or of prose, and from the South, almost daily, letters of insult, profane obscenity, and filth. These are indices to the various estimation in which I am held in the free and servile sections of this Union—indices to the

145. Giddings was back in Washington after having been overwhelmingly re-elected by his constituents. He objected vigorously and publicly to the Second Seminole War, a long-running conflict between the United States and the Seminole Indians and the fugitive African American slaves they had been harboring.

moral sensibilities of free and of slavery-tainted communities. Threats of lynching and assassination are the natural offspring of slave-breeders and slave-traders; profanity and obscenity are their natural associates. Such dross the fire must purge.

June 18, 1842—At the House, Edward D. White, by an explosion of indignant eloquence, and a suspension of the rules, introduced, and drove through by a headlong impulse, a bill taking away the power of holding to bail . . . a debtor, unless upon affidavit of the debt by the creditor. He declaimed about liberty and the natural inalienable rights of man, as if there was not a slave in his State or in this District. If I had said one word about slavery I should have had the whole pack of Southern doulocracy[146] and Northern servility upon me; produced merely a brawl, and been branded as a firebrand in my own land of the Pilgrims. I retired, in utter disgust, without the bar, and suffered this paroxysm of frenzy for the rights of man, to liberate one Louisiana constituent of Edward D. White from imprisonment for want of bail, leaving six thousand slaves to drag their lengthened chain for life, and as inheritance for their children forever.

July 10, 1842—I attended . . . public worship at the hall of the House of Representatives, where the services were performed by Mr. Maffitt,[147] after an absence of five weeks. It was announced in the Globe[148] last evening that he was to preach on "the moral aspects of the nineteenth century." . . . The discourse was a rhapsodical declamation upon the moral improvements of the age—Sunday-schools, Bible, tract, missionary, and temperance societies; but no abolition—not even colonization. Not one word on the subject of slavery or emancipation.

Even as the seventy-five-year-old Adams contemplated his mortality and found himself inspired by the example of the recently deceased (though much younger) Channing in pursuing "the anti-slavery cause," his best course of action did not seem straightforward to him.[149]

146. Government by slaves.
147. Methodist minister John Newland Maffitt, chaplain of the House of Representatives.
148. The semiofficial Washington newspaper that also published records of congressional debates.
149. Diary, October 8–9, 1842.

September 2, 1842—My mind is in the condition of a ship at sea in a hurricane, suspended by an instantaneous calm. The brain heaves, the head swims, the body totters, and I live in a perpetual waltz. The presentiment of a sudden termination to my life is rather cheering to me than painful, and a man conscious of no sin upon his soul which repentant tears may wash out can dispense with the deprecation of the Episcopal litany against sudden death.[150] The apprehension, however, of such a close to my life ought to and does admonish me to set my house in order, to be prepared as much as a prudent forecast can provide for whatever event may by the will of God befall me. I see my duty, but I procrastinate. . . . I have now on hand a controversial warfare with John Tyler, President of the United States; bitter personal hatred of five of the most depraved, most talented, and most influential men of this country, four of them open and undisguised—C. J. Ingersoll, Wise, T. F. Marshall,[151] and W. Cost Johnson—the fifth under a mask—nameless. . . . The mercy of God is the only anchor of my soul for deliverance from this ordeal.

As Adams learned that key Massachusetts Whigs such as Caleb Cushing had criticized his actions in the House, he worried that Channing's fate of being "deserted by many of his followers" would be his own. This was all key context for why he devoted extra scrutiny to Northern political opinion on slavery in this period, even as he thought expansively about big questions.[152] In the process he recorded some direct thoughts about how he perceived his "cause" at this point in his life.

November 11, 1842—I called at the Emancipator[153] office 32 Washington Street—While I was with him, a boy came in with the first number of a tri weekly newspaper called the Latimer Journal intended for popular excitement on the case of the coloured man named George Latimer, held in prison and claimed as a Slave by James G. Gray of Richmond,

150. The 1789 edition of the *Book of Common Prayer for the United States Episcopal Church* included the prayer: "Good Lord, deliver us . . . from sudden death."
151. Thomas Francis Marshall (Whig, Kentucky).
152. Diary, October 1, 9, November 13, 18, 1842.
153. Joshua Leavitt's political abolitionist newspaper.

Virginia—The affair is taking a turn which will produce great excitement and I pray some good.

November 12, 1842—I received, as usual, a number of letters requesting me to deliver lectures in sundry places, and among them one from Joseph L. Tillinghast, of Providence, Rhode Island, requesting a copy of my lecture upon Democracy, for publication.[154] This has occasioned no small embarrassment in my mind, for the topic is as sharp with quills as the fretful porcupine, and the same opinions which have been very favorably received here may be very obnoxious there. I need a guiding spirit as much as I ever did at any period of my life. My present position is one of great popularity with a falling party, and in falling with them the prospect for me is of a sudden and overwhelming reverse, in which case persecution may come not only upon myself, which I can bear with fortitude, but upon those to whom my good name is not only dear but necessary for their comfort. I have deliberately assumed an aggressive position against the President and his whole Executive Administration, against the Supreme Court of the United States, and against the Commander-in-chief of the army. I am at issue with all the organized powers of the Union, with the twelve hundred millions of dollars of associated wealth, and with all the rabid Democracy of the land. I do not mistake my position nor disguise to myself its perils. But my cause is the cause of my country and of human liberty. It is the cause of Christian improvement, the fulfilment of the prophecies that the day shall come when slavery and war shall be banished from the face of the earth.

Adams entered the Third Session of the Twenty-Seventh Congress with guns blazing against the gag rule, only to be met with "the old game" as played "by the Northern Democratic alliance with Southern slavery."[155] His frustration boiled over in a purple passage about slavery's defenders and Northerners whom he perceived as their unmanly abettors. While Adams still resisted any notion that his opinions and actions had completely merged with those of the

154. Presumably this is John Quincy Adams, *The Social Compact: Exemplified in the Constitution of the Commonwealth of Massachusetts* . . . (Providence, RI: Knowles and Vose, 1842).
155. Diary, December 5–6, 1842.

*abolitionists, he had clearly moved a fair distance along the antislavery spec-
trum. So while his merger of partisanship and antislavery still sought to dif-
ferentiate between the abolitionist and Whig brands of antislavery, that same
move showed how he now saw slavery as touching all of his other priorities.
And there was now at least as much potential for fine distinctions and outright
disagreements between himself and other antislavery Whigs as there had once
been between himself and abolitionists.*

January 2, 1843—Morning absorbed in reading the newspapers of the last
night's mail and the Globe of Saturday evening upon my table. It contains the speeches of John C. Calhoun in the Senate of the United States
last August, in favor of advising and consenting to the ratification of the
Webster and Ashburton Treaty. Calhoun is the high-priest of Moloch—
the embodied spirit of slavery. . . . His speech is remarkable for one of those
glaring, unblushing, dare-devil inconsistencies which, as far as I know, are
peculiar to the doctrinal school of slavery. . . . There is a temperance in his
manner obviously aiming to conciliate the Northern political sopranos,
who abhor slavery and help to forge fetters for the slave.

January 3, 1843—Mr. Kurtz and Mr. Barcroft, of Georgetown, called
on me this morning and stated that they were members of the Society
of Friends, and Mr. Kurtz had a letter from Philadelphia recommending Mrs. Lucretia Mott, who is desirous of obtaining the use of the hall
of the House of Representatives for a religious exercise; and, without
coming directly to the point, Mr. Kurtz gave me to understand that it
was desired that I should make the motion in the House that she might
have the use of the hall.

I desired Mr. Kurtz to say to Mrs. Mott that I remembered with much
pleasure the hospitality which I had once, some years since, enjoyed at
her house, and the social intercourse with which I had at other times
been favored by her husband and other friends; that I should be happy
to see her at my house, and, if she desired it, would make the motion
in the House that she should have the use of the hall. But I observed to
Mr. Kurtz that Mrs. Mott was known as a distinguished abolitionist of
slavery; that there was little difference between her opinions upon the
subject of slavery and mine; but he knew how obnoxious I was here,
both in and out of Congress, for that very thing; and he would consider

whether the application for the use of the hall would not be more likely to succeed if made by another member.

January 6, 1843—Mr. Leavitt ... has published in the Emancipator only a part of my address at Braintree,[156] and for omitting other parts of it alledged [sic] that he did not approve them—I asked him, what were the parts which he disapproved. He said the parts which had a political party aspect. I said they all had indirect reference to the Slavery questions—

January 13, 1843—Mr. Leavitt was here this morning, and read to me an article which he has prepared to publish in the Emancipator, explanatory of the charge by him in a former number of that paper against members of not having supported me upon my trial. Six of the members of the delegation, Briggs, Hudson, Burnell,[157] Winthrop, Baker, and Saltonstall, with a concurring signature of Calhoun,[158] have written me a letter requesting me to furnish a statement ... to repel the imputation in the Emancipator that they did not support me.

The joint resolution from the Senate proposing a new rule to abridge the right of petition. Parmenter[159] opposed it, to my surprise, for he had yesterday voted against laying it on the table. Giddings, equally to my surprise, supported it. He is Chairman of the Committee of Claims, much annoyed by their multitude, and does not see the lurking stab to the right of petition.

While other Northern Whigs and Northern Democrats sought to shore up ties with like-minded Southerners to preserve national parties in this sectionalizing era, Adams's interest in such things actually decreased. He put his energies into convincing as many people as possible that slavery was the defining issue of their times.[160]

---

156. John Quincy Adams, *Address of John Quincy Adams, to His Constituents of the Twelfth Congressional District, at Braintree, September 17th, 1842* (Boston: J. H. Eastburn, 1842). It was a vigorous assault on the Democrats and the Tyler administration, centered on but ranging beyond their Texas policy.

157. Barker Burnell (Whig, Massachusetts).

158. William B. Calhoun, that is, the Massachusetts Whig congressman.

159. William Parmenter (Democrat, Massachusetts).

160. See also Diary, April 11, 17, 1843.

February 15, 1843—Before going to the House, I had a quarter of an hour's conversation with Cushing, and told him there was a war now in parturition between Freedom and Slavery throughout the globe; that it would be a war for the abolition of slavery, at the head of which would be Great Britain; that in this war I could take no part—I was going off the stage; but he was coming on to it; and I conjured him, as he cherished his own and his country's honor, not to commit himself, in this great controversy, to the side of slavery; and to return to the cause of liberty, from which he had not yet irrevocably strayed.

He heard me without taking offence, but apparently without conviction.[161]

February 25, 1843—Mr. Daniel Whitaker, agent for the proprietors of the revived Southern Review, published at Charleston South-Carolina, came to solicit my subscription, and if agreeable, my contribution to it, both of which I declined.

February 27, 1843—I had prepared resolutions to be offered to the House, with a view to call the attention of the people of the free States to the disproportion of slave-holding Judges on the bench of the Supreme Court of the United States.[162] . . . I asked leave to present my resolutions respecting the slave-holding and free State Judges on the bench of the Supreme Court. Multitudes of objections were heard. I asked a suspension of the rules, and the yeas and nays. The Speaker said the House had voted to go into committee, and my resolutions were returned to me. I gave them to Stansbury to be published in the National Intelligencer.

161. Cushing would indeed grow stronger and stronger in his Southern sympathies until he took a rather extreme pro-Southern position in the years surrounding the Civil War. See John M. Belohlavek, *Broken Glass: Caleb Cushing and the Shattering of the Union* (Kent, OH: Kent State University Press, 2005). That became apparent to Adams when less than two weeks later, Cushing cast a "Northern servile, or dough-face" vote on Texas annexation (Diary, February 28, 1843).
162. The significance of this disproportion came home to him within days of this resolution, as he read the Supreme Court decision on *Prigg v. Pennsylvania*, an important fugitive slave case, as evidence of "the transcendent omnipotence of slavery in these United States" (Diary, March 10, 1843).

Further evidence of how much had changed for Adams came in his response to Tyler administration officials' allegation that Texas must be annexed to protect it and the United States from British abolitionist designs on the young republic. Given Adams's own attitude toward British abolitionists twenty years earlier, one can imagine that these 1843 diary entries on this subject would have cast different groups as the villains. And when he did evince distrust for Britons in power, it was for the opposite reason from what it had been years previously.[163]

April 1, 1843—In them [letters of Jacksonian schemers in 1835] originated the project of enlarging the encroachment upon Mexico, from the mere acquisition of Texas, to embrace all New Mexico. . . . The root of the danger is in the convulsive impotence of Mexico to maintain her own integrity, geographical, political, or moral, and the inflexible perseverance of rapacity of our South and West, under the spur of slavery, to plunder and dismember her.

April 4, 1843—The spirit of encroachment upon Mexico is stimulated and nourished by this settled and too well founded conviction of her helpless weakness, in conflict with the gigantic energy of our national avarice and ambition. When I contemplate the prospect before us, my heart sinks within me for the cause of human freedom and for our own. At the Department of State, too, I found matter for gloomy anticipations in the instructions of 13th January last to the Consul at the Havanna, Robert B. Campbell, which discloses great alarm at the Havanna, and thence instigated here, at the supposed design of the British Government to take possession of the island of Cuba—and a real design at the Havanna, to urge us to be beforehand with Britain by taking it ourselves. The Secretary of State tells the Consul, in a very trenchant tone, that we shall not permit Great Britain to take possession of Cuba. The real fact I suppose to be that the British Government are turning the screws upon the importation of slaves into the island, and that they can no longer in defiance of all law and all treaty openly

163. For more on his activities and thoughts relative to Texas in these weeks, including teaming up with eleven other antislavery congressmen to address the free states on the issue, see Diary, April 28, 1843. For other similar thoughts on British abolitionists and the British government, see Diary, May 13, June 7, August 7, 11, 21, September 9, 1843; April 7–8, 14, 1844.

gorge their markets with twenty-five thousand ... negroes every year. The Havanna has been and is one of the last inexpugnable haunts of the African slave-trade pirates.

April 14, 1843—Texas is swelling with incredible rapidity into a formidable slave State, which Mexico can never recover, and from the contamination of whose slavery nothing can save this Union short of a special interposition of Providence.

May 8, 1843—I went to the Emancipator office, and had a long conversation with Mr. Leavitt. He is to embark next Tuesday in the steamer for Liverpool, to attend as a delegate from the American Anti-Slavery Society the second triennial meeting of the World's Convention for the Promotion of the Abolition of Slavery and the Slave-Trade throughout the earth.

I urged him very earnestly to observe with unremitting care the movements of the British Government with regard to Mexico and Texas. I told him I distrusted them altogether; I believed their real policy far from desiring to favor the abolition of slavery, either in our Southern States or in Texas. I suspect, on the contrary, that for a suitable equivalent they will readily acquiesce both in the annexation of Texas to this Union and to the perpetuation of slavery here, to weaken and to rule us.

May 31, 1843—Mr. Lewis Tappan and Mr. [Stephen P.] Andrews visited me this morning. ... Mr. Andrews is a native of Massachusetts, but at present an inhabitant of Texas. ... He is now about to embark in the steamer Caledonia, tomorrow, for England, with a view to obtain the aid of the British Government to the cause [of emancipation in Texas]. Mr. Tappan asked me if I would furnish him with letters of recommendation; which I declined, having no correspondent in England with whom I could take the liberty; but I bade him God speed, and told him that I believed the freedom of this country and of all mankind depended upon the direct, formal, open, and avowed interference of Great Britain to accomplish the abolition of slavery in Texas; but that I distrusted the sincerity of the present British Administration in the anti-slavery cause.

Even as the political climate in the North seemed to be shifting in his favor due to the unpopularity of the gag rule and Texas annexation, Adams remained unsure of his course. His "inclination" grew so antislavery that he read even a presidential visit to Boston through the lens of slavery, and searched for a way to leave his own antislavery legacy. Moreover, he had moved to almost a complete rapprochement with abolitionists both American and British. But he remained torn by a commitment to "decorum" and the Constitution.[164]

June 12, 1843—I answered a letter from William Pitt Fessenden, a member of the last Congress from Portland, Maine, who has been charged in an abolitionist address to the people of that State with lukewarmness in support of the right of petition.[165] He wrote to me requesting my testimony as to his course in the House. I have given him my testimony. The abolitionist charges against him are unjust; but zeal in support of the right of petition can do nothing in the Congress of the United States. I wrote this answer with great difficulty, much hesitation, and not a little imprudence in lifting up one corner of the curtain which covers the hideous reality of the slave ascendency in the Government of this Union—the double representation of the slave-owners in the House of Representatives and in the Electoral Colleges for the choice of President and Vice-President. Semper ego auditor tantum?[166]

June 13, 1843—... I received this morning a letter from Asa Walker and two others, a committee of correspondence for a public meeting of the citizens of Bangor and vicinity, holden on the 27th of last month, and at which a resolution was adopted to observe the 1st of next August as the anniversary of West India emancipation, by a public address and other suitable exercises, and the committee appointed to carry the resolution into execution invite me to deliver the address. The temptation is almost irresistible, but must be resisted. My time is not yet come. How shall I answer this letter?

The same question is of more than daily recurrence. I have, for example, an invitation, dated the 19th of April, from a committee of the directors of the Bunker Hill Monument Association, to unite with them in celebrating the completion of that monument, by a civic and military procession, and an address by the Hon. Daniel Webster.

164. See also Diary, August 19, 1843.
165. John Quincy Adams to William P. Fessenden, June 13, 1843, Adams Family Papers, MHS.
166. Will I always be only a listener?

Upon this pageant has been engrafted another, to bedaub with glory John Tyler, the slave-breeder, who is coming with all his court, in gaudy trappings of mock royalty, to receive the homage of hungry sycophants, under color of doing homage to the principles of Bunker Hill martyrdom. I answered this invitation, declining to attend, with a struggle between inclination and decorum to suppress the most imperative motive for my absence—the disdain to be associated with the mouth-worship of liberty from the lips of the slave-breeder. I succeeded but indifferently in veiling my emotions, and touched upon the martyrdom of Bunker Hill only by transparent generalities, which will yet provoke censure.[167]

June 17, 1843—This was the day of the great celebration of the completion of the monument on Bunker Hill. ... What a name in the annals of mankind is Bunker Hill! what a day was the 17th of June, 1775! and what a burlesque upon them both is an oration upon them by Daniel Webster, and a pilgrimage of John Tyler, and his Cabinet of slave-drivers, to desecrate the solemnity by their presence. And then a dinner at Faneuil Hall in honor of a President of the United States, hated and despised by those who invited him to it, themselves as cordially hated and despised by him.

I have throughout my life had an utter aversion to all pageants and public dinners, and never attended one when I could decently avoid it. ... But now, with the ideal association of the thundering cannon, which I heard, and the smoke of burning Charlestown, which I saw, on that awful day,[168] combined with this pyramid of Quincy granite, and Daniel Webster spouting, and John Tyler's nose, with a shadow outstretching that of the monumental column—how could I have

167. It was indeed a terse letter in which Adams wrote vaguely about his regret that his health would prevent him from "manifesting my adherence to the principles" of the Declaration of Independence that "the blood of martyrs on that hill" had defended. He also wrote in veiled terms that during "this renewal of that Covenant," he would be praying for the global "triumph of those principles." See John Quincy Adams to Joseph Buckingham et al., June 15, 1843, Adams Family Papers, MHS.

168. Referring to his memory of having witnessed the Battle of Bunker Hill from a distance as a boy. Already at age eighteen Adams recorded his discomfort with "Pleasure and festivity" on the anniversary at the site "where the immortal Warren fell." Diary, June 17, 1786, in David Grayson Allen et al., eds., *Diary of John Quincy Adams* (Cambridge, MA: Belknap Press of Harvard University Press, 1981), 2: 50–51.

witnessed all this at once, without an unbecoming burst of indigna-tion, or of laughter? Daniel Webster is a heartless traitor to the cause of human freedom;[169] John Tyler is a slave-monger. What have these to do with the Quincy granite pyramid on the brow of Bunker's Hill? What have these to do with a dinner in Faneuil Hall, but to swill like swine, and grunt about the rights of man?

June 26, 1843—I continued, without finishing, my answer to the invitation from Bangor to deliver there an oration on the 1st of August, in celebration of the emancipation of slaves in the British West Indies. This answer will be instead of the oration itself; but it is already too long, and must be much longer to be worthy of the theme. I shall prob-ably not send it, after all; but I feel an irremissible duty to bear my testi-mony once more, before I go hence, against slavery. To select the time, the place, and the manner is a subject of great consideration, and must be neither precipitated nor too long delayed. My ideas are yet crude, indigested, and confused. I will begin to collect and assert them in this letter, with the firm resolve to persevere in the pursuit.

August 10, 1843—I received this morning by the mail the Bangor Courier . . . containing my letter of 4th July last to Asa Walker, Charles A. Stackpole, and F. M. Sabine.[170] It is announced as a letter from John Quincy Adams on slavery, with a statement that it was read at the meet-ing on the 1st of August, without one word of comment upon it. I have expected the publication of this letter, and expect to be held to severe responsibility for writing it. Before my lamp is burnt out, I am desir-ous that my opinions concerning the great movement throughout the civilized world for the abolition of slavery should be explicitly avowed and declared. God grant that they may contribute to the final consum-mation of that event!

169. He felt this way due to the stances Webster had taken as Tyler's secretary of state, such as on the Creole incident.
170. Adams in this letter arraigned slavery as a violation of the Declaration of Independence's principles and lamented therefore that the British had in the intervening years gone well beyond the Americans in the cause of emancipation. The recent trend in American policy toward a proslavery position—illustrated by such things as the gag rule and the government's designs on Texas—was even more troubling. The contrast between the British and American records on slav-ery was therefore to his beloved country's shame. See John Quincy Adams to Asa Walker et al., July 4, 1843, Adams Family Papers, MHS.

August 11, 1843—I received this morning, forwarded from New York by Lewis Tappan, a letter from Thomas Clarkson . . . [enclosing] a full exposition of the proceedings of the second World's Convention, at which no very conspicuous person attended, excepting Lord Morpeth.[171] His speech to the Convention on taking the chair was firm, moderate, and discreet. The resolution honorary to me which he offered, and which was unanimously adopted, is an indication of personal respect for my character, beyond the Atlantic, which ought to fill my soul with humility and with fervent gratitude to God. These events, occurring at the same period with the manifestation of kindly feeling towards me from the people of the State of New York, and with the invitation from Cincinnati to lay the cornerstone of their Observatory, seem temptations of prosperity too great for frail human nature to resist, or to bear with impunity. I pray for the calmness and sensibility suited to justice and to the true estimate of worldly honors.

August 12, 1843—The Boston Courier of this morning republishes, from the Bangor Courier, my letter of the 4th of July last to the Bangor Committee for celebrating the anniversary of the emancipation of slaves in the British West India Islands. . . . Not a word of comment upon the letter is in either of the papers. I expected the publication of that letter, and wrote it for the purpose of exhibiting in as brief a compass as possible my principles, feelings, and opinions relating to the abolition of slavery and the slave-trade throughout the world. I meant it as a note of defiance to all the slave-holders, slave-breeders, and slave-traders upon earth. As the experiment of summons to the whole freedom of this Union in its own defence, I sent it forth alone to try its fortune in the world, and made it purposely bold and startling, to rouse, if possible, both friend and foe. The two publications without comment give no promise of a rally for the support of freedom. As yet, there is no hostile notice of it abroad. It may remain altogether unnoticed—which is the worst fate that can befall it; for, if I can but raise a controversy by it— that is, an adversary worthy of being answered—it shall be, if my life and health will admit, a text-book for future enlargement and illustration for the whole remnant of my toilsome days.

---

171. George Howard, Viscount Morpeth, a moderately prominent British statesman and abolitionist.

August 26, 1843—I went to the town hall, and heard Wendell Phillips deliver a second Anti-slavery Address. . . . His argument was [that] the incumbent duty of every abolitionist is to trample underfoot the article of the Constitution which requires the surrender of fugitive Slaves—He assumes the position that this is null and void; as a compact contrary to the Law of Nature and of God—He thanked God that he was not a citizen of the United States—and goes the extremest lengths of the abolitionists—After his lecture he came and spoke to me, and I told him I could not concur in his doctrines. He took me home in his carry-all—His auditory was small.

During the break between the Twenty-Seventh and Twenty-Eighth Congresses, Adams became aware of new evidence that slaveholders would stop at nothing when he learned that pro-Southern government officials had falsified the 1840 census returns to exaggerate the proportion of insanity among the free black population.[172] As he contemplated the policy agenda of the new Congress, he broke out afresh with bitterness about how "the slave oligarchy" had "systematically" put down measures that would enact the Whig agenda of Improvement.[173] As the new Congress met he determined to go to the root of it all.

November 29, 1843—I made this morning the draught of a Resolution, which I propose to offer to the House of Representatives at the approaching Session of Congress—A Session at which a trial of character more severe than I ever before experienced awaits me; and from which may the Mercy of God deliver me to the judgment of the after age, pure and unsullied. Clouds and darkness are before me. . . . My resolution is for the appointment of a Committee to ascertain the number of slave owners throughout the Union, and the value of the property represented by members in the house and a proportional number in the electoral Colleges.

December 3, 1843—The slavery questions are, in my estimation, more important than [the issues currently being discussed,] . . . and the

172. Diary, October 14, 1843.
173. Diary, November 24, 1843.

aspect of the slavery questions is appalling. The most imminent of my dangers is the loss of my temper—from which I fervently pray I may be preserved.

December 10, 1843—I spent this evening in preparing for the duties of the coming week, and in meditating purposes never to be performed— On full deliberation I conclude that the whole course of my conduct in this Congress must be defensive, even of the cause of Liberty, and above all things to endure mortification.

Although Adams entered the Twenty-Eighth Congress with his now-standard pessimism, as he studied early votes on his motion to revoke the Gag Rule he found the result not discouraging. He also sensed a certain level of "desperation" in the maneuvers of "the slave-power" to preserve the Gag. The Gag was clearly not going quietly away. But the fact that Gag supporters would have to resort to "chicanery" and "every species of subterfuge" gave Adams a sense that the momentum might finally be on his side of this contest. He pursued this fragile opportunity with nervous energy. But he also had all the discipline of a true political manager, including a determination to stay focused on this debate rather than taking slaveholders' bait to engage with gratuitously divisive extraneous issues.[174]

December 21, 1843—In the House, the life-and-death struggle for the right of petition was resumed. The question of reception of the petition from Illinois was laid on the table—ninety-eight to eighty—after a long and memorable debate.

I then presented the resolves of the Massachusetts Legislature of the 23d of March, 1843, proposing an amendment to the Constitution of the United States, making the representation of the people in the House proportioned to the numbers of free persons, and moved it should be read, printed, and referred to a select committee of nine. And now sprung up the most memorable debate ever entertained in the House, in the midst of which the House, at half-past three, adjourned. I can give no account of it. . . . The crisis now requires of me coolness, firmness, prudence, moderation, and fortitude, beyond all former example.

174. See also Diary, December 16–17, 19, 22, 24, 26, 1843; January 3, 5–6, 11, 13, 19, 27, 30–31, February 5, 15–17, 27–28, March 22, 1844.

I came home in such a state of agitation that I could do nothing but pace my chamber.

January 1, 1844—I begin the new year, as I closed the old one, with praise and prayer to God—with grateful thanksgiving for the past, with humble supplication for the future. ... Tomorrow recommences the struggle, which, for me can terminate only with my life. May the Spirit from above in life and death sustain me!

January 2, 1844—Before the quorum was formed this morning, Beardsley[175] told me that he thought the House would not confirm the vote of the committee to strike out the gag-rule, and he intimated that Davis,[176] of Indiana, had changed his opinion, and would move to reverse the decision of the committee. But Davis did not attend. The members present, after a final cursory revisal of the whole report, instructed me to present it this day to the House, and to move that it be printed, and made the order of the day for this day week. I told Beardsley that the action of the House upon the gag would depend entirely upon the perseverance of the twenty-seven members of the New York delegation, and that I was told the Richmond Enquirer had threatened that if they did persevere, Van Buren's claim to the Presidency would be forfeited.

He admitted the fact, and said that he hoped the members would not be moved by any such consideration; two or three weak-minded men might be.

January 22, 1844—Giddings presented several anti-slavery and abolition petitions; among the rest, one from three hundred and eighty-one citizens of Hampshire County, Massachusetts, praying Congress by law to prohibit the officers of the United States from assisting to arrest persons suspected of being fugitives from slavery.

There was much fluttering among the slavers. The Speaker decided that this petition was not within the twenty-fifth rule; from which decision Black, of Georgia, appealed. I called for the yeas and nays. ...

Jameson[177] enquired if laying the appeal on the table would carry the petition with it. The Speaker said no. ... Payne[178] moved to lay the appeal on the table; carried—one hundred and thirteen ayes. He

175. Samuel Beardsley (Democrat, New York).
176. John W. Davis, a Democrat.
177. John Jameson (Democrat, Missouri).
178. William W. Payne (Democrat, Alabama).

then made the question of reception, and Cave Johnson moved to lay that on the table. This is the wooden-nutmeg form of rejecting a petition without refusing to receive it. The question to lay on the table was lost—eighty-five to eighty-seven; and then the question to receive was lost—eighty-five to eighty-six. In the interval between the two takings of yeas and nays, Freedom lost two votes, Slavery gained one, and the majority was changed.

Beardsley presented a petition praying for the repeal of the Act of February, 1793,[179] and Weller moved to lay it on the table. Beardsley moved a call of the House, and Hopkins moved to adjourn, and it was carried. Another slip of the rattlesnake Slavery from the grasp of Freedom.

February 7, 1844—At the House, before the Chaplain appeared, Mr. Hudson came to my seat, and told me that he had heard the Democracy had in a mere caucus determined to take immediately the question on the restoration of the gag-rule; that Dromgoole[180] would withdraw his motion to recommit the report, and will move the previous question. The New York Democrats have been whipped in by the threat that the South will desert Van Buren if his friends join to rescind the rule, with a promise of Calhoun and his party to support Van Buren if the rule is retained and the tariff broken down.[181] I have been prepared for this reverse, and must bear it with patience. . . .

I had an evening visit from Mr. Murray, of New York, with Mr. Charles Butler, a brother of Benjamin F. Butler's, the sometime Attorney-General of Mr. Van Buren. He told me that he was a Loco-foco, but warmly and anxiously with me on the right of petition.

February 22, 1844—This day, at the House, Mr. Kennedy[182] introduced John M. S. Causin, member from the First, and Francis Brengle, from the Second Congressional District of Maryland, who were sworn and took their seats. J. A. Preston, the member from the Third District, also afterwards came in. James Dellet, of Alabama, a Whig

179. The Fugitive Slave Act.
180. George C. Dromgoole (Democrat, Virginia).
181. This all refers to Van Buren's ambitions to return as Democratic nominee for the presidency.
182. John Pendleton Kennedy (Whig, Maryland). The new members he introduced were likewise Maryland Whigs.

slave-monger, made an hour speech for the gag, and against Giddings and me, full of frothy eloquence and invective. The slavers have become bolder with the arrival of the Maryland delegation, and, having now ascertained that they will carry the restoration of the gag, the three successive speeches of Campbell, Burt,[183] and Dellet have exhibited a regular ascending gradation of overbearing insolence and bullying. To leave it all without reply would be tame submission. To reply in the same tone might breed a brawl; for which I should be held responsible by the public. To say just what will be proper, and nothing more, requires counsel from above. May it not be withheld!

February 24, 1844—Dromgoole's object now is to conjure up debate upon many other points, and mingle them with the gag question, and entangle them all together, so as to evade the direct question upon the gag alone, of the issue of which, so taken, he is afraid. Numbers of the Northern Democracy, afraid of their constituents if they vote for the gag, and afraid of losing the vote of the South for Van Buren if they vote against it, suffer Dromgoole to lead them by the nose to relieve them from voting directly upon that question at all.

March 26, 1844—The Commissioner of Patents, H. L. Ellsworth, came, with Jeremiah E. Cary, of Cherry Valley, member from the Twenty-First Congressional District of New York, Otsego and Scoharie, and delivered to me a letter from himself, with one from Julius Pratt & Co., manufacturers at Meriden, Connecticut, and a present of a milk-white ivory cane, one yard long, made of one elephant's tooth, tipped with silver and steel, with the American eagle inlaid in gold on its top, and a ring under the pommel, inscribed with my name, and the words, "Justum, et tenacem propositi virum."[184] The letter requests that on the day when the gag-rule shall be finally abolished I will insert the date after the inscription on the ring.

After expressing my deep sensibility to this testimonial of kindness and approbation of my public conduct, I promised a written answer to Mr. Pratt's letter, and, alluding to my custom of declining valuable presents from individuals for public service, I accepted the cane as a

183. Armistead Burt (Democrat, South Carolina).
184. Just, and a man of firm purpose.

trust to be returned when the date of the extinction of the gag-rule shall be accomplished.[185]

This heady sense of momentum suffered a major setback when Texas annexation advanced while the cause of internal improvements retreated. As with previous reverses, however, these seem only to have confirmed Adams's heroic self-image as a martyr for a truly glorious cause.

April 22, 1844—This was a memorable day in the annals of the world. The treaty for the annexation of Texas to this Union was this day sent in to the Senate; and with it went the freedom of the human race. In the House it was a no less disastrous day. McKay,[186] Chairman of the Committee of Ways and Means, made his long fore-announced motion, to suspend the rules to go into committee of the whole on the state of the Union to take up his Anti-Tariff bill; and after a call of the House, upon which one hundred and ninety-four members answered to their names, the motion was carried by a vote of one hundred and four to ninety-four, the majority consisting of that floating class of Janus-faces who decide all great and critical questions by holding themselves at market till the last hour, and then let the hammer fall to the highest bidder. The vote against reconsidering the passage of the Western Harbor bill had been seventy-three to one hundred and eleven. The number voting on the motion to take up the Anti-Tariff was one hundred and ninety-eight—probably the largest vote of the session. The standing supremacy of the slave-representation is one hundred and twelve, a bare majority of the whole House, consisting of eighty slave-holders and thirty-two free-trade auxiliaries. This is the average, allowing eight slave-holders for occasional defection from their iron rule, and an equal number of Laodicean freemen, neither hot nor cold,[187] and ever wavering between slavery and freedom.

185. For more on this cane, including the elaborate procedure by which Adams handed over the cane to a government agency for safekeeping, see Diary, April 23, 1844.
186. James Iver McKay (Democrat, North Carolina).
187. This is a reference to Revelation 3:14–16, where John quotes Christ as warning the church in Laodicea that "because thou art lukewarm, and neither cold nor hot, I will spue thee out of my mouth."

May 4, 1844—. . . the treaty for the annexation of Texas to the United States, with the President's message transmitting it to the Senate, and the accompanying documents, prematurely published, and the conflicting opinions of the leading men of the Union, disclosed in letters and speeches at public meetings, all indicate the immediate crisis of a great struggle between slavery and freedom throughout the world. I must retire from this contest, or perish under it, probably before the close of the present year, or even of the present session of Congress.

May 29, 1844—It is impossible for me to describe the anxieties under which my soul is oppressed, and which I am compelled to suppress, with reliance only upon superior power to relieve me from them, and with no hope of other relief than from the close of life, and the transition to another state of existence. The deepest of my afflictions is the degeneracy of my country from the principles which gave her existence, and the ruin irreparable of them all, under the transcendent power of slavery and the slave-representation.

Such was Adams's solicitude on the Texas issue that he recorded the names on both sides of the 35-16 Senate vote against consenting to the treaty of annexation. It was a high point on the roller coaster of emotions surrounding Texas, a ride Adams knew was far from over.

June 10, 1844—I record this vote as a deliverance, I trust, by the special interposition of Almighty God, of my country and of human liberty from a conspiracy comparable to that of Lucius Sergius Catilina.[188] May it prove not a mere temporary deliverance, like that, only preliminary to the fatally successful conspiracy of Julius Cæsar! The annexation of Texas to this Union is the first step to the conquest of all Mexico, of the West India Islands, of a maritime, colonizing, slave-tainted monarchy, and of extinguished freedom.

June 17, 1844—The first shock of slave Democracy is over. Moloch and Mammon[189] have sunk into momentary slumber. The Texas treason

188. Known most often in English as Cataline, this Roman senator was implicated in a failed conspiracy to overthrow the Roman Republic in the first century BC.
189. Biblical terms that had become bywords for idolatry (Moloch) and greed (Mammon).

is blasted for the hour, and the first session of the most perverse and worthless Congress that ever disgraced this Confederacy has closed.

The distance Adams had traveled from his earlier prioritization of Anglophobic anti-abolitionism and statesmanlike prudence was further confirmed in a mid-1844 diary entry. He still believed that American abolitionists were apt to "ruin" their "excellent cause" "by mismanagement" and extremism. But he served as a consultant to the legal team defending Washington abolitionist Charles T. Torrey and seemed to take pride in Kentucky abolitionist Cassius M. Clay citing Adams as an influence on his career.[190] For all that ambivalence, his shift in tone toward support of British antislavery was total.

July 1, 1844—I told Mr. Pakenham[191] that I had seen with great pleasure in the Parliamentary papers of 1839 and '40, lent me by Mr. Fox, the avowal by Lord Palmerston, in a dispatch to Lord Howard de Walden, that to promote the abolition of slavery throughout the world was a fixed and settled system of the British Government. I had seen in the newspapers the negotiations with all Europe and all America, especially with the Pope and the Bey of Tunis, all tending to the same result. I told him of the visit of Andrews, the Texan, and Lewis Tappan, to me before they went to England last summer; that Mr. Andrews had communicated his designs to me, and I had expressed to him my doubts of his success. I had expressed the same doubt to Mr. Tappan, and told him I thought the British Government would, in this case, sacrifice their principles to their policy. Mr. Lewis Tappan, without authority from me, had apprised Lord Aberdeen of this opinion of mine, and Lord Aberdeen had protested against it; but it had proved correct. The abolition of slavery in Texas, without war or bloodshed, had been completely within the power of Great Britain, but her Government had failed to carry out their own principles. They disclaim and concede too much. They parry, carte and tierce,[192] to avoid the issue tendered

190. Diary, July 4, 1844; August 19, 1845; for Torry and Clay, see Diary, July 11, September 24, 1844; August 23, 1845.
191. Sir Richard Pakenham, British minister to the United States from 1843 to 1847.
192. Fencing terms.

them, and which they must meet. This was not the general character of English diplomacy. It was usually bold, open, explicit, stubborn. . . .

Mr. Pakenham took no offence at what I said, and spoke with much caution and reserve in return. He seems afraid of the English principles themselves, and fearful that the use of them would be to put edged tools in the hands of children.

The tension of the Texas question led Adams to indulge in even more severe rhetoric than normal against the "slave-mongers" (by far his new favorite term for Southern representatives) and more generally against "the Southern Democracy, which is slavery, and the Western Democracy, which is knavery." He was certain that "Southern Disunionists" had hatched a "conspiracy" to annex Texas.[193] *He was ready to distrust seemingly reasonable Southerners. He also continued in a vindictive vein in his reflections on the February 1844 explosion of a massive cannon aboard the USS* Princeton, *which killed proslavery Secretary of State Abel Upshur, among other Tyler administration officials.*[194] *His reading of the South as one solid sectional interest also emerged in a conversation with an antislavery lecturer about the impact of the Constitution's three-fifths clause on Southern power in Congress.*

July 6, 1844—I met Mr. Thompson[195] at the Intelligencer office, and had a long conversation with him and Mr. Gales on the subject [of Texas annexation]. Thompson is a South Carolina planter, owner of one hundred slaves, and religiously believes that slavery was made for the African race, and the African race for slavery. He opposes the annexation of Texas on Southern grounds as a Southern man. So did Calhoun, so did McDuffie, so did Hamilton all now rabid annexationists.[196] Thompson will be converted like them. . . . He is as cunning as four Yankees, as sly as four Quakers, and just now admires the people of

193. Diary, April 17, 24, May 7, 10, 17–18, 21, August 22, 1844.
194. Diary, February 28, March 14, 1844.
195. Presumably this is Waddy Thompson, the former South Carolina Whig congressman who had recently finished two years as the US minister to Mexico.
196. Calhoun was now secretary of state. The others here are George McDuffie (Democrat, South Carolina) and most likely James Hamilton Jr., former governor of South Carolina.

Massachusetts too much. I hope his letter will be eminently useful at the present crisis, and devoutly pray that he and Benton[197] and the "Princeton" gun may be instruments for the deliverance of my country.

July 24, 1844—[The three-fifths clause adds] 21 members [to the Southern state delegations]. But as an element of power, the whole delegations from the Slave holding States, and each member represents the whole slaveholding interest, and the whole mass of Slave owners—The number of their members therefore is not 21 but 88 knit together by one interest and that interest the ascendancy of slavery.

A conversation with a young Harvard student about the presidential election of 1844 gave Adams an opportunity to elaborate on why he could not support the Liberty Party's candidate. The other candidates were the Whig chieftain Henry Clay and the Democratic dark horse James K. Polk. And as Adams stood for re-election that year, this attitude toward the Liberty Party was hardly limited to presidential politics. Thus, while the differences between Adams and political abolitionists may seem slight to us, they were both significant (enough that he lavished two entries on laying them out) and personal to him.

August 27, 1844—He assigned two motives for his call to see me—one, as a manifestation of personal respect for my character—The other to ask my opinions upon some scruples which troubled him with regard to his voting at the presidential election—He was an abolitionist in principle though not of the abolition party; nor of any abolition society. He was also a whig and strongly desirous of voting for the whig candidate. But the Liberty party charged him [Clay] with being an avowed duelist—and not only a slaveholder, but a decided partizan for perpetual slavery—a gambler—intemperate, and otherwise a loose licentious life—There was no satisfactory refutation of these charges made public, and he was much perplexed what to do. He needed advice and came to ask it of me—I said that his doubts were of no easy solution. That I took no part as a partizan in the presidential election[.] I deemed it my duty to abstain from convassing for any one for that office, and to leave it to the people to fix their choice for themselves—But as to matters

197. Thomas Hart Benton (Democrat, Missouri), who was an expansionist but opposed as dishonorable the Tyler administration's annexation tactics.

of fact I would say what I knew or believed and as to principles what I think—Mr. Clay is a Slave holder and supporter of Slavery. I believe him in error upon those points and hope he will revise and reform his opinions. He is a man of the world of self-indulgent habits; but not as I believe a gambler or intemperate. He abhors dueling, and has been engaged in several duels—A rigorous puritanical principle of morals cannot be applied to the exercise of the right of suffrage—There must be some reference to the result—Mr. Clay's chief competitor is mostly more exceptionable than he—To vote for a third candidate who cannot be elected is in effect to vote for the worst of the three—

October 1, 1844—... members of the Liberty party of the Eighth Congressional District of Massachusetts . . . visited me this morning. They have appointed this day week for a Convention to nominate a candidate for election to the House of Representatives of the United States in the Twenty-Ninth Congress. They have heretofore not nominated a candidate against me; but they will at this time, and it is highly probable will defeat the election. They were, however, to me this day peculiarly courteous and civil. Mr. [M. M.] Fisher said they had no disposition to dictate opinions to me, nor to ask any pledge of me which it might be disagreeable to me to give, but they had come to the conclusion that they were under obligations of duty to vote exclusively for persons who entertained certain opinions on the subject of slavery, and, as they were fully aware of the great and frequent services that they were indebted to me for in support of the cause which they had so much at heart, they wished for this friendly interview to ascertain my opinions on certain points upon which there was considerable diversity among those generally opposed to slavery.

I told them that I would cheerfully give to them my opinions as they were sincerely entertained, upon any and every point interesting to them; that I had no motive to conceal or disguise any of my opinions upon subjects of public concernment; that I had lived seventy-seven years, and served in various offices, and never asked or solicited, directly or indirectly, the vote of any man, and thought it not worth while to commence the practice now. I answered all their questions, discussed with them the points upon which we did not concur; the vote for President, upon which I should not be partisan of any man. We considered the abolition of slavery in the District of Columbia and the Territories, and the prohibition of the inter-State slave-trade.

They declared themselves perfectly satisfied with the interview. One of them said he should vote for me with pleasure; another said he did not know but what he should. The rest were silent. . . . Mr. Fisher said they expected at this election to cast from fourteen to sixteen thousand votes.

October 2, 1844—My visitors yesterday from the committee of the Liberty party were apparently not of one mind when they came, nor yet when they left me. My opposition to the immediate abolition of slavery in the District of Columbia and in the Territories they all disapprove; and Mr. [Appleton] Howe, the late Senator from Norfolk County in the State Legislature, pressed me specially with the question whether Congress have not the power to repeal the laws of the District which allow and sanction slavery. With regard to the inter-State slave-trade, I told them I had no doubt of the power of Congress to prohibit that, and would vote for a bill to that effect to-morrow, though it would not be possible to prevail upon the House to receive such a bill. I told them I regretted that I could not concur with them in all their opinions, and still more the dissensions prevailing among themselves the Colonization Society, the Anti-Slavery and Abolition Societies, the no-government, non-resisting, and women-membered societies. I grieved also at their classing in the same level of exclusion the Whig and Democratic parties. I thought there was a great difference between them, and that placing them on the same level was to secure the triumph of the worst party. This tendency of all private associations to settle into factious cabals is the besetting sin of all elective governments.

October 28, 1844—Of the letters that I received this day, there was one from Abbott Lawrence,[198] enclosing two to him from David S. Brown and Charles W. Churchman, both of Philadelphia—Brown is a Quaker—both dated the 24th, stating that Daniel L. Miller, Junr., a respectable young Quaker, and also abolitionist, would write me that same day a letter of enquiries about Polk, and Clay, and Texas, and entreating Mr. Lawrence to urge me to answer Miller's enquiries, because many Quaker and abolition votes would depend upon my answer.

By the same mail there came to myself a letter from Joseph R. Chandler, Charles Gibbons, President of the National Clay Club,

198. A prominent Massachusetts Whig.

A. J. Lewis, Nathan Sargent, and Charles W. Churchman, notifying me of this letter of enquiries from Daniel L. Miller, Junr., and urging me to answer it. Then two letters from Miller, both of the same date, one giving me notice of the other, which contains three questions for my opinion: 1. Whether the election of H. Clay would defeat the Texas annexation. 2. Whether the election of Polk would insure it. 3. Whether the annexation of Texas would advance or retard the abolition of slavery. I wrote a joking answer, but know not how he will take it. I could not with propriety write any other. It is curious how the polecat rascals work upon the Quakers, and to what base uses electioneering is turned.

Polk's victory over Clay plunged Adams into a crisis and set him to seeking out the causes of this stunning result.[199]

November 8, 1844—I understood the meaning of the guns fired last night on receipt of the election returns from the western counties of New York by the train of cars from Albany. They settle the Presidential election, and James K. Polk, of Tennessee, is to be President of the United States for four years from the 4th of March, 1845. What the further events of this issue may be is not clear, but it will be the signal for my retirement from public life. It is the victory of the slavery element in the constitution of the United States. Providence, I trust, intends it for wise purposes, and will direct it to good ends. From the sphere of public action I must, at all events, very soon be removed. My removal now is but a few days in advance of the doom of nature, and gives me time, if I have energy to improve it, which will not be lost.

November 25, 1844—I walked out for exercise, and at the National Intelligencer office saw Mr. Gales in deep distress at the issue, totally unexpected, of the Presidential election. He is in despair, and foresees that it must prove his irretrievable ruin. It has been accomplished by fraud through the slave-representation. The partial associations of Native Americans,[200] Irish Catholics, abolition societies, Liberty party, the Pope of Rome, the Democracy of the sword, and the dotage of a

199. See also Diary, February 14, 1845.
200. The rising anti-immigrant element in American politics.

ruffian,[201] are sealing the fate of this nation, which nothing less than the interposition of Omnipotence can save.

Adams's gloom was certainly not strong enough to divert him from his crusade against the gag, which he resumed at the beginning of the Second Session of the Twenty-Eighth Congress. It would prove to be yet another extreme change in emotion for him, one he still reveled in nearly a month later. And months after that, he triumphantly "directed the date 3 December 1844 to be engraved" on the ivory cane supporters had given him in anticipation of this victory.[202]

December 3, 1844—In pursuance of the notice I had given yesterday, I moved the following resolution: "Resolved, That the twenty-fifth standing rule for conducting business in this House, in the following words, No petition, memorial, resolution, or other paper praying the abolition of slavery in the District of Columbia or any State or Territory, or the slave-trade between the States or Territories in which it now exists, shall be received by this House, or entertained in any way whatever, be, and the same is hereby, rescinded." I called for the yeas and nays. Jacob Thompson, of Mississippi, moved to lay the resolution on the table. I called for the yeas and nays on that motion. As the Clerk was about to begin the call, the President's message was announced and received. A member called for the reading of the message. I said I hoped the question upon my resolution would be taken. The Clerk called the roll, and the motion to lay on the table was rejected—eighty-one to one hundred and four. The question was then put on the resolution; and it was carried—one hundred and eight to eighty. Blessed, forever blessed, be the name of God!

January 1, 1845—Great numbers of members of both Houses of Congress were here, and among them several of the bitterest political opponents that I have in the world. The personal hatred of the Southern slave-holders against me is evidently much envenomed by

---

201. These last two points seem to be bitter reflections on the ongoing influence of Andrew Jackson in American politics.
202. Diary, March 17, 1845.

the extinction of the petition gag-rule, and my position as the head of the anti-slavery movement in this country, disavowed by the whole body of abolitionists, and bound hand and foot and chained to a rock as I am, by the slave-monger brood linked together with the mongrel Democracy of the North and West.

Renewed momentum toward the annexation of Texas put Adams into another drastic patriotic mood swing, even as some Northern representatives explored ways to mitigate the impact it would have on the sectional balance of power. Adams was more apt to contemplate Texas annexation in a global context, and it and events like Andrew Jackson's death led him to cry out in his journal, "Oh Lord, how long" will it be "until Slavery shall be abolished on the earth?"[203]

January 22, 1845—Till this Texas question is decided, I can think of nothing else; I am crushed between the upper and the nether millstone, of the question to speak or not to speak in this debate. If possible, speak I must. Yet I make no progress in my preparations. . . .

Orville Robinson, a New York Van Burenite, asked leave to introduce a bill for the annexation of Texas to the United States. I called for the reading of the bill, and, upon its being read, quite a commotion rose among the Southern members. Payne, of Alabama, objected to its reception.

It proposes to admit so much of Texas now as will constitute one slave-holding State, and no slavery in all the rest of the Territory, nor slavery but by the consent of Congress hereafter. Payne was frantic about it. Andrew Stewart,[204] on the other side, moved to reject the bill at the first reading, to make an issue with the slavers. The House refused to reject the bill, by yeas and nays—sixty-eight to one hundred and nineteen. The bill was referred, with all the rest, to the committee of the whole on the state of the Union.

February 27, 1845—The Senate, this evening, by a vote of twenty-seven to twenty-five, adopted the resolutions of the House of

203. See Diary, June 17, 25, 28, July 3, 9, 1845.
204. A Pennsylvania Whig.

Representatives for admitting Texas as a State into this Union, with two additional resolutions giving the President an alternative as to the manner of consummating this transaction. This addition was proposed by Robert J. Walker, Senator from Mississippi, and is, in substance, the plan of Thomas H. Benton. It is a signal triumph of the slave-representation in the Constitution of the United States.

July 7, 1845—We have the first news that the Congress of Texas, assembled on the 17th of last month, immediately and by unanimous votes of both Houses accepted the terms prescribed by the joint resolution of the Congress of the United States of the 1st of March last for annexing Texas to the United States. . . . If the voice of the people is the voice of God, this measure has now the sanction of Almighty God. I have opposed it for ten long years, firmly believing it tainted with two deadly crimes: 1, the leprous contamination of slavery; and, 2, robbery of Mexico. Victrix causa Deo placuit.[205] The sequel is in the hands of Providence, and the ultimate result may signally disappoint those by whom this enterprise has been consummated. Fraud and rapine are at its foundation. They have sown the wind. If they reap the whirlwind, the Being who left to the will of man the improvement of his own condition will work it out according to His own good pleasure.

Adams's final diary entries relative to slavery and the politics thereof, written as he neared the age of eighty, demonstrated what had changed and what had not. He continued to thoroughly distrust the motives of and resent the power of the "slave-mongers," and to read seemingly unrelated bills as triumphs or defeats for the "anti-slavery cause."[206] But he had reconciled sufficiently with the Liberty Party to contribute pieces to its newspaper, and when leading antislavery politicians in Boston invited him to preside at a protest meeting against a fugitive slave rendition, he seemed to truly regret that his poor health kept him from doing so.[207] Still, this entry reflects how he retained his partial, careful aloofness from the abolitionists, along with his sense of having failed to secure the defeat of slavery and all it had come to represent, to the very end.

205. The victorious cause was pleasing to God.
206. Diary, March 18, May 28, August 6, November 7, 1846,
207. Diary, September 14, 23, October 24, November 3, 1846.

October 31, 1846—There has perhaps not been another individual of the human race, of whose daily existence from early childhood to fourscore years has been noted down with his own hand so minutely as mine. At little more than twelve years of age I began to journalize, and nearly two years before that, on the 11th of February, 1778, I embarked from my maternal uncle Norton Quincy's house, at Mount Wollaston, on board the Boston frigate, Captain Samuel Tucker, then lying in Nantasket Roads, and bound to France. I was then ten years and seven months old, and the house whence I embarked had been built by my great-grandfather John Quincy, upon his marriage with Elizabeth Norton in 1716. There he lived to the age of seventy-seven years, and there he died on the 13th of July, 1767, the day after I had received his name in baptism.

If my intellectual powers had been such as have been sometimes committed by the Creator of man to single individuals of the species, my diary would have been, next to the Holy Scriptures, the most precious and valuable book ever written by human hands, and I should have been one of the greatest benefactors of my country and of mankind. I would, by the irresistible power of genius and the irrepressible energy of will and the favor of Almighty God, have banished war and slavery from the face of the earth forever. But the conceptive power of mind was not conferred upon me by my Maker, and I have not improved the scanty portion of His gifts as I might and ought to have done. May I never cease to be grateful for the numberless blessings received through life at His hands, never repine at what He has denied, never murmur at the dispensations of Providence, and implore His forgiveness for all the errors and delinquencies of my life!

November 4, 1846—There was a steady and soaking rain all morning which ... confined me to the house, and I forgot the invitation of Mr. Edmund Quincy to the meeting of the Norfolk County Anti-Slavery Society held at the Town Hall—It was my intention to have attended—I have no communion with any Anti-Slavery Society and they have disclaimed all confidence in me; but I sympathize with all their aversion to Slavery.

ACKNOWLEDGMENTS

PRIDE OF PLACE AND THE biggest thanks must go to the Massachusetts Historical Society and the Adams Papers Project, and especially C. James Taylor, for granting permission to publish and for putting the entire John Quincy Adams Diaries manuscripts online.

David would like to thank Matt for joining him on this journey into John Quincy Adams's many, many words; for the conversations it spawned; and for being such a quick draw on email.

Many of the ideas for this volume emerged in conversation with students in History 3296, "John Quincy Adams's America," a seminar for junior history majors at Temple University in 2013 and 2014, for which each student read twenty to thirty pages of the Adams diary every other week.

Matt would like to thank David for inviting him on board, and for being an ideal collaborator, from the point of view of both responsiveness and exciting exchanges regarding Adams and surrounding issues. His thanks also go to the students in his US political history course in summer 2015, who read draft versions of the chapters. That helped guide us on what needed explaining, and the class discussions of Adams's twists and turns helped us refine the volume conceptually.

Miriam Liebman has been an essential sounding board and editorial consultant, and her assistance with transcriptions and proofreading has also been invaluable.

Nancy Toff guided this project from proposal to publication at OUP, and we relished her enthusiasm, her patience, her professionalism, and her line-editing mojo. (Can we buy an adjective?)

INDEX